Heidegger and Rhetoric

SUNY series in Contemporary Continental Philosophy

Dennis J. Schmidt, editor

Heidegger and Rhetoric

Edited by
Daniel M. Gross and Ansgar Kemmann

STATE UNIVERSITY OF NEW YORK PRESS

Published by
State University of New York Press, Albany

Printed in the United States of America

For information, address State University of New York Press,
194 Washington Avenue, Suite 305, Albany, NY 12210-2384

Production by Marilyn P. Semerad
Marketing by Anne M. Valentine

Library of Congress Cataloging-in-Publication Data

Heidegger and rhetoric / edited by Daniel M. Gross and Ansgar Kemmann.
p. cm. — (SUNY series in contemporary continental philosophy)
Includes bibliographical references and index.
ISBN 0-7914-6551-9 (hardcover : alk. paper)—ISBN 0-7914-6552-7 (pbk. : alk. paper)
1. Heidegger, Martin, 1889–1976. 2. Rhetoric. I. Gross, Daniel M., 1965– II. Kemmann, Ansgar. III. Series.

B3279.H49H346 2005
193—dc22 2004027568

10 9 8 7 6 5 4 3 2 1

Contents

1

Daniel M. Gross

Introduction

Being-Moved: The Pathos of Heidegger's Rhetorical Ontology

> Tradition has long ago lost an understanding of rhetoric—such was the case already in the Hellenistic and Early Middle Ages inasmuch as rhetoric became merely a school discipline. The original meaning of rhetoric had long since vanished. Insofar as we forget to ask about the concrete function of Aristotelian rhetoric, we lose the fundamental possibility of interpreting it and making it transparent. Rhetoric is nothing less than the discipline in which the self-elaboration of *Dasein* is expressly executed. *Rhetoric is no less than the elaboration of Dasein in its concreteness, the hermeneutic of Dasein itself.*
>
> Die Tradition hat längst das Verständnis für die Rhetorik verloren, sofern die Rhetorik einfach eine Schuldisziplin wurde, schon im Hellenismus und Frühmittelalter. Der ursprüngliche Sinn der Rhetorik war längst verschwunden. Sofern man vergißt, nach der konkreten Funktion der aristotelischen Rhetorik zu fragen, begibt man sich einer Grundmöglichkeit, diese so zu interpretieren, daß dabei durchsichtig wird, daß die Rhetorik nichts anderes ist als die Disziplin, in der die Selbstauslegung des Daseins ausdrücklich vollzogen ist. *Die Rhetorik ist nichts anderes als die Auslegung des konkreten Daseins, die Hermeneutik des Daseins selbst.*
>
> —Martin Heidegger, SS 1924[1]

"Heidegger and hermeneutics" trips off the tongue. But "Heidegger and rhetoric"? This story has not been adequately told, despite Heidegger's intense conviction expressed above.[2] Indeed it is often assumed that the rhetorical sensibilities of a Ricoeur, Derrida, or Foucault developed primarily in the wake of that other specter of modern German philosophy, Friedrich Nietzsche. The year 1872 would thus mark the emergence of modern rhetorical theory—the year that Nietzsche taught his modest course on Ancient rhetoric and began to formulate a notion of truth grounded in "a mobile army of metaphors."[3] But now this source story doubles. In the summer semester of 1924 Martin Heidegger, then a young professor at the University of Marburg, delivered an idiosyncratic series of lectures on Aristotle's rhetoric under the course title "Grundbegriffe der Aristotelischen Philosophie" ("Basic Concepts of Aristotelian Philosophy") and referred to, among other places, in Karl Löwith's transcript as "Aristoteles: Rhetorik II."[4] Like Nietzsche's course on classical rhetoric, Heidegger's could mark the emergence of modern discourse theory.

When *Being and Time* was published in 1927, rhetoric as a discipline had been substantially absorbed into the body of Heidegger's existential analytic, never again to fully resurface. The "hermeneutics of facticity" that predated SS 1924 by at least two years reemerged as the only way in which the basic structures of Being could be made known.[5] Subsequently projects in a Heideggerian vein have recognized only a distant relationship to the rhetorical tradition, if any. But Theodore Kisiel has suggested how we can draw a direct *genetic* link between Heidegger's reflections on rhetoric and *Being and Time*, his philosophical masterwork. Indeed SS 1924 can be seen as a formative moment in Heidegger's lifelong project of grounding metaphysics. As Kisiel describes it, SS 1924 is one of Heidegger's "greatest courses, breaking ground not merely in Greek philosophy but also for his entire path of thought."[6] During these Marburg years Heidegger had been trying to get a book out on Aristotle and thereby secure a university chair. The book never appears, but ripens instead into the first draft of *Being and Time*. As such Kisiel posits, SS 1924 "provides us with perhaps our best glimpse into how that book on Aristotle might have looked."[7] In fact the list of concepts molded in part or in whole during Heidegger's ruminations on rhetoric does read like a glossary of key terms from *Being and Time*, though the explicit connection to SS 1924 has been lost. One purpose of this book is to trace the rhetorical genealogy of some of these key terms: Being-with (*Mitsein/koinōnia*), belief (*Glaube/doxa*), Being-in (*Lage*), care (*Sorge*), mood (*pathos*), moment (*Augenblick/kairos*), ecstacy (*ekstasis*), fear (*Angst/phobos*), deliberation (*Überlegung*), articulation (*logos*), and decision (*Entschluß/krisis*). For it turns out that Heidegger's general description of how we move from concernful understanding to theory, and back—a cornerstone of the *Being and Time* project traceable through the succession of these terms—is worked out first in his elaboration of basic concepts in Aristotle's *Rhetoric* (BT 158).

Certainly we understand Heidegger's philosophy better when we consider his engagement with rhetoric. But much can be gained as well by looking at SS 1924 from the perspective of the rhetorical tradition per se. Four important aspects of that tradition are radically revised by Heidegger in new philosophical terms, and these revisions help compose the substance in which contemporary rhetorical theory moves.

1) Though Heidegger gives the classical rhetorical subject *elocutio* only modest attention, what he does say is innovative, and ties into the explicit focus of SS 1924: conceptuality. Troping appears as poetic logos; it provides the nontheoretical distance necessary to see how we are in our everyday situations and how we are moved. Setting Aristotle against Plato, Heidegger claims for instance that if the "good" man were not already transformed by a trope such as the "good" thief, the concept "good" would be unrecognizable (as would be any univocal Platonic Idea). Without the ambiguous turn in language measured out in a trope, human expression would be one dimensional, like the yelp of a dog. We would lose the unique capacity we have as speaking beings to disclose ourselves against the world, to see always that "things might be otherwise." So tropes are neither ornaments to a univocal core of language, nor are they "originary" in the manner described say, by Nietzsche. Instead a trope, acting in concert with its staid manifestation as a concept (*Begriff*) marks the contours of contingency.

2) Heidegger sees language neither as an ideally transparent means of communication between minds nor as an arbitrary system of differences, pace Saussure. Instead language is understood discursively, that is to say rooted in shared moods, human institutions, and the nonchronological history these institutions compose. In this regard there is also an important relationship between Heidegger's early thoughts on language—its use and abuse, its emergence and silence—and the later Heidegger of *Unterwegs zur Sprache*. Reversing the traditional "art of speaking," Heidegger describes rhetoric as the art of listening. What this vivid redescription does is efface the facile image of a Cicero or a Demosthenes: ingenious orators molding words that either elicit from an audience the intended passion or dissolve before a structure of logical reasoning. Heidegger describes instead a being who, insofar as that being can hear, is constituted as someone among others, someone in a particular situation that demands action. In his later essays Heidegger describes the art of listening to language constitutive of *Gelassenheit*, the attitude of "releasement" that accepts the contingency and partiality of our understanding of Being and just lets "beings be." Thus the art of listening in SS 1924 obviously has a more practical orientation than does later Heideggerian poetics. But what remains throughout is an insistence on language as medium, not means. Following Foucault we tend now to call

language so described "discourse." But SS 1924 demonstrates that Heidegger laid early tracks to a language part and parcel of human institutions and their histories.

3) Anticipating rhetorically minded theorists of the constructed subject, Heidegger shows how human beings simultaneously compose discursive institutions and are composed by them. *Heidegger thus relocates rhetoric at the heart of his fundamental ontology.* We are human insofar as we can generate shared contexts, articulate our fears and desires, deliberate and judge in the appropriate terms of our day, and act meaningfully in a world of common concern. Moreover, in all such activities we are simultaneously agent and patient, mover and moved (to use Aristotle's terminology). The critique of Heidegger as a radical antihumanist and deconstructor of human agency thus falls short of its mark. Moreover, Heidegger's rhetorical ontology is important in terms of the history of the discipline: he departs from the epistemology of tropes popular during the Enlightenment (for example, Dumarsais and Fontanier) and from the critique of ornamental style (Ramus and the Port Royalists through the eighteenth-century British Elocutionary movement). At the same time Heidegger manages to dissociate rhetoric from the romantic tradition that tended to make rhetorical invention a matter of individual genius and passion a matter of individual psychology.

4) Finally, Heidegger characterizes pathos (variously "passion," "affect," "mood," or "emotion") as the very condition for the possibility of rational discourse, or logos. No cynical and crowd-pleasing addition to logos, pathos is the very substance in which propositional thought finds its objects and its motivation. Without affect our disembodied minds would have no heart, and no legs to stand on. We would have no grounds for concern, no time and place for judging, no motivation to discourse at all. No doubt the priority of pathos does have a vibrant tradition in theology running from Augustine through the Christian Grand Style of the Renaissance to Luther's Reformation theology, the latter being a tradition with which Heidegger was deeply engaged during his Marburg years.[8] What Heidegger emphasizes in the tradition like none before is the fact that without others, pathos would remain unarticulated (as it does in nonhuman life) and rational discourse would never get off the ground. Here is the theme that this introduction follows in most detail: the passions are actually phenomena constitutive of social life.

Heidegger's conception of language and Mitsein are densely entwined in contemporary philosophy. Despite the reevaluation that the terms undergo over the course of Heidegger's career, language and Mitsein are essentially conceived in terms of rhetoric. Thus rhetoric, to state my broadest argument in the form of a syllogism, lies at the heart of much contemporary philosophy, especially in its "continental" and poststructuralist strains. Most immediately, SS 1924 was one of a series of courses on Aristotle that influenced generations of philosophers in Germany, including Hans-Georg Gadamer, Hannah Arendt, Walter Bröcker, Herbert Marcuse, and Ernst Tugendhat. This notable set of names is a first indication that SS 1924 exerted some force on twentieth-century German philosophy in particular. But Gadamer and Arendt are typically thought to have elaborated their most important work in the wake of *Being and Time*. In the following section I will emphasize instead the connections between ideas developed in SS 1924 and the philosophies of Gadamer and Arendt, suggesting that Heidegger's unique spin on the rhetorical tradition lies at the heart of a political philosophy articulated in the shared places and common concern of the body politic. But this is no static analysis of how things are. A true political philosophy must also analyze change. Hence the central role Heidegger gives pathos in his political philosophy—key to the art of moving people.

Why, finally, if so productive, does Heidegger drop rhetoric as the antidote to metaphysics? Why, in other words, do hermeneutics subsume rhetoric after 1924? A close reading of the course offered in this book will provide us with responses that go to the heart of Heidegger's politics, including his subsequent Nazism. SS 1924 turns out to be a complex discourse on rhetoric and politics crucial to understanding Heidegger's own life work, as well as communitarian politics broadly conceived.

I. Hermeneutics or Rhetoric?

When we move from rhetoric to hermeneutics we suffer a political and ethical loss. But this loss is not absolute. In making the move, we solidify a formal and universal method of interpretation unavailable to rhetoric practiced in ad hoc fashion as a proactive art. Second, though cast in a new guise, hermeneutics rearticulates crucial rhetorical insights. By looking briefly at the best known work of Hans-Georg Gadamer, we can see both how this gain can be maximized and the ways in which rhetoric—and Heidegger's rhetoric in particular—has left a deep impression upon Anglo-European philosophy. Moreover, in typical and instructive fashion, Gadamer downplays the political loss suffered when rhetoric gives way to hermeneutics.

It is well known that *Truth and Method* is a work indebted to Heidegger's temporal analytics of Dasein. And the rhetorical bent of Gadamer's masterwork is also no secret: he acknowledges that a review of the first edition of *Truth and Method* by the romanticist Klaus Dockhorn led to significant revisions of the second edition in a rhetorical vein.[9] Gadamer's rhetorical turn has had an afterlife, moreover, inspiring for instance Germany's top contemporary university program devoted to the discipline, the Seminar für Allgemeine Rhetorik in Tübingen. So we have Heidegger, and we have rhetoric. But what about *Heidegger's rhetoric*? Is there any evidence that Heidegger's lectures on the rhetoric of Aristotle had any lasting effects on the work of attendee Gadamer (see chapter 2)? What happens when we read *Truth and Method* with these lectures in mind? If we can plausibly identify some characteristic features of Heidegger's rhetoric residual in the work of Gadamer, then the argument for influence begins to take shape, and we can begin to see how the priority of pathos was depoliticized with the turn to hermeneutics.

Broadly conceived, Aristotle's rhetoric is the discipline that allows Heidegger to establish logos as a derivative mode of construing the world, a mode grounded in everyday, pathetic situations ("der *logos* in den *pathē* selbst seinen Boden hat" [177]).[10] This is a fundamental reversal of the philosophical hierarchy inherited from Plato, in which particular human dispositions and momentary passions only obscure the logic of good judgment. Like Heidegger, Gadamer places his philosophical hermeneutics firmly in the tradition of a Platonism—if not turned on its head, at least taken in a heretical direction. "In both rhetoric and hermeneutics," Gadamer insists, "theory is subsequent to that out of which it is abstracted; that is, to praxis."[11] And Aristotle's "anthropological foundation for the art of speech," that is his *Rhetoric*, is identified by Gadamer as a primary source of this insight.[12] As Gadamer tells the story, Heidegger broke ground when he situated Aristotle's insight in a counterhistory of transcendental philosophy and thereby revealed a new way to understand practical life. "I must have ground under my feet" [Ich muß Boden unter den Füßen haben]: this is Aristotle's imagined cry to Plato over the course of SS 1924 (37). Our everyday doings and sayings need not be abstracted in order to retain their wonder. Praxis need only be grounded and subject to time—at which point the very distinction between praxis and theory dissolves in its Platonic form.

But Plato's *Phaedrus* or Aristotle's *Rhetoric* are for Gadamer not quite enough on their own if one is to develop a modern understanding of language, even if these works are read sympathetically. Nor is Heidegger on himself the end of the story. For in his self-explanatory statements Heidegger denied what Gadamer calls "the significance of the Humanist tradition" and thus was blind to the very medium in which his most radical insights developed.[13] We will see that Heidegger does indeed provide a genealogy for his reflections on the derivative nature of rational discourse, and that genealogy is most definitely not secular humanist. Rather it is essentially theological. What the theological tradition running from Augustine through Luther to August Hermann Francke provides is an account of pathos as the ground of rational discourse (logos) and not simply its supplement. It is nevertheless useful to play out in some detail Gadamer's account of the secular humanist tradition and the sympathy he finds there with Heidegger's project. Such an account will allow us to specify later precisely where Heidegger leaves this tradition behind in his treatment of rhetoric during the course of SS 1924.

Humanism, exemplified for Gadamer in the figure of the early eighteenth-century Italian rhetorician Giambattista Vico, defended the *sensus communis* against the encroachment of Cartesian critical science. And in doing so, humanism returned in a new fashion to Aristotle's breakthrough: social phenomena are neither random nor perfectly predictable, but they are subject to a socially constituted practical knowledge, or *phronēsis*, manifest above all in the Aristotelian triad of politics, ethics, and rhetoric (see chapter 7).

> Practical knowledge, phronēsis, is another kind of knowledge. . . . Primarily, this means that it is directed towards the concrete situation. Thus it must grasp the "circumstances" in their infinite variety. This is what Vico expressly emphasizes about it. . . . The Aristotelian distinction refers to something other than the distinction between knowing on the basis of universal principles and on the basis of the concrete. Nor does he mean only the capacity to subsume the individual case under a universal category—what we call "judgment." Rather, there is a positive ethical motif involved that merges into the Roman Stoic doctrine of the sensus communis. The grasp and moral control of concrete situations require subsuming what is given under the universal—that is, the goal that one is pursuing so that the right thing may result.[14]

But the concept of the sensus communis was "emptied and intellectualized" by the German Enlightenment culminating in Kant, who made practical sense a general faculty in all men. Vico's radical concept of a "sense that founds community" was thereby digested and transformed.[15] But via Dilthey, the rhetorical conception of sensus communis would burst onto the scene once again, and as Gadamer tell the story, it would come in the form of Heidegger's historicism.

This is what Gadamer calls Heidegger's "fresh beginning." "Understanding," which is Dasein's essential mode of being according to Gadamer, is described as a composite of prejudices and projections that are always subject to change.[16] In other words fore-having, fore-sight, and fore-conception—the famous SS 1924 triad of the hermeneutic situation—establish the horizon in which our everyday doings and sayings can make sense.[17] But once realized, "sense" tends to crystallize into concept, superimposing a theoretical *telos* upon the world of multiform activity. Words would be used as simple indicators of things or fixed concepts, and human behavior could be rationalized. This is what Gadamer calls the "Enlightenment slogan," perpetuated by the likes of Habermas: "to dissolve obsolete prejudices and overcome social privileges through thought and reflection." But in Gadamer's view, the Enlightenment thinking that still dominates our technological age underestimates the "affections" that motivate the human mind, as well as the historical contingency of ideas.[18] Such historicism is also undeniably a factor for the Marburg Heidegger: "I actually see a being-there in its Being when I see it in its *history*." [Ich sehe ein Daseiendes eigentlich in seinem Sein, wenn ich es in seiner *Geschichte* sehe (35).]

Reforging Heidegger with the humanist tradition, Gadamer makes the bold claim that rational-scientific discourse is a special case of language generally conceived in terms of rhetoric.[19] And what rhetoric builds, hermeneutics understands. But this general rhetoric could never be described in terms of a purified theory, as a system of interlocking communication rules abstracted from empirical data, pace Searle or Habermas. It could never take structuralist form (Group μ) or the form of a systematic treatise on rhetorical *technē*. Aligning himself implicitly with the Marburg Heidegger, Gadamer suggests instead that rhetoric is a manifestation of human being in its historicity. It reveals the force that historically sedimented language quietly exerts on who we are and what is possible, and gives an account of what makes any particular human expression either resonant or forgettable. It is a phenomenology of language capable of relating passions, change, and nothingness to expression that would be purely instrumental. The medium in which hermeneutic understanding takes place is language, rhetorically conceived.[20] And following Heidegger, Gadamer insists that understanding comes before any pragmatic or theoretical interest. Now science's concept of objectivity appears to be a "special case" while both the human and the natural sciences can be seen "as achievements of the intentionality of universal life—i.e., of absolute historicity."[21]

But in claiming in *Truth and Method* that "understanding" and not "affect" comes before any pragmatic or theoretical interest, Gadamer overlooks a crucial element of Heidegger's Marburg project, ceding ground thereby to the very rationalists he sets out to criticize. To think in terms of "organizing a perfect and perfectly manipulated information" is to pave over the immediacy of discourse—its affective context most of all. And as Gadamer sees it, this is a turn that modern rhetoric seems to have taken, Jürgen Habermas leading the charge. But unlike Heidegger, Gadamer chooses not to reclaim for rhetoric the doctrine of affections (*Affektenlehre*) as taught by the likes of Luther or Schleiermacher. Instead he cedes that, in the age of the written word, communication no longer depends on the orator and his ability to suspend critical examination, arouse the emotions, and "carry the listener away."[22] Communication now depends more on a productive understanding, which Gadamer calls "hermeneutics." However we will see in the next section that rhetorical art according to the Marburg Heidegger in no way suspends critical judgment and certainly cannot "carry the listener away." In fact pathos provides the very ground for critical judgment (krisis), first moving the listener to be realized in some form. In other words, Heidegger might object that Gadamer's masterwork ultimately portrays rhetoric from a rationalist perspective, thereby rendering it a vulnerable and inviting target for rational reconstruction of a Habermasian bent. For only if Gadamer had already lost a fundamental understanding of rhetoric could he conclude that the sense of mutual interpenetration of rhetoric and hermeneutics had faded away, "leaving hermeneutics on its own."[23] Significantly, in our interview (chapter 2) Gadamer radically revises the pessimistic understanding of rhetoric voiced in *Truth and Method* and aligns more closely with the position Heidegger takes in SS 1924.

Heidegger's conception of language and Mitsein has become the golden goose for a communitarian political philosophy contrary to liberal individualism. But for some, communitarian thinking depends on recovering Heidegger's "more originary sense of hermeneutics" obfuscated by the likes of Gadamer and Ricoeur. This makes less sense in light of SS 1924. True, Gadamer takes Heidegger's hermeneutics ever further from its proactive origins, which as we have seen entails a certain loss. As Christopher Fynsk puts it in his introduction to Jean-Luc Nancy's *The Inoperative Community*, "the *hermeneuein* of existence . . . consists not in the interpretation of a prior meaning to which Dasein would have access, but in the opening of meaning that occurs as Dasein projects for itself a horizon of significations."[24] Hermeneutics, in other words, is not supposed to be just reception of a tradition (though it is that also), but is as well a kind of "performance" that is simultaneously the instantiation of tradition and an expression of freedom. And it is this traditional difference (or *partage des voix*) measured out in a plurality of voices that is the articulation of a community—a community logically prior to the logos in which it is expressed. SS 1924 shows that rhetoric is the discipline that most comfortably lays out possibilities for concrete being. A return to a more originary sense of rhetoric, and not hermeneutics, would with only slight adjustments provide precisely the account of performative discourse constitutive of a pluralistic community that Fynsk and Nancy seek. And what the rhetorical tradition provides any political philosophy that hermeneutics cannot is an account of how people are moved, as well as the specific institutional context in which human passions are constituted.

This brings us to another supposed champion of the communitarian cause and another student at Marburg, Hannah Arendt.

Dana Villa has argued that Arendt appropriates both Heidegger's "general description of human existence" as articulated in *Being and Time* and the distinction between authentic and inauthentic disclosedness. Arendt's innovation, according to Villa, is that she "spatializes" the distinction in such a way that the public realm—now the arena of agonistic politics—could be seen as the proper venue for authentic disclosure of who we are. Arendt's political space is contrasted to Heidegger's lonely venue of uncanny works and poetic words.[25] On Villa's reading then, Heidegger "denies a priori any relation between the disclosure of Being and *politics*," while Arendt's contribution to modern political philosophy lies precisely in affirming this relation.

SS 1924 proves Villa wrong. The lecture course in fact reveals an original Being-with obfuscated by *Being and Time*, and practically invisible in Heidegger's later work—as Villa rightly points out. Nevertheless it appears that Heidegger's reading of Aristotle leaked into Arendt's political philosophy, even though she did not arrive in body at Marburg until the winter semester of 1924 (see chapter 6). Although what Dana Villa has called the *topos* of political being is described differently by the two philosophers—Arendt's plural space indeed contradicts the more rarefied authenticity-unto-death of Heidegger's later essays—it would appear that Arendt's conditions of authentic politics is quite close to that of the Marburg Heidegger. Arendt's "speech" is for all intents and purposes, Heideggerian/Aristotelian "rhetoric."[26]

Briefly, here is where the two concepts meet. "Speech," Arendt proclaims in *The Human Condition*, "is the actualization of the human condition of plurality."[27] Without speech we might be able to assess a situation and grunt a warning to others, but we would be incapable of constituting ourselves as a particular kind of person capable of acting virtuously. For Arendt speech discloses individuals by rendering actions salient and meaningful in a life story as well as in a shared history. In the Aristotelian tradition described by Heidegger, "judicial rhetoric" is the kind of speech that similarly provides a perspective on "what has happened." To draw a classic example from Aristotle, an act (say a sacred vessel is stolen from a private house) is defined in a particular manner (theft or sacrilege) and the act is then ascribed to an agent (the man is a thief; he can be punished accordingly).[28] Though Arendt does not concentrate on legal discourse, both she and Heidegger submit that linguistic disclosure of the past helps constitute who we are. But both reject a world without freedom or a world in which we would be the self-possessed authors of our actions. We constitute and are subject to those institutions in which our acts make sense. Outside of a world with religious laws and objects, an act of sacrilege, for instance, is unthinkable.

The rhetoric of praise and blame, or *epideictic*, gets short shrift in Heidegger's course, as it does in Aristotle's text (see chapter 4 in this volume). But Heidegger does extensively gloss what he calls the heart of the discipline: "deliberative" rhetoric. Traditionally this form of logos allows an advocate addressing a political assembly to characterize a problem, lay out concrete possibilities for future action, and forge a common opinion regarding what is to be done (124–125). Arendt seems to recall Heidegger's terms when she describes the speech that allows humans to "plan for the future and foresee the needs of those who will come after them."[29] So when we test the link between Arendt and Heidegger's political philosophy outlined in SS 1924, we find one fundamental bond. Each of these basic possibilities for meaningful speech—judicial and deliberative rhetoric—reveals a political community: "Being-with." There can be no agent or patient, no speaker or hearer, unless one presumes a shared domain of past and potential meaning. And it is in Aristotle's *Rhetoric* that Being-with, or koinōnia, is given its definitive form. Gadamer and Arendt draw upon this particular Aristotle, but critical elements were also left behind—the priority of pathos first among them. To understand the importance of what has been lost, we turn now to Heidegger's odd reinvention of the *Rhetoric*.

II. Physis, Polis, and Heidegger's Style

We have recently seen a revival of interest in Aristotle's *Rhetoric*, now consistently placed alongside the Roman rhetorical works of Cicero and Quintilian.[30] The philosopher's reaction has been quick and covetous: "It is time to reclaim the *Rhetoric* as a philosophic work."[31] This is a characteristic protest of Amélie Oksenberg Rorty in her preface to a collection of essays on Aristotle's most misunderstood legacy. Eugene Garver insists in the same tone that Aristotle's *Rhetoric* be read "as a piece of philosophic inquiry, and judged by philosophic standards."[32] In fact quite a bit of attention has been given recently to Aristotle's *Rhetoric*—and most of it in the name of philosophy. But SS 1924 shows Heidegger preparing for this philosophical counterthrust: "That we have the Aristotelian *Rhetoric* is better than if we had a philosophy of language." [Daß wir die aristotelische *Rhetorik* haben, ist besser, als wenn wir eine Sprachphilosophie hätten (117).] And in a fashion so provocative that it elicits a question mark of apparent disbelief from auditor Bröcker: "the philosophers are the real Sophists" [die Philosophen sind die rechten Sophisten (136)]; this because,

Heidegger explains, philosophers are supposed to know the limits of knowledge, like the true Sophists (136). Then finally by way of sarcastic understatement: "It would be welcome if the philosophers would decide to reflect upon what it actually means to speak to others." [Ich weise nur darauf hin, daß es vielleicht angebracht wäre, wenn die Philosophen sich entschließen würden, zu überlegen, was es überhaupt heißt, zu anderen zu sprechen (169–170).] Of course the art of rhetoric is all about speaking to others.

Heidegger's reading of Aristotle flies in the face of conventions old and new, and does so in telling fashion (see chapter 3 in this volume). As passages like these show, the course is polemical and unconventional, and in it Heidegger makes claims that are far-fetched. But as is often the case with Heidegger's provocations, hasty dismissal can be a missed opportunity for thought. Such is the case, for instance, with Heidegger's holistic treatment of Aristotle's corpus. Over the three-month course Heidegger treats in holistic fashion Aristotle's *Metaphysics*, *Politics*, *Nichomachean Ethics*, *Rhetoric*, *Topics*, *De anima*, *De motu animalium*, and *Physics*. Pathos, a key term in the rhetorical tradition, provides the transfer point between social and naturo-physical phenomena. And it is this pathos at the heart of Heidegger's ontology that grounds philosophy in a new way.

The *Rhetoric* was given very little attention in late antiquity, where it was viewed as a logical tool rather than a practical or productive art. Symptomatically the editor Alexander of Aphrodisias (AD 200) situated the *Rhetoric* in the *Organon*, following the *Topics* and preceding the *Poetics*. Though preserved intact, the *Rhetoric* received equally meager attention from writers in the Roman empire and the early Middle Ages. In contrast when it resurfaced as an important text in the fifteenth century as a result of George of Trebizond's new Latin translation (1472), Aristotle's *Rhetoric* was recast as an authoritative treatise on the passions and practical wisdom. Italian humanists read it primarily for its political and moral teachings, and the first English translation (1637) was provided by the political philosopher Thomas Hobbes.[33] This is largely how we find the *Rhetoric* situated today—in the recently reexamined domain of practical reason (phronēsis), where rhetoric is purged of its sophistic ambiguities and reconstructed as a philosophy of everyday language.[34] We are now urged to "philosophize" about social phenomena, but without the scientism that would treat these phenomena as natural objects.

The *Naturwissenschaft-Geisteswissenschaft* distinction is then read back into Aristotle. Even the synthetically minded Aristotle scholar Richard McKeon underscored Aristotle's distinction between the practical human sciences, and theories of "natural" things: the first treats changeable human habits, skills, and institutions, while the second treats physical phenomena subject to precise definition and knowledge. Indeed it is a distinction that McKeon calls "sharp and unbreakable" despite the "easy analogies which had been found even in the time of Aristotle between social and physical phenomena."[35] Shattering centuries of interpretation of Aristotle while staying stubbornly in character, Heidegger takes such analogies seriously. Heidegger treats Aristotle's practical and naturo-theoretical writings holistically, and by doing so he relocates the long misplaced discipline of rhetoric. According to Heidegger's reading of Aristotle, Being-with-one-another turns out to be only one way of being among many—living and nonliving, human and nonhuman. The shared ontology of all Being, claims Heidegger, is grounded in the categories of Aristotle's *Physics* (284). The pathos of a stone allows it to become part of a wall, the pathos of a plant to grow, the pathos of an animal to perceive imminent danger and to shriek a warning to others. Unique to human pathos is a dependence on *nous poiētikos*: the human faculty that allows us to extend into every domain of being and be moved even by things that are not there in body. Thinking allows us to be with others in a manner unattainable for other animals ("In diesem Denken-daran bin ich mit ihm" [326]). Though only human being is moved to discourse, or logos, Being-moved is essential to all (*Sein-in-Bewegung*). What we share with things of all sorts is body-in-movement, a movement characterized by pathos. Heidegger sees this as one of Aristotle's most profound insights into the nature of rhetoric: Being-moved—the heart of rhetorical thought—necessarily exceeds the rational psyche because people have bodies of a certain sort. We are there, we grow and decompose, we can be damaged or excited, mobilized or dispersed. "When Being in a *soma* belongs to a living thing, then soma also belongs to the right understanding of the basic phenomenon of the pathē, and the *physikos* is disclosed in this bringing-forth." [Wenn zum Lebenden mitgehört das Sein in einem *soma*, dann gehört auch zur rechten Erfassung des Grundphänomens der *pathē* das *soma*, und der *physikos* ist mitbeteiligt an dieser Herausstellung (226).] Being-moved in a human way is thus a continuous function of physiology and shared minds. What we have here is "embodied philosophy" at its most literal.

Significantly, this aspect of Heidegger's philosophy drops out before 1927—with political consequence. Already wary of a technological orientation that posits things in the world and its inhabitants as equipment "standing-in-reserve," the Heidegger of *Being and Time* is intent on demonstrating the derivative nature of Being-in-space. "Dasein is never present-at-hand in space, not even proximally. Dasein does not fill up a bit of space as a Real Thing or item of equipment would." Indeed to talk about Dasein's real embodiment would be "ontologically inappropriate," for where we are is a matter not of substance in space, but rather of where we care to be (BT 418). More appropriate would be to talk about Dasein's essential "place." If Dasein cannot be understood by asking where it is on a spatial grid posited by modern physics; it can be understood by asking where it stands relative to everyday equipment and things of potential concern, social institutions (*das Man*) and a limit such as death: "Because Dasein as temporality is ecstatico-horizonal in its Being, it can take along with it a space for which it has made room, and it can do so factically and constantly. With regard to that space which it has ecstatically taken in, the 'here' of its current factical situation [Lage bzw. situation] never signifies a position in space, but signifies rather the leeway of the range of that equipmental totality with which it is most closely concerned—a leeway which has been opened up for it in directionality and de-severance" (BT 420).

Our brief discussion of Heidegger and Arendt suggests that this *Being and Time* "situation" is in fact a substantial development of rhetorical context and rhetorical genres: judicial, deliberative, and epideictic. But at this point I would like to highlight what drops out—namely the special materiality of human Dasein and the way that this materiality determines how we encounter others. In Heidegger's 1924 discussion of Aristotle, the extension of naturo-physical phenomena comes explicitly into question: "Must the physicist research the Being of life in all its possibilities and entire breadth, or is his subject only a particular aspect of life relative to its Being?" [Hat der *physikos* das Sein des Lebens in allen seinen Möglichkeiten und seiner ganzen Erstreckung zu erforschen, oder ist für den Physiker nur ein bestimmter Ausschnitt des Lebenden hinsichtlich seines Seins Thema? (233).] And as indicated above, Heidegger's answer is also clear: Aristotle's basic ontology is grounded in the physical categories. Moreover, these categories do not just ground individual beings as such, but social being: *Miteinandersein.*

Heidegger sets out this argument in the style that had already made him something of a cult figure by 1924. In order to get a sense of how this style works, it is helpful to take an extended look at the dense and mantralike passage in which the argument is made. Heidegger is insistent: Socrates put physis in the background when treating social phenomena, and Aristotle saw this as a fundamental mistake. Physis and *polis* are in fact essentially bound because we are there concretely for each other—simultaneously subject and object. This passage should also give readers a good sense of Heidegger's style of appropriating classical texts for his own purposes. It is clear that Heidegger is doing much more than a simple historical treatment of forgotten philosophical problems. Heidegger's revisionism puts Aristotle to immediate use, moving into a sarcastic attack on the *Lebensphilosophie* popular in Germany during the 1920s.

> Socrates advanced the project of treating the things themselves—in fact during this period general interest in the *zetein peri physeōs* slackened. People turned to the *politikē* while the *physei onta* re-

ceded into the background. But this turn was not the result of simple omission, as if the human sciences were simply studied more than the natural sciences. Rather it was a fundamental oversight. The concepts of Being-in-the-polis also have their foundation in the concepts of nature. Aristotle saw this and shifted the weight of his work initially to the investigation of physis as Being. He thereby established the foundations for an investigation of Being as such.

Our take on the characteristic Being of living things has shown us that living means Being-in-a-world. This determination now becomes *ambiguous*:

1) The Being of this living nature is determined in its *eidos* as the *dynamis* of Being-in-the-world—that is to say it is determined in the first instance as eidos, as the *determination itself of the Being of Beings* [and]

2) as *an encounter from out of this world.* The living thing is in the world then in a second sense: it belongs *to the world.* My Being is Being-in-the-world while simultaneously it belongs to the world in such a way that I can be encountered in the world by another, like a chair.

For the Greeks both are eidos. The Greeks knew nothing about the difference between an interior and an exterior viewpoint. When we consider this we gain a broader sense of the fundamental interconnection of the Being of living things. Now I would like to point out that *Being-with-one-another* has been subject to *a more precise determination*:

1) Beings with one another are Being-with-one-another in such a way that all are Being-in-the-world for themselves. *They are there in such a way that encountering another is Being-there for another, so that each Being that is for another is in the world.* The one who encounters is in the world of the encountered—there for another Being.

2) In Being-with-one-another we have with an Other the same world. Being-with-one-another is at the same time *having the same world with an Other.*

When someone writes a book on epistemology it is presupposed that pertinent questions can still be posed in the required manner.

Answers can be left up to the epistemologist himself. Now we hear that a fight rages among the philosophers whether philosophy should be "philosophy of life." One side claims that philosophy cannot be philosophy of life, the other that it must indeed be so. But "philosophy of life" is like "plant botany"! The emphatic claim that botany has to do with plants is just as strange and senseless as the reverse.

[Sokrates hat die Aufgabe, mit den Sachen selbst sich zu beschäftigen, gefördert, allerdings ließ in dieser Zeit das *zetein peri physeōs* nach, man wandte sich ab auf die *politikē*, die *physei onta* kamen in den Hintergrund. Das ist nicht ein beliebiges Versäumnis, etwa so, daß sie mehr Geistes- als Naturwissenschaften getrieben hätten, sondern es ist ein fundamentales Versehen; auch die Begriffe vom Sein-in-der-*polis* haben ihre Grundlagen in den Naturbegriffen. Aristoteles sah das und verlegte das Hauptgewicht seiner Arbeit zuerst auf die Erforschung der *physis* als Sein. Von daher hat er den Boden gewonnen für die Seinsforschung als solche.

Aus dieser Betrachtung des Seinscharakters des Lebenden haben wir gesehen: Leben besagt In-einer-Welt-sein. Diese Bestimmung wird jetzt *doppeldeutig*:

1) das Sein dieser lebenden Natur ist in seinem *eidos* bestimmt als diese *dynamis* des In-der-Welt-seins—also einmal als *eidos*, als *Seinsbestimmung selbst des Seinden.*

2) als *Begegnung aus der Welt her*: Das Lebende ist noch in einem zweiten Sinne in der Welt, im Sinn der *Weltzugehörigkeit.* Mein Sein ist In-der-Welt-sein, zugleich im zweiten Sinne in der Welt als zu ihr gehörig, so zwar, daß ich in der Welt für einen anderen begegnen kann, wie ein Stuhl.

Für die Griechen ist beides *eidos*, der Grieche kennt nicht den Unterschied zwischen äußerer und innerer Betrachtung. Dadurch ergeben sich fundamentale Zusammenhänge des Seins des Lebens im weiteren Sinne. Ich weise darauf hin, daß das *Miteinandersein* jetzt eine *schärfere Bestimmung* erfahren hat:

1) Miteinandersein sind solche Seienden miteinander, die jedes für sich In-der-Welt-sein sind. *Das Einanderbegegnen ist Füreinanderdasein, so, daß jedes Seiende, das für das andere ist, in der*

> *Welt ist.* Das Begegnende ist in der Welt des Begegneten, ist da für ein anderes Sein.
>
> 2) Im Miteinandersein haben wir miteinander dieselbe Welt. Miteinandersein ist zugleich: *miteinander dieselbe Welt haben.*
>
> Wenn man ein Buch über Erkenntnistheorie schreibt, ist das Voraussetzung. Ob dann die Fragen noch in der üblichen Weise gestellt werden können, kann man den Erkenntnistheoretikern selbst zu entscheiden überlassen. Dann herrscht heute, wie wir hören, ein großer Streit unter den Philosophen, ob die Philosophie "Lebensphilosophie" sein soll. Von der einen Seite wird behauptet, die Philosophie kann nicht Lebensphilosophie sein, von der anderen, sie muß es ja sein. "Lebensphilosophie" ist wie: "Botanik der Pflanzen"! Die emphatische Behauptung, die Botanik habe es mit Pflanzen zu tun, ist genau so komisch und unsinnig wie das Gegenteil (240-242).]

First to a point about the form of this passage—and its content. What can seem in this passage like tautological nonsense actually performs a critical role in the development of Heidegger's argument about the interconnection of physis and polis. In one respect the argument is classically antiskeptical: to question the existence of "other minds" is nonsensical. If one is situated in a language and a world so deeply that the question can even be asked, then de facto the question has been answered. Or to put the argument back into Heidegger's phenomenological terms, political community and "I" are "equiprimordial" because any subject position I can take presupposes the world of common concern in which and from which I distinguish myself. I am there in the world going about my business (the interior, subjective view) and there in the world as the business of others (the exterior, objective view). But here the antiskeptical argument takes a new stylistic turn. For these are not two moments that can be distinguished in time, nor can they be adequately represented in the spatial configuration implied in a sentence that links two predicated subjects with an additive conjunction (I am this *and* I am that). Hence Heidegger's stylistic dilemma. What Heidegger wants to characterize is the inherent multiplicity in the One, the simultaneity of being active and being passive, the nature of a life at the same time constructive and constructed. Such could be expressed by the Greeks in the middle voice, as many critics of instrumental thinking from Nietzsche to Derrida have pointed out. But despite his reverence for ancient Greek as one of the only two languages in which one could truly think, Heidegger was intent upon exploiting possibilities in the German language to reach new and supposedly more authentic modes of expression. Among the possibilities Heidegger had at his disposal were variations on the verb *sein* and a German language that allows one to nominalize agent and patient in a way that expresses their interanimation: "Das Begegnende ist in der Welt des Begegneten, ist da für ein anderes Sein." Heidegger experimented with these morphological, syntactical, and poetic-associative possibilities throughout his career, with mixed results. But in this case his stylistic stutterings allow him to produce a discussion of Miteinandersein achievable by no other means. This particular achievement, however, has been dramatically misunderstood.

III. Heidegger the Humanist?

At the heart of debate about the politics of poststructuralism lay Heidegger's appropriation of the Greek middle voice and its Derridian consequences. Pressing questions were raised: Does the middle voice leave us completely without political agency and without the ability to recognize ourselves as both subject and object of ethical discourse? Does it lead to bureaucratic apathy—a conservative resignation before the juggernaut of linguistic institutions that call us into being? Or is discoursing in the middle voice inherently progressive insofar as it deconstructs the grammar of activity and passivity, thereby undermining the oppressive illusion of the liberal subject—a subject assumed to be author of his own actions, master of the universe, and perpetrator of his own misfortune? Jacques Derrida, Michel Foucault, Pierre Bourdieu, Paul de Man, J. Hillis Miller, Vincent Pecora, Luc Ferry, and Alain Renaut among others weighed in on this debate about humanism and the death of the subject in the last three decades, and the late Heidegger's discourse on language became both a topic of debate and locus classicus for a (failed?) middle voice. But regardless of their position, advocates on both sides presented Heidegger's discourse on language as the attempt to dissolve passion and action, subject and object. In light of our stylistic reading of SS 1924, we can now see this as a serious error.

Here is Jacques Derrida in 1968 on the middle voice—a passage from *Margins of Philosophy* designed to illustrate a crucial claim about his notorious neologistic gerund, *différance*. It is a key passage insofar as it both recalls Heidegger in no uncertain terms and misreads him famously. And in what seems to be an unintentional, but for our purposes fortuitous allusion, Derrida actually exemplifies the modern middle voice by way of the French translation of *kinēsis* or the German *Bewegung*: *mouvance*.

> Because it brings us close to the infinitive and active kernel of *différer*, *différance* (with an *a*) neutralizes what the infinitive de-

> notes as simply active, just as *mouvance* in our language does not simply mean the fact of moving, of moving oneself or of being moved. No more is resonance the act of resonating. We must consider that in the usage of our language the ending *-ance* remains undecided *between* the active and the passive. And we will see why that which lets itself be designated *différance* is neither simply active nor simply passive, announcing or rather recalling something like the middle voice, saying an operation that is not an operation, an operation that cannot be conceived either as passion or as the action of a subject on an object, or on the basis of the categories of agent or patient, neither on the basis of nor moving towards any of these *terms*. For the middle voice, a certain nontransitivity, may be what philosophy, at its outset, distributed into an active and a passive voice, thereby constituting itself by means of this repression.[36]

No doubt phrases that turn around "announcing" and "recalling" do seem to imitate formally philosophical claims in the rhetoric of late Heideggerian phenomenology—as Vincent Pecora suggests.[37] And Derrida's description of a nontransitive middle voice both inactive and impassive does seem to be the kind of "hyperbolic antihumanism" that Luc Ferry and Alain Renaut attribute to French Heideggerians.[38] However, SS 1924 shows Heidegger to be at most the hyperbolic antihumanist's distant relative.

It is said that Heidegger's "Letter on Humanism" (1946) opened the way for French philosophy of the 1960s—a philosophy that would finally decenter the world from man's point of view and announce thereby the death of the self-constituting subject extending from Descartes to Sartre. It would be the essential antihumanist text. And indeed the "Letter on Humanism" does recall Nietzsche and foreshadow Derrida in its condemnation of a subject/object logic, announcing "the liberation of language from grammar into a more original essential framework reserved for thought and poetic creation."[39] It is a text that claims that ethical evaluations multiply only when original thinking "comes to an end";[40] a text skeptical of man's power to master his environment and critical of Occidental man's reductive *nomomachia* (for example, man = rational animal). Instead of describing language as either a tool or a representation, it is in his "Letter on Humanism" that Heidegger famously proclaims that "language is the house of Being," simultaneously identifying language as a more essential ethical medium (*ethos*, means "abode" or "dwelling place" [Heraclitus Frag. 119]) and describing how man "is" only in being called to language, in being beside himself in ecstasy, in being Other. As Ferry and Renaut argue, it seems only a short step from decentering man, as Heidegger does, to a radical antihumanism that describes in apathetic terms how we come to be. And without agency, Pecora or the neoliberals would add in a Kantian vein, there could be no relationship between a self-determining subject and potentially universal values, and hence no ethical discourse at all. So with the destruction of the subject, the intersubjective dissolves as well, along with the public space in which we hammer out a common destiny. Thus Ferry and Renaut can sarcastically remark that Heideggerian antihumanist philosophy "has some difficulty accommodating itself to the newly rediscovered reference to human rights"—a remark directed at the likes of Althusser, Foucault, Derrida, Bourdieu, Lacan, Lyotard, Lefort, and Castoriadis.[41] But as we have already begun to see, SS 1924 provides a description of humanity and ethical discourse that cannot be called in good faith either neo-Kantian or proto-Derridian. If anything, Heidegger's work in 1924 would be neo-Aristotelian and protocommunitarian. And it is in his middle voice discussion of the kinetic ambiguity of Being-in-the-world that Heidegger comes into his own.

Returning to the long passage above, we pick up an unanswered question: What are then the "concepts of nature" in which the concepts of Being in the polis have their foundation? And do these natural concepts established in Aristotle's *Physics* submit willingly to Heidegger's stylistic liberties? Not only do they, but they actually seem to anticipate various creative forms of their own abuse. The key lies in the complex relationship between *pathēsis* and *poiētikos*, whose interanimation defines motion (kinēsis) for Aristotle. It is a relationship that Heidegger only addresses explicitly during his final lecture on the last day in July 1924, but one that he says "reaches into the true center of the Greek view of the world and life." [Die Bestimmung der *poiēsis* und *pathēsis* reichen hinein in das eigentliche Zentrum der griechischen Welt- und Lebensbetrachtung. Darin liegt, daß das Verständnis dessen, wie die Griechen das Sein aufgefaßt haben, daran hängt, wie man die *kinēsis* versteht (326).] And it is this passage that in retrospect seems to spark Heidegger's deepest insights into the relationship between rhetoric, politics, and Being as such. Here is the relevant passage from the *Physics,* first in Greek, then in the Hardie/Gaye English translation, and finally in Heidegger's German:

> 1) "Kinēsis: entelecheia tou dynamei poiētikou kai pathētikou he toiouton" (202b23).
>
> 2) "Alteration is the fulfilment of the alterable as alterable (or, more scientifically, the fulfillment of what can act and what can be acted on, as such)."
>
> 3) "Bewegung ist immer Bewegung eines Bewegten, das durch ein anderes Bewegendes bewegt wird." (322)

Here in even greater relief is an example of Heidegger's unique morpho-syntactical stylistics and its innovative role in the appropriation of Aristotle's philosophy. Once again unable to exploit the middle voice construction of the Greek, Heidegger recreates the ambiguity of activity and passivity in three signature steps. First, to one of Heidegger's favorite German roots, *weg* (way), is added the prefix *be* that indicates change undergone. Then *bewegen* is morphed through four variations: a passive verb form *bewegt wird*, and three forms of the verb's nominalization: *Bewegung*, *Bewegen*, and *Bewegendes*. And these three terms indicate respectively apparent neutrality (motion), a passive object (the moved), and an active subject (the mover). But by uniting different Greek terms—*kinēsis, dynamis, poiētikos,* and *pathētikos*—in one German root, Heidegger makes a strong stylistic point that one can make grammatically in Greek: passivity and activity are fundamentally interanimate. Heidegger then underscores this point when he ambiguously qualifies the thing moved as that which is moved by another mover (*ein anderes Bewegendes*)—not *a* mover but *another* mover. So is the moved also a mover or is it moved by a mover that is its Other? Significantly, this question is left unanswered. Finally the definitional copula is used in a nearly but not quite vacuous manner: "Bewegung ist Bewegung." What this does is immediately confound our expectations about Aristotelian definition that we have inherited from his scholastic interpreters: a definition need not describe a thing in terms of *genus* and *differentia specifica* ("Man is a featherless biped") nor must one assume that the thing to be defined (*definiens*) is somehow distinct from that which defines it (*definiendum*). So in this case Heidegger makes the point emphatically and repeatedly that a thing that moves should not be determined in its Being according to the degree to which it participates (*methexis*) in motion, motion in turn understood as existing like a Platonic Idea beside the world of things human and natural. Instead kinēsis should be understood as a fundamental way that Dasein *is* ("Die *kinēsis* ist eine Weise des Seins des Daseienden selbst" [288]).

Heidegger would later pit a germanized middle voice against the illusion of a purely descriptive definition by leaving out the copula altogether. His late essay on language follows up on the impersonal *es gibt* by simply saying, "die Sprache spricht," apparently inviting neoliberals to condemn with even more force his disregard for agency. For if language speaks and not people, then crucial liberal-democratic ideals such as consent and free discussion seem foreclosed. But read with SS 1924 in view, even this radicalization by Heidegger preempts the liberal critique. In his essay entitled "Language" (1959) Heidegger warns us:

> If attention is fastened exclusively on human speech, if human speech is taken simply to be the voicing of the inner man, if speech so conceived is regarded as language itself, then the nature

> of language can never appear as anything but an expression and an activity of man. But human speech, as the speech of mortals, is not self-subsistent. The speech of mortals rests in its relation to the speaking of language.[42]

So language does speak, finally. But humankind also speaks insofar as we "listen" and "respond" (*ent-sprechen*) to the jarring linguistic difference (*Unter-schied*) that calls things into the world.[43] Compare with this passage from SS 1924 on the rhetor as speaking animal:

> When the Greeks say man is a living thing that speaks they do not mean that in a physiological sense, that he produces a particular sound. Instead man is a living thing *that has his authentic Dasein in dialogue and discourse.* The Greeks exist in discourse; the rhetor is the one who has actual power over Dasein. *Rhētorikē peithous demiourgos*: Being able to speak makes possible the actual authority I have to persuade people—to determine how people are with one another.
>
> [Wenn die Griechen sagen: Der Mensch ist ein Lebendes, das spricht, so meinen sie das nicht im physiologischen Sinne, daß er bestimmte Laute von sich gibt, sondern: Der Mensch ist ein Lebendes, das *im Gespräch und in der Rede sein eigentliches Dasein hat.* Die Griechen existierten in der Rede. Der Rhetor ist derjenige, der die eigentliche Macht über das Dasein hat: *Rhētorikē peithous demiourgos*, das Redenkönnen ist diejenige Möglichkeit, in der ich über die Überzeugung der Menschen, wie sie miteinander sind, die eigentliche Herrschaft habe (108).]

It is worth comparing these passages in terms of the role Heidegger attributes to the subject, and for documentary purposes as well. That is to say, the comparison helps us answer a pressing question raised when we try to separate Heidegger's philosophy circa 1924 from his interpretation of ancient philosophy. Throughout this introduction I have naturally tried to distinguish between what Heidegger says and what Heidegger says Aristotle says. I have done this according to scholarly convention: noting a shift in tense, vocabulary (say from Greek to German), or person (say from "they" to "I"), locating conceptual and historical consistencies or inconsistencies (Aristotle could not be a *Lebensphilosoph*), and of course looking for the points at which Heidegger himself says that he is doing something innovative. But one looks for these latter points in vain. Nowhere in SS 1924 does Heidegger stop explicitly to disagree with Aristotle and set himself apart on some conceptual point. Quite the contrary; the very last utterance is "It is worth nothing to say something new; it is only worth saying that which the Ancients already knew." [Es gilt nicht Neues zu sagen, sondern das zu sagen, was die Alten schon meinten (329).] Aristotle is in fact presented over the course of SS 1924 as an object of adoration: everything one would want to find in him is there already. Plato on the other hand is cast as villain. And Heidegger's passionate assessment of both hero and villain seems characteristic of his pedagogy at the time. It is when he moves on to subsequent projects that Heidegger's affect seems to change, the ax falling on former favorites. In the very next semester (WS 1924–25) Heidegger was lecturing enthusiastically on Plato's dialogues and as is well known, both Plato and Aristotle wound up playing villainous roles in the history of the forgetting of Being (metaphysics). But of course Heidegger's claim that he had said nothing not already said by the Ancients is merely an intellectual conceit; Heidegger's appropriation of Aristotle actually verges on the cavalier. *Ousia* is Dasein? What, after all, is more Heideggerian than this?

Separated by thirty-five years, these analogous passages show concretely how Heidegger appropriates the Greek view of language and develops his own complex understanding of agency. In both passages Heidegger approaches the issue by stating explicitly what language is not: namely a physiological function that produces the sounds or utterances (*Laute*) treated by linguistic science. Nor is language a tool that man uses to express his thoughts and feelings, externalizing what is internal. Both passages then turn on the pronouncement that human beings speak insofar as they can hear, that human being is in language and not the other way around: "The Greeks exist in discourse;" "The speech of mortals rests in its relation to the speaking of language." This is not to say that the two passages are identical. The first passage is put in terms of the Greeks, the second in universal terms. The first is concerned with living, existing, and Being-there in discourse, the second with language and Being-unto-death. The second was written after the meaning of being was grounded in Being and no longer in Dasein. The first was written before this, Heidegger's *Kehre*. So it is no surprise that the passage from SS 1924 can summon the power that the rhetor holds over both Dasein and Miteinandersein while the passage from 1959 has an air of *Gelassenheit*, or detachment. But it is nevertheless a mistake to describe the (Heideggerian) middle voice as "an operation that cannot be conceived either as passion or as the action of a subject on an object, or on the basis of the categories of agent or patient, neither on the basis of nor moving towards any of these *terms*," as Derrida might have. For although human being is in language and not the other way around, passion and action, subject and object, agent and patient are there as constructed and interanimate terms. In 1924 a subject can act insofar as the shared language in which that subject is constituted presents possibilities for further movement. And when Heidegger claims in 1959 that "the speech of mortals resides in its relation to the speaking of language," he says precisely the same thing. Whether in ancient Greece or elsewhere, a speaking being can size up an immediate mood, redescribe the world in creative and persuasive terms, come to a radical decision (given the circumstances), and act in concert upon it. In 1924 the rhetor illustrates this role for Heidegger, in 1959 the poet. No doubt this change does not come without losing sight of the institutional weight of politics in everyday life, the physis of the polis. But in any case Heidegger's experiment with a German middle voice in no way kills the author. Rather it describes in new terms how the author is rhetorically constituted.

Now that Heidegger's middle voice has been distinguished from its antihumanist echo, we are ready to understand the special materiality of Being-with that lies at the intersection of physis and polis, and to focus once again upon his rediscovery of a profound pathos at the heart of the rhetorical tradition. Let us remember that Heidegger was working on the "political body" at a moment in German intellectual history run through by the Naturwissenschaft/Geisteswissenschaft distinction. Once again, this is a distinction that divides the practical human sciences from theories of natural things, the first treating changeable human habits, skills, and institutions, the second physical phenomena subject to precise definition and knowledge. It was a distinction Heidegger thought overextended, despite the intellectual debt he felt toward those who promoted the distinction: Dilthey and Husserl. To say that the Ancients favored Geisteswissenschaft over Naturwissenschaft would be not only anachronistic, as Heidegger indicates in the long passage cited above, but indicative of a fundamental mistake. This mistake is put in relief when Heidegger asks a scientific materialist, a humanist, and a true Aristotelian "physicist" the question, "What does a house look like?"—a question, ingeniously chosen to interrogate the very kind of thing that lies at the intersection of supposedly autonomous natural and human worlds.

Heidegger would agree with critics of scientism such as Dilthey and Husserl that it is incorrect to construe bodies of any kind merely in terms of material substance—where a house would be described only in terms of stone, brick, and wood—or in terms of pure mathematical extension, surface area, and weight. In fact Heidegger warns us, "When we translate soma with 'body' we must be aware that for the Greeks *corporeality* did not mean materiality. 'Soma' means instead a particular *obtrusiveness* of a being, a being-there . . . that belongs to me, stands immediately available to me, is there for me in its specific obtrusiveness and self-evidence." [Wenn wir *soma* mit 'Körper' übersetzen, so ist zu beachten, daß *Körperlichkeit* für den Griechen nicht Stofflichkeit oder Materialität bedeutet, sondern *soma* meint eine eigentümliche *Aufdringlichkeit* eines

Seienden, eines Daseienden . . . ein Seiendes, das mir gehört, zu meiner Verfügung steht, was für mich in dieser Aufdringlichkeit und Selbstverständlichkeit da ist (28).] But neither can a house be accurately described merely as it presents itself to us, in its eidos—what I am calling the "humanist" description—being that Heidegger defines "eidos" in the following terms: " 'what is seen; what is sighted'; the 'appearance'; that which 'makes a being stand out'; what I see and determine as Being-there uniquely on hand. If it distinguishes itself as a chair, it is a chair for the Greeks." ["was gesehen, gesichtet wird," das "Aussehen," das "Sichausnehmen" eines Seienden. Was ich hier sehe und als daseiend eigenständig vorhanden feststelle, nimmt sich aus wie ein Stuhl, ist—für den Griechen—also ein Stuhl (33).] This humanist perspective would only give us, for instance, a shelter in which we seek protection from harmful elements such as wind, rain, and heat (205).

So in Heideggerian terms the true Aristotelian physicist turns out to be the one whose very rendering of the house in its self-presentation reveals whence it has come materially, practically, and conceptually speaking. ("Derjenige ist der rechte *physikos*, der das Haus so anspricht, daß er es anspricht auf das Aussehen, das in sich selbst Bezug hat auf das, woraus das Haus besteht" [205].) With this definition in mind we finally get a pointed answer to the question, "What does a house look like?" We also see a fine example of Heidegger as *rhētor poiētikos* realizing a body of Greek philosophical work in his unique language of phenomenology. It runs as follows: A house appears in wood, stone and brick, so as to produce the necessary protection and shelter; it is a "being-built" carried out in light of a shelter being there. ("das Aussehen, *eidos*, dieses Hauses in Holz, Steinen, Ziegeln und dieses wegen der Schaffung des benötigten Schutzes, des Obdachs (ein Gebautsein, das geführt wird im Hinblick darauf, daß da sein soll das *skepasma*") [205].) Material is construed in terms of its realization in a thing (for example, not merely "wood" but a "wooden chair" or "wooden door") and human intention is construed only as it moves into concrete form. In short, we don't envision an abstract house as such, but rather some wooden or brick house, say, in some particular place. Material is realized as it takes shape (pathētikos) and the realization takes place in becoming concrete (poiētikos).

Thus Heidegger sums up Aristotelian physics: "The *Being of nature* as it presents itself to us is not determined solely in material, but rather *in its Being-moved.*" [Das *Sein der Natur* ist in seinem Aussehen bestimmt nicht einfach durch die *hylē*, sondern *primär durch das Bewegtsein* (205).] And because material things must always be construed in terms of a human world and the human world in terms of its materiality, Aristotle's "nature" is everywhere, as is the movement that it embodies. Heidegger thus deconstructs the Naturwissenschaft/Geisteswissenschaft distinction by way of a return to Aristotle. Moreover, Heidegger realizes that this general description of nature in motion has radical consequences for any discussion of moving people—a traditional goal of rhetoric, along with pleasing and teaching (*movere, delectare, docere*). If one wishes to know what means of persuasion are available to us as rhētor poiētikos, the *pathē* must be considered in a human context. And pathē are not merely psychological emotions that unhappily rule those animal-like individuals who suffer from insufficiently trained minds. They are not abstract (there is no such thing as pure fear, detached from a person), nor are they simply physical-material alterations ("boiling blood," or a "cold sweat"). Rather the pathē indicate possible ways of being-moved that tie humans in a unique way to their embodiment. They do so not by providing a definite material body upon which to work, but rather by determining the possibilities for moving about a shared world:

> A Greek does not see a line in itself—instead *gramma* is always the limit of a surface, surface the limit of a body. The surface has no Being without the body—here again we have inseparability. So also the eidos of fear draws primarily upon a body's condition. The difference lies in the fact that the particular condition of the body (being, say, brown or scratched) plays no role in mathematical inseparability, while for the pathē Being in such and such a condition is essential. Both are *logoi enyloi*, but in quite different senses of the term.
>
> This is the foundation upon which, in the *Rhetoric*, the pathē are considered with respect to eidos. What is important is that Aristotle does not achieve the basic determination of a living thing from physiological considerations. The eidos of the pathē is a disposition toward other humans, a Being-in-the-world.
>
> [Der Grieche sieht eine Linie nicht primär an sich, sondern *gramma* ist immer die Grenze einer Fläche, Fläche die Grenze des Körpers, die Fläche hat kein Sein ohne den Körper—also auch hier ein Nicht-abgetrennt-werden-Können. So hat auch das *eidos* des Fürchtens die primäre Bezogenheit auf ein Sichbefinden des Leibes. Der Unterschied liegt darin, daß die bestimmte Beschaffenheit der *somata* bei der mathematischen Nicht-Abtrennbarkeit keine Rolle spielt, etwa das Braun- oder Zerkratztsein des Körpers, während für die *pathē* das so und so beschaffene Sein wesentlich ist. Beide sind *logoi enyloi*, aber in einem ganz verschiedenen Sinn.
>
> Dies ist der Boden für die Betrachtungsart der *pathē* in der "Rhetorik" hinsichtlich des *eidos*. Wichtig ist, daß Aristoteles die

> Grundbestimmung eines Lebenden nicht gewinnt aus physiologischen Betrachtungen. Das *eidos* der *pathē* ist ein Sichverhalten zu anderen Menschen, ein In-der-Welt-sein (206–207).]

Heidegger's treatment of pathos in his 1924 course thus marks a turning point in the history of modern philosophy and in the history of the rhetorical tradition as well. As Heidegger states explicitly in *Being and Time*, the second book of Aristotle's *Rhetoric* "must be taken as the first systematic hermeneutic of the everydayness of Being with one another," and SS 1924 is where this discovery was made public for the first time. Here one finds worked out in detail Heidegger's famous *Being and Time* treatment of mood, fear, and anxiety and their role in grounding the theoretical attitude, and it is this portion of *Being and Time* that has spawned important works in the phenomenology of perception and the philosophy of emotions. But as one might expect, Heidegger's treatment of pathos in 1924 and in *Being and Time* is no wholesale appropriation of the traditional discourse codified by the Stoics, wherein emotions are conditions of the soul or the psyche. Nor is pathos ancillary to rational human discourse, as the Ciceronian tradition would have it. According to Heidegger, Aristotle's discussion of the pathē treats "the *disposition of the living in his world,* how he stands to something, how he lets something affect him." The affects indeed play "a fundamental role in the determination of Being-in-the-world, of Being with and to others." [Diese *pathē,* "Affekte" sind nicht Zustände des Seelischen, es handelt sich um eine *Befindlichkeit des Lebenden in seiner Welt*, in der Weise, wie er gestellt ist zu etwas, wie er eine Sache sich angehen läßt. Die Affekte spielen eine fundamentale Rolle bei der Bestimmung des Seins-in-der-Welt, des Seins mit und zu anderen (122).] Heidegger thus rearticulates a neglected moment in the rhetorical tradition in which pathos goes beyond a psychology of the autonomous subject. Aristotelian pathos, he argues in his unique phenomenological language, serves as the very foundation for logos, or social discourse.

IV. The Priority of Pathos

Supposedly volatile and even blinding, the emotions have always been treated with caution by those who would hail the virtues of rational discourse aimed at truth. And since Plato such caution is the symptom of a profoundly divisive political philosophy separating experts from the masses. As Socrates suggests in the *Gorgias*, Plato's famous diatribe against rhetorical art, the rhetorician might have some luck arguing to the ignorant about something like the causes of health and sickness, but among those who know, the diagnosis of a trained doctor will carry more weight.

However, this is not simply because of the doctor's authoritative character (ethos) or an ability to excite listeners via pathos. Rather the doctor is more convincing because he is familiar with the technical domain at issue, and based on this knowledge, the doctor can construct a reasonable verbal depiction that corresponds to the facts in a self-evident manner. The doctor's argument is thus ideally transparent, and only convincing insofar as it is aimed at equals and reveals the true order of nature. So ultimately the Platonic scientist persuades his colleagues of nothing, moves them nowhere. What he does is illuminate the truth by means of self-negating logos, thus making the foundation upon which he and his colleagues already stand that much more secure. The sophistic rhetorician on the other hand "has no need to know the truth about things but merely to discover a technique of persuasion, so as to appear among the ignorant to have more knowledge than the expert" (459c). And as the Roman rhetoricians would later insist, the most powerful persuasive technique entails manipulating the passions of a mass audience.

In typical Roman fashion, Cicero acknowledges that it is important for a man involved in civic affairs to give human emotions voice, but only in order to make proofs exciting to those who might otherwise remain apathetic. As Cicero expresses in *De oratore* through the character of Antonius, intellectual understanding might have a direct line to the truth, but that line will usually remain untapped unless some external motivating force is applied. Thus a civic leader must work the emotions of his colleagues and subjects, and eloquent speech provides the means to do so. In the words of Antonius, "That passionate style searches out an arbitrator's emotional side rather than his understanding, and that side can only be reached by diction that is rich, diversified and copious, with animated delivery to match. Thus concise or quiet speakers may inform an arbitrator, but cannot excite him, on which excitement everything depends" (2.52.214). Eloquence is more powerful than a dry appeal to the facts, and thus it often is the only means of persuasion available, even to the well-meaning orator. Quintilian would reluctantly defend eloquence two generations later with the following words: "Appeals to emotion are necessary if there are no other means for securing the victory of truth, justice and the public interest" (*Institutio oratoria* 6.1.7).

Obviously lurking in the Roman defense of eloquence is the fear that emotional appeals present a danger to civil society. Indeed Cicero asserts through the voice of Catulus that an orator can be trained to manipulate human emotions for his own ends, rather than for the general good. Note the language of seduction, which quickly turns to aggression.

> When setting about a hazardous and important case, in order to explore the feelings of the tribunal, I engage wholeheartedly in a

> consideration so careful, that I scent out with all possible keenness their thoughts, judgments, anticipations and wishes, and the direction in which they seem likely to be led away most easily by eloquence. If they surrender to me, and as I said before, of their own accord lean towards and are prone to take the course in which I am urging them on, I accept their bounty and set sail for that quarter which promises something of a breeze. If however an arbitrator is neutral and free from predisposition, my task is harder, since everything has to be called forth by my speech, with no help from the listener's character. But so potent is that Eloquence, rightly styled, by an excellent poet, "soulbending sovereign of all things," that she can not only support the sinking and bend of the upstanding, but, like a good and brave commander, can even make prisoner a resisting antagonist (2.44.186–187).

Cynical sentiment such as this makes it seem plausible to Quintilian that Athenians actually tried to forbid emotional appeals in the lawcourts, futile though that seems. And Quintilian has no doubt that philosophers deemed susceptibility to emotion a vice, thinking it "immoral that the judge should be distracted from the truth by an appeal to his emotions and that it is unbecoming for a good man to make use of vicious procedure to serve his ends" (6.1.7). So logical reason by itself escapes the common man, and a thoughtless appeal to the emotions of an audience is subject to abuse. The Roman solution to this dilemma was to add pathos to logos, to join reason and eloquence—and this by sheer fiat. Perhaps the most influential statement to this effect is furnished by Cicero in the opening pages of *De inventione*: Since "wisdom in itself is silent and powerless to speak," wisdom in the absence of eloquence is useless. What is needed "if a commonwealth is to receive the greatest possible benefit" is *ratio atque oratio*, powerful reasoning allied with powerful speech.[44] So an appeal to emotions is considered unavoidable in the real world, but logical reason has a monopoly on the prestige of truth. Hence logos and pathos must be joined as a pragmatic compromise oriented toward the true and the common good. But this compromise and its orientation are by no means necessary: rather it is a posteriori and contingent upon the arduous training in virtue expected of a Roman citizen. One should read, say, the *Institutio Oratoria* and be convinced thereby that an appeal to emotions should keep the true and the good in mind. Weak motivation indeed.

Even today, those who would wish to extricate logos from pathos concede that in the real world when arguing before real people it is often best that the two sides of discourse be bound. Commenting on the "ethical dimension of Aristotelian Rhetoric" for Rorty's anthology, Troels

Engberg-Pedersen expresses this sentiment in typically condescending fashion: "Since he is addressing the many, the accomplished orator must . . . be concerned with creating an emotional state (pathos) in his audience." "There is nothing intrinsically obnoxious in this," Engberg-Pedersen continues, "as long as one remembers that these various strategies are adopted within a general framework of *Wahrheitsfindung* but are also addressed to people who are like most human beings, with hardly more than a general understanding of the matter and with all the normal moral failings." The strategy of eliciting pathos is thus "regrettably necessary" when a mass audience is involved. When not, one may presume, the account of human emotion often added to rational discourse as a pragmatic afterthought may be unceremoniously dropped.[45] The priority of logos over pathos thus corresponds to the Enlightenment priority of knowledge over belief, rationality over the irrational. And despite Aristotle's similar denigration of pathos in his treatise on rhetoric, it is Aristotle whom Heidegger uses to overturn precisely this prejudice.

Like Plato before him and like those who followed in the wake of Cicero and Quintilian, Aristotle condemns in the strongest possible terms an art of speaking that would neglect logical argument—the "body" of persuasion—in favor of "matters external to the subject" such as human emotion: "Verbal attack and pity and anger and such emotions of the soul do not relate to fact but are appeals to the juryman." As such an emotional appeal warps the outcome of a court case or a debate in the assembly. So that, in the words of a famous Aristotelian analogy, to appeal to the emotions of a jury in order to stimulate clear judgment is "as if someone made a straightedge rule crooked before using it" (*Rhetoric* 1354a). In the first chapter of book 1 at least, Aristotle's conception of rhetorical art seems clear and essentially Platonic. But Heidegger finds a very different Aristotle in book 2, where pathos provides the very condition for the possibility of judgment, or krisis. In fact pathos is a critical concern for nearly a month of Heidegger's lecture course, a topic opened with the following promise: "With the demonstration of the fundamental role that the pathē play in *krinein*, we realize at the same time the possibility of seeing more concretely the ground of logos itself." [Mit dem Aufweis dieser fundamentalen Rolle der *pathē* im *krinein* selbst bekommen wir zugleich die Möglichkeit, den Boden des *logos* selbst konkreter zu sehen (169).] The pathē are no mere afterthought. They are, one could say, before-thought.

Heidegger situates pathos in conjunction with doxa, a term usually translated into English as "belief." As Heidegger describes it, doxa reveals authentic being-with-one-another in the world ("Die *doxa* ist die *eigentliche Entdecktheit des Miteinanderseins in-der-Welt*" [149]). It is a pretheoretical "being-for" (*Dafürsein*), a "being-positioned" relative to the thing ("ein

Gestelltsein zu der Sache"). Doxa is characterized by a particular kind of protolinguistic disposition or nonreflective perspective (*Ansicht*): that of "Yes" ("Ja-sagen . . . kein Untersuchen, Reflektieren" [136–137]). For example Thales, by saying "yes" in some preconscious way to the water surrounding him, fashioned out of doxa the first theoretical ontology: the *archē* of Being is water. Not yet a fully realized mind-set, doxa might seem a simple way of being which we could share with other animals. And indeed, anticipating his *Being and Time* criticism of Dasein fallen into the "They," Heidegger warns us in 1924 that the seductive power of the Other constituted in doxa can be strong, and what should be a fundamental affirmation of our being-in-the-world can be flattened into received opinion. This is where we return, in a certain undesirable sense, to a nonhuman state. What makes doxa a distinctly human revelation of being is its provisional status, its "openness" (*Offenheit*), its "yes" *that could always be otherwise* ("Es könnte auch anders sein" [137]). And it is pathos that provides doxa with dynamism. As we just saw, the Roman compromise assumes that enlightened humanity would communicate via pure logos in a perfect world, leaving behind the pathē for good. Heidegger sees this fantasy as wildly misguided. If we could imagine living in a world without pathos, that world would leave anything but pure reason behind. Without human emotion what we would be left with is apathy and unexamined belief. And without the dynamism that only pathos can provide, doxa would remain frozen and inarticulate. It is pathos and pathos alone that draws logos out of doxa.

No doubt the capacity for speech resides already in doxa, as does the possibility that one can change one's mind, see things from another perspective (hence doxa is already a way of being beyond inarticulate animals):

> Doxa is thus set out as the ground and motive for *speaking-with-one-another, negotiating-with-one-another*. For although it has a certain fixity, in doxa still lies the possibility of speaking about one's orientation. It could be otherwise. The tendency of doxa is to leave discussion open. The pathos—a negotiation over doxa—is always latent; in the doxa a bringing-to-language is always ready to spring forth. The doxa is precisely that out of which speaking-with-one-another emerges, from which it takes its motivation, and at the same time it is that which is itself negotiated. The doxa is thus ground, source, and motive for speaking-with-one-another.

> [Damit ist zugleich die *doxa* herausgestellt als der Boden wie als der *Antrieb zum Miteinanderreden, Miteinanderverhandeln*. Denn obzwar die *doxa* eine gewisse Festigkeit hat, liegt es doch in ihr,

daß man darüber, worüber man einer Ansicht ist, immer noch reden kann. Es könnte auch anders sein. Ihr Sinn ist, eine Diskussion offen zu lassen. Der *logos*, das Verhandeln darüber, ist ständig latent; in der *doxa* ist das Zur-Sprache-Bringen ständig auf dem Sprung. Die *doxa* ist es gerade, woraus das Miteinandersprechen erwächst, woraus es seinen Antrieb nimmt, und zugleich auch dasjenige, woraus es das nimmt, worüber verhandelt wird. So ist die *doxa* Boden, Quelle und Antrieb für das Miteinanderreden (151).]

In doxa we are already "there" in the world with others in some essential, but ultimately provisional way. Out of doxa we can articulate the common concerns of a community, and upon doxa we can build a proof (*pisteis*). For example, the syllogism depends upon a stable belief stated in the major premise:

All men are mortal
Socrates is a man
—
Therefore Socrates is mortal

But even the theoretical propositions that can be drawn out of shared belief remain falsifiable, Thales's claim included. Doxa is finally some particular orientation, always subject to revision. And it is precisely the "ontological" bracketing of any particular doxa that makes humans human: uncertain, unfinished, and subject to desire. We must make do in a world of the merely probable and thus we are always susceptible to affect and change.

Now we are squarely back in the domain of rhetoric. When we talk about the essential uncertainty of belief and consequent motivation to discourse, we return to the first and most famous defense of rhetoric against the age old charge made by philosophers that rhetoric neglects the truth. In Gorgias's *Encomium of Helen* human frailties give rise to the first probabilistic epistemology and to an eloquent defense of the art of speech: "All who have and do persuade people of things do so by molding a false argument. If everyone, on every subject, had memory of the past and knowledge of the present and foresight of the future, speech would not do what it does, but as things are, it is easy neither to remember the past nor consider the present nor predict the future, so that on most subjects most people take opinion as counselor to the soul."[46] If humans were omniscient, all speech would be true and there would be no need for eloquence or passion. But of course if humans were omniscient, speech in any form would be unnecessary—we would have nothing to discuss, nothing to describe, nothing to debate. It is precisely our limits that make us human (not God or simple animal) and motivate us to eloquence. We live in a world of the more or less probable, and we cannot take for granted that everyone shares the same beliefs. Nor can we assume that our own beliefs are unassailable. *Moving and persuading people is thus an essential human activity.* In a world of probabilities the rhetor does not have arguments at his or her disposal that are guaranteed "true." Hence Gorgias's provocative claim: "All who have and do persuade people of things do so by molding a false argument."

But couldn't the pathos "latent" in doxa be probabilistic and still dispassionate? If we cannot discuss human affairs in terms of absolute truths, couldn't we at least devise some method for assessing probabilities without prejudice or pathos? Such is the fantasy of some statisticians working in the human sciences today. It is the task of rhetoricians to demonstrate why this fantasy too is impossible, and here Heidegger's SS 1924 lectures again prove instructive. It has been suggested that "in the doxa a bringing-to-language is always *ready to spring forth*" (my italics). But logos cannot spring forth from belief like the Christ child—conceived in abstraction and born into a divine plan. Something mundane must motivate this event in language and give it a human voice. Logos is nothing without a human body and a shared situation in which it can be heard, no matter how messy such practicalities may be. Thus runs the reasoning Heidegger finds in the second book of Aristotle's *Rhetoric*. It is also a way of thinking that lies at the heart of certain Christian theology—a tradition in which Heidegger was deeply immersed in 1924, and which he cites explicitly in his genealogy of the Affektenlehre.

In Heidegger's historical introduction to the concept pathos the secular humanist tradition is largely avoided and along with it the manipulative psychology that ties emotions to the untrained mind. Instead pathos is described in the tradition running from Aristotle to Luther, where a basic emotion such as fear makes our collective existence concrete and moves us in our fundamental beliefs.[47] Luther's early writings are mentioned, the *Sermo de poenitentia* in particular. Other figures cited in this intriguing genealogy are Augustine (*De civitate Dei* and the "Pelagianische Schriften"), Johannes Damascenus (*De fide orthodoxa II*), Gregory of Nyssa, Nemesius, pseudo-Dionysius Areopagita, and Dilthey ("Weltanschauung und Analyse des Menschen seit Renaissance und Reformation"). It would be a fine project for an intellectual historian to reconstruct and comment on Heidegger's genealogy of pathos, but that will not be my project here (see bibliography). Instead I wish to measure the impact of one central tenet on Heidegger's rhetorical philosophy: pathos alone has the power to provide logos with a critical moment, kairos. I wish to point out that when Heidegger remarks that logos would be unable to "spring forth" from doxa without some concrete motivation, it is not from the Greek tradition alone that he draws. Clearly he has in mind a notion of concrete divinity as well: without pathos belief would remain unreceptive to God's word. Indeed a theological conception of rhetorical pathos is critical to important strains of modern German philosophy.

No one argued this point with the mastery of romanticist Klaus Dockhorn. According to Dockhorn it is Luther's Affektenlehre that grounded Enlightenment philosophy, opening the way for what would later become the "hermeneutics of facticity" practiced by both Heidegger and Gadamer. Luther insists that without affect the Word of the Holy Ghost would remain a dead letter. If such apathy were possible the (past) historical Passion of Christ would be intangible, and the fear of God's wrath (future) would remain abstract. Summarizing Luther's view, Dockhorn concludes the following: "Belief realizes itself in affect—must complete itself in affect—because reason is incapable of making past and future present."[48] It can thus be said that Heidegger's and Gadamer's hermeneutics of facticity—also a method for tracing the folds of past and future in the present—secularizes Luther's rhetorical Affektenlehre. I will bring the body of this introduction to a close with Heidegger's concrete analysis of one such affect: fear (phobos). It is analysis that clearly draws upon this Lutheran tradition while rewriting its residual metaphysics. A review of SS 1924 shows that logos and doxa can be bound by way of fear. When touched by fear, our belief is mobilized: community and its Other are defined, we ask "What is to be done?" and we can be moved to action. But for Heidegger it is not fantasy of future misfortune represented by the rhetor that moves the audience in its belief, as suggested in the Roman tradition and reiterated by Luther. We can appeal to the intentional mind only after the fact. Instead belief and its articulation are composed in a fearsome situation made immediate (kairos). We are moved ultimately not by fantasy, but by concrete possibilities contoured by experience.

In the Roman rhetorical tradition people can only be moved by the power of a fantastic motor running on the fuel of an advocate's passion. Cicero insists that "it is impossible for the listener to feel indignation, hatred or ill-will, to be terrified of anything, or reduced to tears of compassion, unless all those emotions, that the advocate would inspire in the arbitrator, are visibly stamped or rather branded on the advocate himself" (*De or.* 2.44.189). And despite the fact that "emotion is not in our own power," we are nonetheless able to generate emotions in ourselves by way of *phantasia*, whereby "things absent are presented to our imagination with such extreme vividness that they seem actually to be before our very eyes" (*Inst. or.* 6.2.29). When otherwise unoccupied, the mind becomes absorbed by fantastic visions that in a practical context can be turned to some profit. With this in mind Quintilian imagines that he is prosecuting a man accused of murder: "Shall I not bring before my eyes all the circumstances which it is reasonable to imagine must have occurred in such a connexion? Shall I not see the assassin burst suddenly from his hiding-place, the victim tremble, cry for help, beg for mercy, or turn to run?" (6.2.31). For this is how we can stir in ourselves the emotion needed to present a murder scenario with the proper *energeia*, or vividness. In the Roman tradition then, passions are the product of individual mentation. Heidegger reverses this scheme, arguing that in fact individual mentation is the product of passion.

To summarize, we have so far discussed three states of being that would be nonhuman: embodied, but lacking the capacity to believe (a dog); believing, but lacking the capacity to change (a dogmatist); and perfectly rational, but disembodied (Descartes). What the two latter ways of being would share is the certainty that comes with immobility. Perhaps we can conjure a being beyond the world of probabilities and contingency, but the price we would pay for such a trick comes in terms of time (see chapter 5). In a world of belief where things could not be otherwise or in a world mirrored by pure logos, Being itself would be frozen. And as we have seen, it is pathos that gives Being its dynamism and motivates the historical process continually rearticulating belief. We would expect then that pathos is characterized by uncertainty, or even confusion. And indeed this is precisely how Heidegger describes being overcome by fear: it is fundamentally "unsettling" (*Unruhe*), "confusing" (*Verwirrung*), and "mixed-up" (*Durcheinandergeraten*) (183). Here pathos is described in terms of fear:

> "Pathos is a sudden change and hence a transformation to . . . out of a previous situation, but not a sudden change that would take its own course. Instead, it is a way of disposing oneself toward the world that stands at the same time in a possible relation to *hexis*. This change into another condition and the new being composed from the old has in itself the possibility of being-seized, being-suddenly-overcome. This way of losing composure, being-made-to-lose-composure, is done in such a way that composure can be regained; I can compose myself again. I am in danger at a particular moment, in a moment of terror, composed. I can draw to this disposition through the condition marked by terror by way of a possible being-composed-for."
>
> [*Pathos* ist ein "Umschlagen" und demnach ein bestimmtes "Werden zu . . ." aus einer früheren Lage, aber nicht ein Umschlagen, das für sich einen eigenen Verlauf hätte, sondern eine Weise des Sichbefindens in der Welt, die zugleich in einem möglichen Bezug steht zur *hexis*. Dieses Umschlagen in eine andere

> Verfassung und das Sein in der neuen von der alten her hat in sich selbst die Möglichkeit des Ergriffenwerdens, Überfallenwerdens. Die Art und Weise des Aus-der-Fassung-Kommens, Aus-der-Fassung-gebracht Werdens ist dem Sinn nach so, daß sie wieder gefaßt werden kann; Ich kann mich wieder fassen, ich bin einen bestimmten Moment, in einer Gefahr, im Moment des Schreckens, in Fassung. Ich kann die durch den Schrecken gekennzeichnete Befindlichkeit beziehen auf ein mögliches Gefaßtsein dafür (171).]

Here Heidegger would seem to agree with Roman rhetoricians that pathos confuses clear-headed rationality, and the self-possession that comes with fixed belief does seem vulnerable to the destabilizing power of passion. But for Heidegger the fact that we are subject-to-movement in our belief is precisely what defines us as human. Without pathos, ultimately, we would have no traffic between inside and outside, self and Other, individual and community. Or using Heidegger's terminology from the passage just cited, an "old" form of being could never be superseded by one that is "new." Perhaps there would still be a world of data around each of these impossible beings, but that world would have no affective contours. Nothing would be appealing or repelling, frightening or attractive; indeed nothing and nobody could elicit either our love or our hate. In fact Merleau-Ponty and others working in the phenomenology of perception would argue that in such a state no thing would appear at all—we would be effectively deaf, blind, and mute. And in such a state, Heidegger would tell the rationalists, logos would be the last thing on one's mind. Besides the unimaginable isolation such a state would entail, living without pathos would also seem poisonous to our collective well-being. For living being requires selective traffic with an environment, and for a human being that environment is articulated collectively. Without pathos we would lack not only the sympathies and antipathies that define community, but also the capacity to absorb the past experiences and future possibilities critical for survival within community.

Thus it is not an image or fantasy that makes past and future present and provides the motivation to act. It is rather a decisive moment (krisis) that folds past experience and future possibilities into a provisional present. Heidegger calls this "Being-there-for," manifest, say, in the belief that someone is now going to make something happen to me ("das *Dafürsein*, *Glauben*, daß ich das und das zu erwarten habe, das mir von diesem Menschen jetzt etwas passiert" [259]). Not surprisingly the passionately contoured world that Heidegger draws out of Aristotle's *Rhetoric* is indeed teeming with wily and threatening people just waiting to do something unpleasant. You have nine kinds of fearsome people falling under three categories: those who are "ill disposed" (*von schlechter Gesinnung*), those who are always looking for the advantage (*auf eigenen Vorteil*), and those who are cowardly (*feige*). Note the relational aspect of such affect: I fear being at the mercy of someone who, for instance, knows that I have committed a crime and hence could betray me; when weak, I fear someone who has power over me; when strong, I fear the *ressentiment* of the weak; when wronged, I present the fearsome possibility of retribution, and when perpetrator, I remain fearsome insofar as I anticipate retribution and present the threat of a preemptive strike (256–257). But I fear these people not because I can imagine the damage they could do (I can equally imagine the threatening qualities of Atilla the Hun), but rather because my concrete relationship to this person—past and present—positions me unfavorably with respect to his or her capacity to harm me in the near future. ("Es muß 'sich zeigen' als so und so, aber doch nicht als eigentlich da. Für das Fürchterliche ist charakteristisch die *Möglichkeit*, das *Möglichsein*, aber im Sinne des *Unbestimmten*. Das Moment der Unbestimmtheit steigert gerade die Möglichkeit, daß es kann" [253].) Hence the most fearsome person is not only capable of harming me in some indeterminate way but also stands in an uncertain relationship to me: those who are "reserved" and "ironic" appear to Heidegger as the most dangerous types ("die Zurückhaltenden, die Ironischen" [257].)

So in a world where other human beings present the possibility for both self-realization and for self-destruction, pathos is essential for glory as well as survival. And it is the rhetorician who is trained in the art of making pathos immediate (kairos), thus inspiring us to judge and act. Political events are characterized in a threatening manner ("die politischen Ereignisse als gefährlich hinstelle"), a decision is taken, leading to collective action. In fact fear above all other manifestations of pathos brings us to language. It is thus a critical factor in the formation of human Dasein. (Heidegger describes fear as "diejenige Befindlichkeit, die zum Sprechen bringt" [261].) Indeed the very lack of composure brought on by terror forces us to decide who is with us and who is against us, and then to articulate our concerns. Out of Aristotle we get for the first time a story about the genesis of language told not in terms of God or Nature, but in terms of human Dasein: "Wenn uns unheimlich ist, fangen wir an zu reden. Das ist ein Hinweis für die *daseinsmässige genesis des Sprechens*: wie das Sprechen zusammenhängt mit der Grundbestimmung des Daseins selbst, die durch die *Unheimlichkeit* charakterisiert ist" (261). Pathos, Heidegger concludes, is the ground of logos, providing the mood and motivation necessary for the speaking animal to emerge and find its place in the world. Heidegger's summary:

> In what follows we will come to understand how fear and the pathē stand in relation to logos, insofar as logos is taken as

> speaking-with-one-another, as that which effects the elaboration of Dasein in its everydayness. In so far as the pathē are not the annex of psychological events, but compose instead *the ground upon which language grows and to which expressions return*, the pathē provide *the fundamental possibilities in which Dasein finds itself and orients itself*. This basic Being-oriented, the lighting of Being's being in the world, is no *knowledge*, but is instead a *finding-oneself* variously determined, depending upon the ways Being can be there. Given first among these characteristic ways of finding-oneself and being-in-the-world is the possibility of speaking about things stripped of the appearance with which they are most closely associated. Thus we are presented with the possibility of coming to a particular *matter-of-fact* that, in a certain sense, returns to the way the world is seen as prefigured by the pathē.
>
> [Wir werden uns im folgenden noch kurz zu verständigen haben, wie die Furcht und die *pathē* im Zusammenhang stehen mit dem *logos*, sofern der *logos* genommen wird als Miteinandersprechen, das die Funktion hat, die Auslegung des Daseins in seiner Alltäglichkeit zu bewerkstelligen. Sofern die *pathē* nicht nur ein Annex der psychischen Vorgänge sind, sondern *der Boden, aus dem das Sprechen erwächst und in den hinein das Ausgesprochene wieder wächst*, sind die *pathē* ihrerseits *die Grundmöglichkeiten, in denen das Dasein sich über sich selbst primär orientiert*, sich befindet. Das primäre Orientiertsein, die Aufhellung seines Seins-in-der-Welt ist kein *Wissen*, sondern ein *Sichbefinden*, das je nach der Daseinsweise eines Seienden verschieden bestimmt sein kann. Erst innerhalb des so charakterisierten Sichbefindens und In-der-Welt-seins ist die Möglichkeit gegeben, über die Dinge zu sprechen, sofern sie entkleidet sind des Aussehens, das sie im nächsten Umgang haben. Es entsteht jetzt die Möglichkeit, zu einer bestimmten *Sachlichkeit* zu kommen, die in gewisser Weise die Art, die Welt zu sehen, wie sie durch die *pathē* vorgezeichnet wird, zurückstellt (262).]

A world seen and prefigured by the pathē. What would it mean for passions to "see" and "prefigure" the world of things stripped of their most immediate qualities? A puzzling and incomplete passage indeed, but one that is also highly suggestive. Certainly we can imagine by now the process that finds an emotional and chaotic situation demanding expression—expression that in turn motivates human subjects to act. And having reviewed SS 1924 we should also understand what Heidegger is getting at when he says that logos presumes community. But to what extent is an emotional situation or a world without language actually prefigured by the pathē? And to what extent does such prefiguration have the structure of a primitive language, or a sketch? A close reading of SS 1924 suggests that emotions might be treated as structuring "turns" that, like tropes, constitute a domain of mental perception that make language possible. But this line of thought will have to wait for another occasion.

Whatever happened to this more agreeable Heidegger who seemed at one time to be working on the very sort of pluralism Arendt would later characterize as the antidote to Heideggerian politics? Theodore Kisiel (chapter 6) will venture a psychohistorical explanation situated in the particularities of Weimar politics and the French occupation of the Ruhr. But if we compare Heidegger's nascent pluralism in 1924 to his 1930s reading of Nietzsche on "Will as Affect, Passion, and Feeling," one sees also an internal logic to the ominous developments in Heidegger's political philosophy.

> Affect: the seizure that blindly agitates us. Passion: the lucidly gathering grip on beings. We talk and understand only extrinsically when we say that anger flares and dissipates, lasting but a short time, while hate lasts longer. No, hate and love not only last longer, they bring perdurance and permanence for the first time to our existence. An affect, in contrast, cannot do that. Because passion restores our essential being, because it loosens and liberates in its very grounds, and because passion at the same time reaches out into the expanse of beings, for these reasons passion—and we mean *great passion*—possesses extravagance and resourcefulness, not only the ability but the necessity to submit, without bothering about what its extravagance entails. *It displays the self-composed superiority characteristic of great will.* [italics added][49]

The body politic, in other words, is subordinated to the so-called great will. Ominous words indeed. With a shallowness typical of his political activity, Heidegger in fact moves in his 1933 speeches and writing from the resolute Freeman to resolute nation revealing authenticity in the face of French rationalism and American cultural imperialism, and justifying among other things German withdrawal from the League of Nations and adherence to the German *Führer*. A far cry from the rhetorical pluralism that characterized Heidegger's nascent political philosophy in 1924.

Remember that Heidegger's treatment of Aristotle's corpus shows that authentic speaking emerges only from a political community, and without pathos, the community would remain mute: "The determination of Being-with-one-another in politikē founds that which rhetoric brings to language." [Die Bestimmung des Miteinanderseins in der *politikē* berührt mit das, was in der Rhetorik zur Sprache gebracht wird (127).] According to the Marburg Heidegger then, Being-with-one-another in the world is a fundamental way of being human. An original and isolated encounter with the world is in fact unimaginable, because the very perceptions that would compose such an encounter depend on shared dispositions (doxa) and common concern for what is good and bad, just and unjust, honorable and blameworthy. We humans thus have political existence (*bios politikos*) insofar as our actions are coordinated in a common world. Ethics show us how Being-in-the-world is differentiated, and rhetoric how Dasein's articulations are situated in time and place.

Already when *Being and Time* was published, suspicion of *das Man* and his sociality had grown, while the domain of authentic Being-with had withered. The hermeneutic method was to penetrate to yet a more formal and universal level of Being, and the Aristotelian triad of politics, ethics, and rhetoric were to be revealed as derivative social phenomena. Now within the horizon of hermeneutical understanding, "ethics" is reconstrued according to the more primordial structural totality of "care," which comes before every factical situation—political action included (BT 238). A primordial phenomena such as guilt is formalized so that ordinary phenomena related to the law or social values—phenomena related to our concernful Being with Others—would "drop out" (BT 238). This done, Heidegger's existential analytic of Dasein did gain new scope, taking thereby the great leap forward into what we know as Heidegger's philosophical masterpiece. Yet in taking this leap, Heidegger dropped his convictions that public speaking could authentically emerge from political community and that such an emergence would be motivated by pathos. Now "only by authentically Being-their-Selves in resoluteness can people authentically be with one another" (BT 344). This was Heidegger's other critical turn, and one that has significant consequences for how we understand Heidegger's politics—whether present-at-hand in the most obtrusive way (the Rector's Speech of 1933)—or conspicuously absent (the late Heidegger's silence about Auschwitz). In *Being and Time* Heidegger does make the half-hearted suggestion that people can be authentically bound together "when they devote themselves to the same affair in common" (BT 159). But Heidegger's conception of authentic Being had already moved decisively out of the emotional public sphere and into the rarefied domain of the resolute Freeman (BT 434).

SS 1924 thus marks at the same time the rhetorical turn in twentieth-century philosophy and a fundamental revision of the rhetorical tradition itself. Between 1924 and 1927 Heidegger artfully coaxed elements of the rhetorical tradition from their ethical and political home to be incorporated in an account of "fallen" discourse and poetic speech acts. And this move by Heidegger represents a general trend in the modern territorial struggle between rhetoric and philosophy. It was once a rhetorician's responsibility to understand what one did in speaking and what changes in the world one could thereby effect. Locutions and their legalities were left largely to logicians and grammarians. In this century rhetorical theory is for the first time relieved of the sole responsibility for providing analyses of these "illocutionary" and "perlocutionary" dimensions of a speech act. That task has been taken over by philosophers of language such as Grice and Searle, Habermas and Sperber. With these philosophers everyday language is still analyzed in context, but that context usually extends no further than the pragmatic presuppositions implicated in speech acts or to an unevaluated background of unarticulated predispositions. Then into this amorphous background is swept the power manifest in discursive histories, and rhetoric is depoliticized. Ironically Martin Heidegger's early work on Aristotle's rhetoric allows us to reconsider how political, ethical, and emotional context is in fact constitutive of everyday language.

Notes

1. Martin Heidegger, *Grundbegriffe der aristotelischen Philosophie: Marburger Vorlesung Sommersemester 1924*, Gesamtausgabe vol. 18, ed. Mark Michalski (Frankfurt: Klostermann, 2002), 110, hereafter cited as GA 18. Henceforth all page references not otherwise specified are to this text, and translations are my own. An English translation of GA 18 is forthcoming from Indiana University Press under the title *Basic Concepts of Aristotelian Philosophy.* In this passage I in fact follow the Bröcker transcript which diverges from GA 18 in one important respect: where the Bröcker transcript reads, "Sofern man vergißt, nach der konkreten Funktion der aristotelischen Rhetorik zu fragen," GA 18 editor Mark Michalski follows instead the Schalk transcript, which reads "Sofern man vergißt, nach der konkreten Funktion der aristotelischen Logic zu fragen." In context I believe that the Bröcker transcription makes more sense.

2. Typical is Ramsey Eric Ramsey, "Listening to Heidegger on Rhetoric," *Philosophy and Rhetoric* 26 (1993): 266–277. Like most who have written on the topic, Ramsey was unaware of Heidegger's SS 1924 lectures at the time. His analysis takes off from the following well-known remark from *Being and Time*: "This work of Aristotle (the *Rhetoric*) must be taken as the first systematic hermeneutic of the everydayness of Being with one another." Martin Heidegger, *Being and Time*, trans. John Macquarrie and Edward Robinson (New York: Harper & Row, 1962), 178, hereafter cited as BT. For a major exception see P. Christopher Smith, *The Hermeneutics of Original Argument: Demonstration, Dialectic, Rhetoric*

(Evanston: Northwestern University Press, 1998). See our bibliography on the topic "Heidegger and Rhetoric."

3. Sander L. Gilman, Carole Blair, and David J. Parent, ed., trans., *Friedrich Nietzsche on Rhetoric and Language* (Oxford: Oxford University Press, 1989), xii.

4. Karl Löwith, "Aristoteles: Rhetorik (II)," DLA Marbach no. 75.7452.

5. Heidegger, BT, 38; Theodore Kisiel, *The Genesis of Heidegger's* Being and Time (Berkeley: University of California Press, 1995), 16.

6. Kisiel, *The Genesis of Heidegger's* Being and Time, 283.

7. Ibid., 292.

8. See for instance Debora K. Shuger, *Sacred Rhetoric: The Christian Grand Style in the English Renaissance* (Princeton: Princeton University Press, 1988); Klaus Dockhorn, review of *Wahrheit und Methode* by Hans-Georg Gadamer, in *Göttingische Gelehrte Anzeigen* 218 (1966): 169-206; John Van Buren, *The Young Heidegger: Rumor of the Hidden King* (Bloomington: Indiana University Press, 1994).

9. See previous note.

10. With Kisiel's help, we can translate this intervention into the terms of *Being and Time.* In SS 1924 Heidegger develops his radical philosophical methodology that moves between immediate human situations—the *ontic*—and the *ontological* dimension of experience that constitutes situations in terms of time (prejudice and anticipation). Kisiel, *The Genesis of Heidegger's* Being and Time.

11. Hans-Georg Gadamer, *Philosophical Hermeneutics.* ed., trans., David E. Linge (Berkeley: University of California Press, 1976), 21.

12. Ibid., 22.

13. Martin Heidegger, "Letter on Humanism," ed., trans., Frank A. Capuzzi and J. Glenn Gray, in *Basic Writings* (New York: Harper & Row, 1977).

14. Hans-Georg Gadamer, *Truth and Method* trans. Joel Weinsheimer and Donald G. Marshall (New York: Crossroad, 1989), 22.

15. Ibid., 21, 30.

16. Ibid., 259.

17. Ibid., 266; *Vorgriff* (preconception, fore-conception) is first discussed in 1919. It is joined by *Vorhabe* in 1921 and finally *Vorsicht* in SS 1924. See Kisiel, *The Genesis of Heidegger's* Being and Time, 508.

18. Gadamer, *Truth and Method*, 567.

19. Following Schleiermacher, Gadamer calls rhetoric the "inverse" of hermeneutics. Gadamer, *Truth and Method*, 188.

20. Ibid., 384.

21. Gadamer, *Truth and Method,* 259.

22. Gadamer, *Philosophical Hermeneutics*, 25.

23. Ibid., 26.

24. Christopher Fynsk, forward to *The Inoperative Community,* by Jean-Luc Nancy (Minneapolis: University of Minnesota Press, 1991), xxiv.

25. Dana R. Villa, *Arendt and Heidegger: The Fate of the Political* (Princeton: Princeton University Press, 1996), 130.

26. Hannah Arendt, *The Human Condition* (Chicago: University of Chicago Press, 1958), 175–192. On the influence of Heidegger's reading of Aristotle, see also Van Buren, 226; Franco Volpi, "Heidegger in Marburg: Die Auseinandersetzung mit Aristoteles," *Philosophischer Literaturanzeiger* 37 (1984): n. 3. See especially three early studies noted by Van Buren that, on the basis of attendance of Heidegger's courses, work out many details of his reading of Aristotle's practical philosophy: Hans-Georg Gadamer, "Praktisches Wissen" (written 1930), in his *Griechische Philosophie I, Gesammelte Werke*, vol. 5 (Tübingen: Mohr, 1985), 230–248; Helene Weiss, *Kausalität und Zufall in der Philosophie des Aristoteles* (Darmstadt: Wissenschaftliche Buchgesellschaft, 1967; unaltered reprint of the 1942 Basel edition), ch. 3; Wilhelm Szilasi, *Macht und Ohnmacht des Geistes* (Freiburg: Alber, 1946), ch. 2.

27. Arendt, *The Human Condition,* 178.

28. Heidegger writes "Über das, was geschehen ist, soll sich der Richter eine Ansicht bilden" (125).

29. Arendt, *The Human Condition,* 175.

30. George A. Kennedy, *Classical Rhetoric and Its Christian and Secular Tradition from Ancient to Modern Times* (Chapel Hill: University of North Carolina Press, 1980), 81.

31. Amélie Oksenberg Rorty, *Essays on Aristotle's* Rhetoric (Berkeley: University of California Press, 1996), ix.

32. Eugene Garver, *Aristotle's* Rhetoric: *An Art of Character* (Chicago: University of Chicago Press, 1994).

33. George A. Kennedy, "The Composition and Influence of Aristotle's *Rhetoric*," in Rorty, 423. On its marginal status in the west before the end of the sixteenth century see Brian Vickers, *In Defence of Rhetoric* (Oxford: Oxford University Press, 1989), 229, 297; and Lawrence D. Green, "Aristotle's *Rhetoric* and Renaissance Views of the Emotions," in *Renaissance Rhetoric,* ed. Peter Mack (New York: St. Martin's, 1994), 1–26.

34. Rorty, *Essays on Aristotle's* Rhetoric, ix.

35. Richard McKeon, introduction to *The Basic Works of Aristotle* (New York: Random House, 1941), xxvi.

36. Jacques Derrida, *Margins of Philosophy*, trans. Alan Bass (Chicago: University of Chicago Press, 1982), 9.

37. Vincent Pecora, "Ethics, Politics, and the Middle Voice," *Yale French Studies* 79 (1991), 203–230.

38. Luc Ferry and Alain Renaut, *French Philosophy of the Sixties: An Essay on Antihumanism,* trans. Mary Schnackenberg Cattani (Amherst: University of Massachusetts Press, 1990), 22.

39. Heidegger, "Letter on Humanism," 194.

40. Ibid., 195.

41. Ferry and Renaut, *French Philosophy of the Sixties,* 22.

42. Martin Heidegger, *Poetry, Language, Thought* (New York: Harper & Row, 1971), 208.

43. Ibid., 209.

44. Quentin Skinner, *Reason and Rhetoric in the Philosophy of Hobbes* (Cambridge: Cambridgge University Press), 83.

45. Troels Engberg-Pedersen, "Is There an Ethical Dimension to Aristotelian Rhetoric?" in Rorty, *Essays on Aristotle's* Rhetoric, 125.

46. This translation combines that from Rosamond Kent Sprague, *The Older Sophists* (Columbia: University of South Carolina Press, 1972), 52, and George A. Kennedy, in Matsen, Rollinson, and Sousa, eds., *Readings from Classical Rhetoric* (Carbondale: Southern Illinois University Press, 1990), 35.

47. "The Aristotelian doctrine on pathē . . . had a tremendous affect on subsequent philosophers and theologians (*Thomas*'s Affektenlehre). Above all, the pathē are a basic theological question. I should mention that the doctrine of affections basic to theology and philosophy of the Middle Ages is also relevant for *Luther*—in particular *fear*, which played a special roll in the Middle Ages, because the phenomenon of fear stands in a special relationship to sin, and sin is the concept opposing belief." [Die aristotelische Lehre von den *pathē* . . . hat auf die nachfolgenden Philosophen und Theologen sehr gewirkt (*Thomas*' Affektenlehre). Überhaupt sind die *pathē* eine Grundfrage der Theologie. Da gerade die Lehre von den Affekten innerhalb der Grundfragen der mittelalterlichen Theologie und Philosophie auch für *Luther* relevant ist, erwähne ich das. Es ist vor allem die *Furcht*, die im Mittelalter eine besondere Rolle spielt, weil das Phänomen der Furcht im besonderen Zusammenhang steht mit der Sünde, und Sünde der Gegenbegriff des Glaubens ist (177).]

48. "Time and again, in Luther's *Tischreden* in particular, we hit upon the formula '*Dialectica docet, Rhetorica movet.*' And Luther knows exactly what he means by the *movere* of rhetoric. His convictions can be grasped precisely because he makes it clear from the beginning what happens to the hearer of words when

the Holy Ghost is 'rhetorized' (*'rhetoricatur'*). When it counts, he makes past and future present—that is, when he wants to make each past that matters into experience: the historical Passion of Christ. What is thus made we call *belief.* Belief completes itself in affect—must complete itself in affect—because reason is incapable of making past and future present." Dockhorn, review of *Wahrheit und Methode,* 178.

49. Martin Heidegger, *Nietzsche,* vol. I, trans. David Farrell Krell (New York: Harper & Row, 1979), 48–49.

2

TRANSLATED BY LAWRENCE KENNEDY SCHMIDT

Heidegger as Rhetor: Hans-Georg Gadamer Interviewed by Ansgar Kemmann

I. BIOGRAPHICAL INTRODUCTION

How did you, Professor Gadamer, come to rhetoric—through Heidegger?

When speaking of Heidegger you must, of course, first remember what an enormous task lay before him, considering the dominance of St. Thomas Aquinas. And what was truly amazing is that he was able to revive Aristotle. For me as well—there can be no doubt about it—I was completely enthralled when I came to Freiburg, simply due to the well-known essay on Aristotle, which secured him the call to Marburg.[1]

When I then arrived in Freiburg, through recommendations supported by Natorp and Hartmann,[2] Heidegger was unbelievably friendly to me. Right away he saw me as a messenger from Marburg; probably he had already suspected his chance that a call to Marburg could result from this essay. After his lecture, he invited me, privately and confidentially, to read Aristotle with him alone once a week in the evening. And there I grasped, to my great surprise, that *logos* has something to do with speaking. In Marburg's Neo-Kantianism logos was just "reason." Yes, I was

---

Hans-Georg Gadamer graciously welcomed me (A.K.) into his home several times from 1999 to 2001. The present text, which was in great part reviewed by us together, documents the point our conversation had reached by December 4, 2001.

astonished. And I must certainly say that had a determining influence on me. How Aristotle came alive for me! Also in Freiburg in the 1923 summer semester the Aristotle seminar on *phronēsis* occurred, and that ignited my thinking to a much greater degree.

Allow me now to say a bit about your question—how I came to rhetoric. The general opinion is, of course, always: What else? He had just heard Heidegger's lecture. But that wasn't the case. Rather, in Freiburg I had already realized that I couldn't do anything, that I didn't have the tools, and for that reason I studied classical philology—and under the direction of Prof. Lommatzsch[3] I studied especially rhetoric, both Attic and Roman rhetoric, Cicero and Quintilian.

Lommatzsch had given me Cicero to read so that I could practice my Latin. I diligently did so; after all, we spoke Latin in the seminars! Yes, it was a small seminar, perhaps five people. That I then delved further into rhetoric was my own decision—because rhetoric was closest to philosophy! At that time Friedländer[4] also began to concern himself with topics from the time of Hellenism and to ask what was slowly developing between Latin and Greek.

The history of rhetoric belonged to my preparations that permitted me to continue at all. The late rhetoric, especially Quintilian, and an important part was played by Plato's *Symposium*, particularly the last phase where Socrates is told, "You will not understand what I will now say." Isn't it the truth? [*laughs*]—Well, that's the origin of my hermeneutics!

Naturally, while I was studying classical philology, I always participated in Heidegger's seminars and even heard many lectures—not all. Of course, this took place only between 1924 and 1927. So, I am also not in the strict sense a completely well-educated classical philologist in every respect. However, the topic that chiefly interested Heidegger at that time, the *pathē* doctrine, this aspect of Aristotle's rhetoric—that you correctly remark Heidegger especially emphasized then—that topic I did not understand at the time. I was still too immature for that. After the lecture we, the students, seldom discussed it. The development that Heidegger himself achieved is something other than what I slowly accumulated, coming from my completely different starting point.

II. On the Status of Rhetoric

In two recent and published conversations you have again referred to rhetoric and pleaded for the broad concept of rhetoric. To Gudrun Kühne-Bertram and Frithjof Rodi you located historically "the very broad concept of rhetoric" as the post-Aristotelian concept of rhetoric "that contained all the humanities until modern times."[5] *In a similar manner you told Jean Grondin, "Therefore it would actually bring greater honor to the study of the humanities to place it under the old concept of rhetoric, where one deals with believable statements and not with conclusive proofs."*[6]

Your teacher, Martin Heidegger, to the contrary, referred directly to Aristotle and already established rhetoric as the dynamis *of humans. "What does rhetoric really mean? What sense of rhetoric relates to* legein*? Aristotle defined rhetoric (1.2) as dynamis. This definition is to be retained even though Aristotle often designates it as* technē*. This designation is incorrect, whereas dynamis is the correct definition."*[7]

What is at stake in this alternative (technē/dynamis)?

That is a very important question. Technē was a very general expression, if one did not mean mathematics specifically. So the special character of Heidegger's statement is that it is a probing attempt. Concerning this one must see that Heidegger was still using technē, until he began emphatically using the concept of *energeia*. And so he associated the concept of dynamis with the concept of energeia, and missed the other one. That is the reason.

Naturally how Heidegger had ordered these concepts was quite correct. In general, I can only say that it was at least as much of a revelation for me as it can be for younger students today. Although Hartmann carefully read Aristotle, it did not actually transfer to his own thinking; whereas Heidegger accomplished this and fascinated me right away.

Even from today's perspective, I would want, like Heidegger, to characterize rhetoric as more a dynamis. That should indicate that rhetoric belongs to being human and is not just an occasional ability. Actually, everyone is a speaker.

III. The Rhetoric of Philosophy: Using the Example of Martin Heidegger

Concerning rhetoric Martin Heidegger remarks in his lecture of SS 1924, "I only wish to point out that it might be more appropriate if philosophers could decide to consider what speaking to others really means."[8]

Who are the "philosophers" and what led to their losing sight of speaking to someone and conversation?

That is a very general critique. Heidegger was always a rowdy, and this somewhat influenced what he said. In such a case he was referring to, for example, Richard Kroner in Freiburg and Nicolai Hartmann in Marburg and people like them, naturally also Edmund Husserl—although he actually never tried to hide his admiration for Husserl, at least not at that time. However, in Hartmann's case I do not consider him to be very just. Hartmann had a wonderful relationship with his students. Hartmann was also not a bad teacher, but compared to Heidegger, he was, frankly, a knight—so aristocratic and reserved. Naturally, I tried to bring the two together, but that failed completely, whereas it worked with Bultmann and Heidegger. However, with Hartmann—that didn't succeed, and successful teaching was clearly on Heidegger's side.

Did Heidegger take to heart in his own thinking his remark about philosophers?

Heidegger's manner of lecturing was already enormously fascinating—oh yes, rhetorically masterful! I wouldn't say that his written work was equally convincing, but as a speaker he had an enormous radiance. Enormous, you cannot even imagine. We were all awestruck! That Aristotle suddenly became a phenomenologist was exactly what Heidegger accomplished and was quite the exception. He worked so long on Husserl, until Husserl believed him about Aristotle. And it is remarkable how correct Heidegger was, wouldn't you agree? The way Hartmann and all the others, even the philologists, treated Aristotle certainly did not present him as a contemporary opponent! It was pure history. But with Heidegger, Aristotle suddenly came alive.

What does speaking to others concretely mean for Heidegger?

Ah, this question is very interesting. It was very difficult to speak with Heidegger because he wanted to understand step by step. So he did not terribly much like to discuss with me. I understood too quickly. He didn't like that; he needed the steps. In this he was naturally far superior to me and thereby was a much greater thinker in that he continually saw intermediate steps. I mean, I always learned an incredible amount when I listened to him—but it was not a conversation. I must say that until the end of my studies, I still didn't know whether he thought I was any good at all.

His ability to work was enormous. Also how he educated Hannah Arendt, wouldn't you agree? She was an interesting, talented Jewess. I also knew her rather well, but I did not have the slightest idea of their personal relationship. Heidegger conducted it again with unbelievable caution; in the meantime we, of course, know this. Once a friend of mine, Jakob Klein, came to me and said he had heard that there was a relationship between Heidegger and this woman. "But that's totally crazy," he said, "in such a small town everyone would know about it!" He underestimated them.

I came to be completely and positively recognized by Heidegger only through my engagement for him after the war. He was simply thankful for that as a person. Later he often came to Heidelberg, about every second semester, and had discussions with my circle of students. He always looked forward step by step; I really experienced that myself. But I hadn't noticed at all, I must admit it, that my students were actually always disappointed with him, since they were much more used to me as a conversation partner.

At the time I didn't suspect that. I believed all honored him as I did! I remember quite well that I always fell under his spell, but my students did not! They were all angry that he didn't let me speak enough. Now I learn this. I, an old man, am told such things: "Oh Heidegger, that was always terrible."

Heidegger never got beyond that stage, but it is also difficult when one has such a superior intellect. He could easily situate the other within his thinking. For people like us, it is easier to notice that the other could also be correct.

On the other hand, Heidegger could be very humane at the appropriate moment. For example, just before Löwith died, he wrote him such a wonderful letter that Löwith and his wife were completely charmed. Heidegger, therefore, had been able to sanction Löwith's own path as a bold path, although at first when Löwith returned to Heidelberg, he sharply and publicly attacked Heidegger.

What did the possibility of public lecturing mean to Heidegger?

Heidegger certainly hoped that through public lectures others would be able to overcome many of the prejudices in traditional philosophy. Yes, yes, that was always the feeling. He trusted that this could be accomplished through the lecture, and that was also the case.

Naturally it was not an exchange with the audience. He tried too hard to find himself. When I last visited with him, I knew he did not have much longer to live. One could already sense that. He asked me, "Well, you say language is only in conversation?" "Yes," I answered. And then we continued to God only knows what, but it was absolutely unimportant. There just wasn't any point to it.

What characterized his manner of lecturing? To what extent did it reflect his understanding of philosophy?

The originality of his use of language was what was so unbelievably compelling; it was amazing. And its effect was tremendous. When I first heard him lecture, it turned my convictions upside down. I came home from Freiburg to Marburg and did not want to continue any manner of speaking that I had used before. I wanted to directly grasp the words and not use any foreign terms!

I mean, behind all of Heidegger, there was the wish to overcome the Latin elements in the language of philosophy, and justly so. There are only Latin remains in all the foreign words in our discussion. "*Diskussion*"—I can say what I want, but it is, of course, just Latin. Kant had still lectured in Latin, then he translated and finally began to speak German. However, the texts that his students had were always still in Latin. Even for Heidegger this problem with Latin remained, so that he always strove to find the natural German language.

Today I see: that is Europe. Elsewhere it is much smoother—to proceed from Greek, for example with the Japanese—because there, Latin does not constitute such a barrier. The point that is important for all of us is that Latin cannot be applied to the totality of humanity as it can be applied to Europe.

Something very, very peculiar in the younger Heidegger was that he loved polemics and always constructed the polemic in written form. So he always knew what he had said. Therefore, he suddenly had wonderfully developed texts. These he shot out into the lecture room, and when he had made an especially forceful point, he would look out the window, satisfied. Very remarkable. I must certainly say this really enticed me.

What were such polemics?

Any old malice, preferentially against Max Scheler. Scheler was one of his favorite opponents, the one who had understood him the best. So when he lost Scheler, he lost more than the rest of us—in his own perception. I will never forget the moment when he dealt with the death of Scheler.[9] In the meantime I had met Scheler and also had a very strong impression of him, although for me he was very unsympathetic. Scheler is the only one besides Heidegger about whom I must say that his lectures were simply fascinating. He had a demonic radiance, very dramatic. In contrast, Heidegger was very, very modest in his presentation.

The early death of Scheler was a very fateful event for Heidegger. An opponent, who was just beginning to blossom, was lost. Scheler was one, the only one, I would say—we all could not judge ourselves with reference to [Heidegger]—but Scheler, well, he could and [Heidegger] saw this very slowly, only after having for his whole life always and only malicious critical comments to make about Scheler.

I remember the following incident: In this famous lecture, "The Hermeneutics of Facticity,"[10] Heidegger came to speak about Scheler. "On this point Scheler makes this reference: 'Aristotle wrote in *de partibus animae*. . .' " And then Heidegger roared from the lectern, "Now gentlemen, ladies and gentlemen, what has Scheler just quoted? This text doesn't exist." Later I went to him and said, "Excuse me, professor, you have misunderstood something here. You didn't recognize a typographical error. Instead of *anima-e*, there must be an *l*, therefore *animal* period, and then it would be *de partibus animal(ium)*. This text does exist."—"Hum, aha, he's correct." In the next lecture Heidegger explained, "I wish to make a correction; naturally it was thus and so from *de partibus animalium*. I only return to this so that no one would come to the insane idea that I wanted to refute Scheler with the help of a typo." He would become so possessed by something but was also immensely accomplished in extracting himself.

Heidegger even said about the SS 1924 lecture, "The lecture does not aim at something philosophical. It concerns the understanding of basic concepts in their conceptuality. The aim is philological and is to practice somewhat more the reading of philosophers."[11] *The concluding sentence reads, "What is at stake is not to say something new, but to say what the Ancients really meant."*[12]

Does this remark indicate a genuine philosophical point—or does it concern "mere rhetoric"?

The final sentence is very emphatic. What is at stake is not to say something new, but to actually say only what the Ancients meant. That was his colossal demand. However, the first sentences, I would think, are a type of self-defense. He said that in order not to fall into the warranted suspicion that he just wanted to push his own views. That's the meaning. I'm quite sure that's what he wished to say here.

He was not so sure himself how far he would come in his confrontation with Husserl. He naturally avoided this confrontation in Freiburg. There, for reasons of self-preservation, he fulfilled as best as possible the role that Husserl had allotted him. When he was in Marburg the situation was also difficult for him. On the one hand, he had to move Hartmann aside; on the other, there was still Paul Natorp. Natorp had contact with him for another year and a half, and that was in fact an important influence. I am still convinced today that we have not done enough with this, namely to understand the influence the later Natorp had on the younger Heidegger.

In the concluding move of the lecture, Heidegger takes up again the problem of speaking to others—at least in relation to teaching. "Teaching implies, according to just its meaning: to speak to another, approach the other in the manner of communicating. The actual being of a teacher is: to stand before an other and to speak to him, and in such a way that the other, listening, follows him."[13]

Listening follows him!

What then does communicating mean for thinking?

One seeks the correct words. One, so to speak, offers them to the other, and discussing [*Reden*] is similar. For this reason I elevate conversation, since in a conversation one immediately reacts to the offer. A conversation is able to bring both sides closer to one another. One has not just defended one's own position but has also understood the other. A conversation is, naturally, an intimate situation, which one cannot direct wherever one likes.

How much public presentation does thinking need, can thinking tolerate?

I am always asking myself that, and now I am very aware of how much I depend on the audience when I stand behind the lectern. So when I have given a successful lecture, I am always inclined to say, "Your reward, you can thank the audience for its success." That is how it is. A lecture from a lectern is not a public presentation. Of course, it's a public presentation, but not an official one in the sense of a written publication, rather it is much more like a conversation. That is what Heidegger meant here, and I would also support this idea.

That a lecture is spoken from a lectern also means that one might, under certain circumstances and upon reflection, guard oneself more, as Heidegger did when he wrote out all these polemics, since in truth he had become accustomed to very blustery critiques against the most varied people.

However, I would also fully admit that those who conduct their lectures using too much of their rhetorical ability are not the best teachers. I heard something like this in Breslau; it was Eugen Kühnemann,[14] and it was ghastly. [*laughs*] He had too much rhetoric.

How did this "too much" get expressed?

Well, he again and again used rhetorical affectations. To that extent Heidegger was much more substantive.

So affectations that provided for entertainment but didn't add much to clarification?

Yes, yes. We all found them very amusing. It was clearly something different when we heard someone like Hönigswald, who had a carefully considered lecture—a good preparation for Heidegger, whom we did not yet know at that time! I didn't have any problem learning this, since I was much too shy to immediately lecture without a manuscript. I first attempted that in Leipzig.[15] There I suddenly had to teach the whole field of philosophy: Kant and Hegel and Heidegger himself and Husserl—all of it had to be somehow mastered! It was not an unwarranted expectation for me, since, for my continued development, I had to learn how to present material that I didn't have in my head from morning to night. Well, in short, my lectures became always better, and I continue to recognize this effect even today.

I have become a good speaker simply because I carefully notice the reaction of the audience. And when the lighting is dim—there is a very dark auditorium in the chain of auditoriums that I remember lecturing in—and there I believe I spoke poorly because I could not make out the last row!

The conversation with the audience is sometimes present even in written texts. Actually all of my works were spoken. I then changed them with difficulty and effort into a written form that would preserve as much of the spoken character as possible. For that reason they read better, whereas most other peoples' texts do not allow one to notice that one is being addressed.

IV. The Philosophy of Rhetoric in the Universe of Linguisticality [*Sprachlichkeit*]

Rhetoric is not only an aspect of doing philosophy; it is also a topic in philosophy. Concerning this, Heidegger's 1924 summer semester lecture states, "It is better that we have Aristotle's Rhetoric *than if we were to have a philosophy of language. In the* Rhetoric *we have in front of us something that concerns speaking as a basic mode of human being, as being with one another. Therefore, an understanding of this* legein *also presents new aspects concerning the comprehension of the being of being with one another."*[16]

Even the later Heidegger distanced himself from a nominalistic philosophy of language. But, at the same time, in his consideration of "the living of mortals in the speaking of language,"[17] *he avoided returning again explicitly to rhetoric.*

What did Heidegger win, what did he lose, in doing this?

Difficult to say. Naturally also in my case, since my encounter with him was at first so dramatic. Later, a certain distance appeared (between us) due to his political mistake and the way he nevertheless played along, understandably so, for a little bit. However, everybody who was not blind must have known. He erred when he did this. Still, a deficiency in the handling of his case is that no one said clearly, what I, however, say at every opportunity: He was the sole university president who occupied a

German professorial chair, and who did not retain his presidency for even one year.

Did his retreat out of politics contribute to his neglect of nonpoetic forms of speaking?

Yes, I believe so. Concerning poetic forms of speaking, he just had such a trust in his own philosophical fantasy that he did not consider the other forms worthwhile. That he, unfortunately, misunderstood the starting point was not so important to him. Since he had found a connection to his philosophy in poetry, everything was in order.

Heidegger was not to be deterred. Naturally, he could always bring his own good thoughts to any reasonable idea. But one must nevertheless say that poetic interpretation was his weakest area. One can always respectfully note the boldness with which he attacked the project. But almost always falsely. There were simply boundaries to his talent, but they were hardly visible due to the strength of his talent. One had to be as certain as I was that he, and not I, had erred. Finally I won this very high acknowledgement from him: he admitted to himself that I dealt with poems better than he could.

His own poetry—it is better not to talk about it. There were . . . well, you surely know the story about when he came to Bröcker? No? Ah, a wonderful story. Heidegger wrote terribly many poems later, and he occasionally showed guests his full closets with lots of stuff. One day he wanted to visit his friend and student Walter Bröcker. Naturally he was immediately and joyfully invited. He arrived with a packet and said, "Here, I wanted to ask you to look at these; they are my poetic attempts." After dinner he gave them to him and the next day, during a late breakfast, he looked at him with anticipation. And then—true Bröcker—Bröcker said, "Oh yes, that. The fire is over there." And Heidegger was not offended by this!

To what extent do poetic and rhetorical elements of human linguisticality differ? How are they related to each other?

Well, rhetorical speaking can sound much more preceptorial than poetic. I would not, however, as I said, claim that Heidegger's greatness lay in the poetic. He was, to be sure, very receptive, but never quite in the right place. He saw only himself, reflected. That was his weakness. Also the part he played with Celan—he is himself to be blamed. Although it grieved him and he was prepared for complete admiration. But—oh well.

In the 1924 lecture Heidegger especially emphasized "how logos had its ground in pathē."[18] *The pathē are "the fundamental possibilities, by which* Dasein *primarily orients itself, is attuned. . . . The possibility to speak about things is first presented within the so-characterized attunement* [Sich-Befindens] *and being-in-the-world, to the extent that the appearance, which the thing has in its immediate environment, has been removed."*[19] *Greek ontology also took its beginning from a* pathos. (*"The discussion of the being of beings out of a fear that it will at some point no longer be."*[20])

In this context what is the meaning of characterizing pathē as "ground" and "fundamental possibilities?"

That is the distrust of speaking. So speaking *is* not the first! There is still something, which . . . therefore, one makes a decision about something without at the same time being able to say it to others. In this way one can, so to speak, justify what Heidegger said. It makes good sense to say that.

To what extent does such a fundamental possibility of orientation in how one feels [im Befinden] *have argumentative power? It almost sounds like the pathē are a final judge—if one reversed the path and from logos returned to pathos.*

Yes, but with the caveat that it is also—warranted [*bewährt*]. It is not simply a game. This circumstance then leads him to logos. I remember how he said, "logos," and I was completely puzzled that it should mean "language" and not "reason." I was completely puzzled, but then over and again it became very clear.

What is decisive is that logos is able to express something in such a way that what is really intended is transferred to the other. And yet every logos is in some manner incomplete. That was decisive, I believe, also for Heidegger.

And if every logos is incomplete, must each logos justify itself?

Just so, just so.

Nevertheless must not a being-affected [Betroffensein] *already exist, before one can speak about it?*

That is very perceptive. There is no doubt that Heidegger saw that. I mean, my own accomplishment beyond him, if one may call it that at all, goes exactly in this direction! To be sure, I didn't draw this idea from the same subject matter,[21] rather it was clear to me for many other reasons, to which belong also many forms of. . . . Well, in the course of a conversation lots of things surface that disappear again in the end.

Heidegger himself is motivated by an almost childish compulsion in his professional development. One did not see this because he didn't make it very public. In public he would express this in words. In this sense he also saw that words are not the first.

That it is exactly fear that brings one to speak—in the SS 1924 lecture one reads, "When we feel uncanny, we begin to speak"[22]—does this make sense?

Right away I would say this is said in slight mockery. I already recognize him in that sentence. But what I find missing is a sentence like this: This process by which speaking is awakened through fear, is surely and usually not a development from what one actually questions. But rather it is the avoidance of the uncanny itself. The tendency of most people is to try to sneak past the always more radical forms. And naturally for him what is meant by the uncanny is the lifelong question concerning the afterlife. Fear is fear of death!

I believe, however, that there is a certain one-sidedness when he understands coming to speak in this way. It could be so, but it is clearly not true discussion [Reden]. Heidegger can only afford to say this because he immediately turns it over into the vulgar form where one makes excuses. One always slides into this misuse of language in order to remain, so to speak, in a good mood. He found the courage to say everything in this manner, because he had, at the same time, the courage to indict others, because the others, in truth, just chattered, wishing to escape. In approximately such a way he came to express it. Or, at any rate in a similar manner. Yes, that is curious. . . . Hence the lifelong question about the afterlife. In his statement the Christian seeker after God who has not found him speaks. And so it remained until the end. But fear, I believe, is not his last word. That is not stated here[23] but he had the strong desire to say how much one feared in vain.

On the day I saw him for the last time, I still remember that he came toward me in the yard, taking his wife's arm. Five days later he was dead, or eight days, I cannot remember exactly. We were actually very cheerful. He approached so, and there was some sort of approval . . . and also, how he came, guided by his wife's arm, moved me very deeply. That was anything but a hiding from one's own fear. No, it was more, but fear always played a part in Heidegger. In truth he was extremely honest with himself in recognizing that he feared. And nevertheless, he also knew that this was actually unnecessary.

Now in your later years do you consider religious questions more often? Is that a more important theme for you now than earlier?

I would say that the attempt to understand religious questions is less important to me. It is not becoming *more.* Again and again I conclude: *ignoramus* is our function. That is what is correct, and so the idea of knowing about the afterlife is really not a human question. Furthermore, one would then have to include the whole question about what happens before the first cry of birth. So I would avoid both. We cannot understand them any differently than as we, as all humans, similarly deal with all cases of destruction.

How do you yourself see the relationship between linguisticality and attunement [Befindlichkeit]?

Pathei mathos[24] is the decisive statement. One learns through experience. That is not a particularly exceptional idea. I have only recalled this statement because one always views it from epistemological points of view. But in life we do not relate to ourselves according to epistemological perspectives; rather we must live our own experiences.

This circumstance is decisively important for me because in it I see the part that writing plays in the modern world, and now even in all other forms of reproduction. How can one actually communicate what is common, when such an apparatus stands in between? To receive a letter is something completely different than when you understand someone who is a partner in a conversation. And reversed, it is very difficult to write so that one is correctly understood.

And certain things are surely apparent, for example, that some things need to be written by hand, such as letters of condolence. It is, I believe, still customary that one writes longhand and not with a machine. There are things that one cannot simply erase from the world.

In the mentioned lecture[25] *Heidegger stresses "that in fact the body participates in the genesis of pathē." In a conversation with Gudrun Kühne-Bertram and Frithjof Rodi you express yourself similarly: "I have, for some time, come along far enough to know that pointing . . . is also already language and the whole body speaks too, the language of gesture, the language of intonation, and so on. Linguisticality is only an approximating concept. One must go much, much further."*[26]

How far must one then go?

As far as it is at all possible! One can even speak by being silent. That was also one of Heidegger's favorite problems. He said being silent is speaking . . . that even being silent is speaking. He liked that a lot, already in Marburg. And it also strengthened me in my conviction that even in that situation something is said.

Then what does linguisticality [Sprachlichkeit] mean?

Everything that can allow something to be understood. Therefore, hermeneutics; thereby its indefinability. That humans can express themselves in gestures, noises, spoken words, and written words is, however, something external. It is much more important how one moves within linguisticality and that one is always prepared to seek new possibilities that allow the other to speak and that allow you to comprehend what he wished to say.

No one who expresses something says what he really means. Because no one can ever have the last word, everything that one says only tends in a particular direction. And thereby remains vulnerable and understandable. In truth, rhetoric is the overarching concept for everything that has to do with the other.

The interaction with the pathē, Heidegger says, is a question of hexis: "Ethos *and pathē are constitutive of legein itself."*[27] *In a conversation with Jean Grondin, for the "old, honorable concept of rhetoric" you referred to that form of knowledge that is discussed in Plato's* The Statesman, *that is to know how "to find the right word at the right moment."*[28] *Clearly such knowledge requires dynamis as Aristotle defined it. "To be able to see what speaks for a thing," says Heidegger.*[29]

What relationship does the rhetorical dynamis have to the human ability to understand?

It is the same dynamis! We consider what speaks for a thing. But if one does not know that one only says the half of it, then the other can also not understand you. The other needs exactly what one has not said. In this way I would in principle understand every type of education; it is the unexpected reception of what one alone had not even said.

We have understood each other, but that cannot be put into words again. Also, our figures of speech are like that: "I get along well with him." (Literally, "I understand myself well with him"). One cannot then say, "But wait, no one understands that."

One only speaks about understanding when it is not obvious. And when one has understood something, one has not yet agreed to it; rather one now knows what the other meant. Therein lies the winnings. I emphasize this so much, because this is the way we come to understand one another! It consists first in just listening to the other and considering whether he couldn't perhaps also be correct.

What is the status of knowing in rhetoric? Is it technē or phronēsis?

In experience one does not know how to hold these apart. They are intertwined. Basically, I believe that is how one must respond.

Phronēsis is a whole virtue; it is not an ability, but a being, as Heidegger correctly stated. I mean, it is just a fact about phronēsis that one in fact can hardly say, "That is phronēsis!" One notices much more easily when it is lacking.

And so we notice more quickly when a discourse lacks appropriateness, than when it is present?

Yes, but also we cannot express everything, even when it is very moderate. The speaker who is not self-critical is on the wrong path.

Your concluding question in the conversation with Grondin, "Can we revive the old, broad sense of rhetoric?"[30] *remained open. Aristotle, however, appears to have understood rhetoric more narrowly when he placed it as a technē within politics and thereby established it as the practical coming to a decision. Freeing rhetoric from this determination has not necessarily agreed with it. Again and again it is even claimed that the broad sense of this concept leads right away to demanding too much of rhetoric or to surrendering it to complete relativity.*

How do you evaluate this risk? Does rhetoric need to be tied to politics?

Well, you cannot say that in general. It depends. You once read my essay[31] about why the philosopher does not really live for politics. I recall that now with this answer and add: one cannot say that so completely clearly. And here I would also say: already both are there. I am tempted to go into that, yet I must [see the limitations]. And if one does not achieve this perspective that includes both, then politics will just not become politics, but something that is the opposite of politics: that one knows everything ahead of time. The politics that one wanted as politics turns out not to be one. Rather, politics is exactly what one instinctively does and that then takes effect by itself.

Is this perhaps the relationship: if one would bind rhetoric completely within the horizon of politics, then one could not achieve an understanding of what politics is?

Yes.

A philosophical rhetoric would take the political into account, but not be absorbed into the political.

That is it. But it is certainly a very arduous task to correctly use and choose between the broad concept of rhetoric and the one common today.

It is surprising that you never really held a class on rhetoric, although rhetoric often plays a part in your writings.

To be a good defender of my option, it was just not possible. I had always—oh, well, it's so difficult, you know; something like a critique of such a subject matter is so difficult. I do not know how my works came about. They just all came. And many works of others [on rhetoric] disappointed me when I read them. But in the main, the answer is simple: I no longer felt that I was at the apex of my philological knowledge. There were rather heavy demands placed on me. And I wasn't able to do everything, not even then.

What would be most important to you in the revival of rhetoric? How would then the art of speaking stand in the relation to the art of listening?

It always depends on the first five years of life. You must always consider that in these first five years one learns to speak. That's the point; that's the reason I say this. That is why it is so definitive, as definitive as how you can hear where somebody has come from. It has to do with the colossal power of learning to speak—it is the building of the world! I am now a great-grandfather. I now have a great-grandson who is about six years old. When he learns a new word that he correctly uses, he is overjoyed. That surely is what is essential, that one learns to fully express oneself. Everything that one learns in addition builds upon such a basis.

We must learn more languages. That is the main point. English will naturally become the worldwide language of commerce, but there will be mother tongues everywhere. And that is what we must fight for. Every language has a new point of view, and one will become more tolerant when one permits the way the other speaks. I believe that by learning more foreign languages, one will be educated in the end to a greater self-critique. That is also a possible way to achieve world peace. We will also have to learn, to say, that all religions have their partiality and therefore may justify their recognition of the others. I don't know, but I suspect that this must happen if we wish to survive.

But surely it is true that rhetoric is, by far, not yet a possible word for what it itself is. In the end it is a communal listening. That is what my hermeneutics always had in view: there is no last, definitive word. That is given to no one. If the other misunderstands me, then I must speak differently until he understands me. We are all always only underway.

Professor Gadamer, thank you very much for this conversation.

Notes

1. The essay referred to is Heidegger's programmatic work of 1922: "Phänomenologische Interpretationen zu Aristoteles: Anzeige der hermeneutischen Situation," also called the "Natorp Report," printed in *Dilthey-Jahrbuch* 6 (1989): 237–269.

2. Paul Natorp (1854–1924), professor of philosophy at the University of Marburg, next to his teacher Hermann Cohen the intellectual head of the so-called Marburg school of Neo-Kantianism. Nicolai Hartmann (1882–1950), professor of philosophy at the University of Marburg. Influential in the fields of metaphysics, ontology and ethics. In 1925 he left Marburg to succeed Max Scheler at the University of Cologne.

3. Ernst Lommatzsch (1871–1949), professor of classical philology at the University of Marburg.

4. Paul Friedländer (1882–1968), Gadamer's second philology teacher.

5. "Die Logik des verbum interius: Hans-Georg Gadamer in Conversation with Gudrun Kühne-Bertram and Frithjof Rodi," *Dilthey-Jahrbuch* 11 (1997–98): 19–30, esp. 29.

6. "Dialogischer Rückblick auf das Gesammelte Werk," in *Gadamer Lesebuch*, ed. Jean Grondin (Tübingen: Mohr Siebeck, 1997), 280-295, esp. 284.

7. Martin Heidegger, *Grundbegriffe der aristotelischen Philosophie: Marburger Vorlesung Sommersemester 1924*, Gesamtausgabe, vol. 18, ed. Mark Michalski (Frankfurt: Klostermann, 2002), 114, hereafter cited as GA 18. When the conversation reproduced here was held, GA 18 had not yet been published. Hans-Georg Gadamer had, as a text, a copy of Walter Bröcker's transcript of the lectures. A translation of GA 18 is forthcoming from Indiana University Press under the title *Basic Concepts of Aristotelian Philosophy.*

8. GA 18, 169f.

9. Max Scheler died on May 19, 1928. On the following Monday (May 21), Heidegger presented an obituary for him in his lecture. Printed in *Metaphysische Anfangsgründe der Logik im Ausgang von Leibniz*, GA 26.

10. Printed in *Ontologie Hermeneutik der Faktizität,* GA 63.

11. GA 18, 3.

12. Ibid., 329.

13. Ibid., 327.

14. See also Hans-Georg Gadamer, *Philosophische Lehrjahre* (Frankfurt: Klostermann, 1977), 12. In the summer semester of 1918 Gadamer attended the Neo-Kantian Eugen Kühnemann's Introduction to Kant's *Critique of Pure Reason.*

15. Gadamer taught in Leipzig from the summer semester 1938 to the summer semester 1947.

16. GA 18, 117.

17. Compare Martin Heidegger "Die Sprache" (1950) in *Unterwegs zur Sprache* (Pfullingen: Neske, 1959), 9–33, esp. 32.

18. GA 18, 177.

19. Ibid., 262.

20. Ibid., 289.

21. What is meant is the SS 1924 lecture course (GA 18).

22. GA 18, 261.

23. In the lecture course SS 1924.

24. Aeschylus, *Agamemnon*, 177.

25. GA 18, 203.

26. Gadamer, "Die Logik des verbum interius," 30.

27. GA 18, 165.

28. Gadamer, "Dialogischer Rückblick auf das Gesammelte Werk," 292.

29. GA 18, 118.

30. Gadamer, "Dialogischer Rückblick auf das Gesammelte Werk," 295.

31. Hans-Georg Gadamer, "Über die politische Inkompetenz der Philosophie," in *Hermeneutische Entwürfe* (Tübingen: Mohr Siebeck, 2000), 35–42.

3

Mark Michalski
Translated by Jamey Findling

Hermeneutic Phenomenology as Philology

It was quite a surprise when, in the summer semester of 1924, Martin Heidegger began his Marburg lecture course, "Basic Concepts of Aristotelian Philosophy," with the announcement that he would be offering a course neither on philosophy, nor on the history of philosophy, but on philology.[1] In order to understand what is meant here by philology and by a philological approach to Aristotle, it is best to begin by considering two relevant points of intellectual history.

First, Heidegger had by then already spent a few years pursuing the project of laying bare the primordial concern of Aristotelian thinking. He sought to accomplish this project by means of a destructuring (*Destruktion*)[2] of the philosophical-theological systemicity and conceptuality that had been layered upon such thinking in the course of the philosophical tradition, and in particular by Thomas Aquinas, Thomism, and Catholic theology. In this project Heidegger could actually find more solidarity with the Protestant theologian Rudolf Bultmann—who was then striving, in corresponding fashion, to release the authentic *kerygma* of the New Testament from the distorting conceptuality of Greek philosophy—than he could with his more systematically disposed philosophical colleagues Paul Natorp and Nicolai Hartmann. For both Heidegger and Bultmann, it was a matter of penetrating through a long tradition of interpretation,

The translator would like to gratefully acknowledge the suggestions of Rod Coltman and Ted George, which were most helpful in completing this translation.

of pressing through to the interpreted text itself and to the concepts proper to it. Given that both projects dealt with Greek and Latin texts, collaboration with classical philologists was only natural. Hence there developed, in the Marburg of the 1920s, a certain cooperation, which strictly speaking was philological in character, between the instructors and students in the departments of philosophy, theology, and philology. Likewise characteristic of this air of cooperation were the numerous reading circles, which have been related by Hans-Georg Gadamer in a published recollection of his student years.[3]

Second, classical philology in the stricter academic sense had, one year prior to the Heidegger lecture course with which we are here concerned, seen the publication of an extremely significant contribution to Aristotle scholarship, namely, Werner Jaeger's attempt at a reconstruction of the historical development of Aristotelian philosophy. What was remarkable about this attempt was that a new view of Aristotle's philosophy as a whole had actually emerged from precisely that piecemeal work for which philologists are so well known. The result was that specialists in philosophy were placed in the somewhat compromised position of having to argue philologically as well as philosophically in order to contest Jaeger's conclusions concerning the overall meaning of Aristotelian philosophy. Here again, Gadamer's testimony is instructive. In a vita written for his habilitation, Gadamer remarks that Jaeger's book on Aristotle brought home to him, as a philosopher, the need for a thorough training in philology. According to Gadamer, the advance of philosophical interpretation would be impossible if one had "to trust in the results of philological research without any critical resources of one's own. Philosophical and philological questions cannot be posed independently of each other."[4]

In what follows, we will first investigate more precisely the extent to which Heidegger's claim to be doing philology—taken in terms of this assertion of the inseparability of philosophy and philology—can be confirmed. That is, we will examine the extent to which the methods of philology are in fact used, and the results of classical philology taken into account, in the Aristotle lecture course of 1924. However, the matter is not thereby laid to rest. For, in the first place, Heidegger does not actually say anything about *joining* philosophy with philology; rather, he says that he wishes to *replace* philosophy with philology. And, in the second place, he gives a hypothetical formulation: If philology were to denote "passion for the knowledge of that which has been expressed and of its self-expression" [Leidenschaft der Erkenntnis des Ausgesprochenen und des Sichaussprechens], then his aim and his procedure would be purely philological, then what he carries out would be philology (4, 333). Heidegger, then, does not employ some vague concept of philology, nor does he utilize an already established academic concept; instead he determines the concept in terms of a fundamental way of knowing—indeed, one that is rather well suited for disputing the privileged rank of what is traditionally called philosophy. Hence we will, in the second part of the exposition that follows, pursue the question of what exactly is to be understood by the phrase "passion for the knowledge of that which has been expressed and of its self-expression." In this connection, it is also crucial to notice the occasional usage, in this same lecture course, of the term *hermeneutics,* which serves to remind us that this lecture course in fact belongs to Heidegger's attempt to recast the reflexive phenomenology of Husserl as a hermeneutic phenomenology. We are thus faced with the task of grasping philology as a moment in the hermeneuticizing of phenomenology. At the same time, however, we will also need to inquire into the relationship of philology to Aristotle's treatment of rhetoric, which is dealt with extensively in the lecture course under the heading of a "hermeneutic of *Dasein.*"

I. Heidegger as Classical Philologist

Surveying the sources and aids to which Heidegger has recourse for his interpretation of Aristotle, one finds him relying almost exclusively on the texts of Aristotle themselves. Both the interpretation of Aristotle that has developed in the history of philosophy as well as the various forms of philosophical Aristotelianism remain, so to speak, bracketed. To be sure, in connection with the question concerning the essence of the concept and its definition, Heidegger does make reference to Porphyry, Boethius, Kant, and Hegel. But, in typical fashion, he does so only to show that in their scholastic logic a fundamental possibility of speaking has degenerated into a mere thought technique, and that only by virtue of a return to the Aristotelian determination of *horismos* as *logos ousias* can this fundamental possibility be recovered (9f, 15f, 335f). In addition, Heidegger's reference to the treatment of the affects by the Stoics and the church fathers, as well as by Thomas Aquinas and Luther, does not imply that our understanding of Aristotle is to be augmented by a study of this effective history (*Wirkungsgeschichte*); on the contrary, it seeks to show that Aristotle's doctrine of the pathē exerts a tremendous influence on those discussions and therefore represents a necessary basis for their interpretation (177f). The sole exceptions to this tendency are apparently Aristotle's late-classical commentators Themistius and Simplicius, as well as Friedrich Nietzsche. I say "apparently," because Heidegger introduces these figures not so much as philosophers but as philologists. Based on Heidegger's numerous references to the first two, in which he cites brief statements from their commentaries on Aristotle's *Physics* (319, 369, 376, 381, 386, 394), one may conclude that Heidegger carefully worked through at least the parts of those commentaries dealing with chapters 1–3 of the third book of the *Physics*. From Nietzsche, on the other hand, there is simply the aperçu that Greek is the "most speakable of all languages," to which Heidegger then adds "In the final analysis he must have known what it is to be Greek" [was das Griechentum ist (109)]—and which we might then complete as follows: as the natural classical philologist that he was. In any case, what is worth noting here is that Heidegger had undertaken a reading of precisely that lecture on the "History of Greek Eloquence" that is contained in the second volume of Nietzsche's *Philologica*.

What emerges from all of this—namely, that apart from the texts of Aristotle himself no philosophical authorities whatsoever are admitted as interpretive aids, whereas at least a few philological authorities are—may be confirmed by looking at a handful of the contemporary classical philologists to whom Heidegger refers. Most prominent among these is in fact none other than Werner Jaeger, to whom Heidegger returns repeatedly throughout the course. To begin with, Jaeger's book on Aristotle, which had appeared the previous year, is the only text Heidegger recommends to his students as secondary reading. Admittedly, in the course of this recommendation Heidegger lets it be known that this book addresses precisely what he himself proposes *not* to deal with: the personality, that is, the figure of Aristotle, his philosophy in the sense of a system, and his development.[5] But at this point it remains unclear whether Heidegger intends the relationship between Jaeger's approach and his own to be understood merely as complementary or, rather, as conflicting. What cannot fail to be noticed, however, is the switching of labels that takes place: Jaeger, the classical philologist, gives us philosophy; Heidegger, the philosopher, gives us philology. It is tempting to detect here an admonition to not look too rashly and ambitiously for a philosophical system when dealing with the texts of Aristotle, but at least initially to be content with philology for a while—indeed, even to proceed more philologically than does Jaeger, the philologist. Be that as it may, Heidegger does accept certain isolated conclusions of Jaeger's research—specifically, conclusions concerning the literary character, the relative chronology, and the authenticity of the writings contained in the Aristotelian corpus (4f, 37, 107, 239, 323). It is only with regard to the more fundamental issues of Jaeger's work that Heidegger speaks disapprovingly, and in such cases his arguments are altogether philological—as, for example, when he says that one ought not to use vague conjectures concerning the relation of certain portions of a text to other texts for the purpose of dating them "and from the relations of the treatises write a developmental history of Aristotle. It is my conviction that this effort is altogether hopeless" (299). All in all, however, one cannot avoid the impression that Heidegger actually saw himself quite seriously challenged by this effort—which is perhaps why he gave such a rigorous examination in the subject to his student Gadamer, whose professional commitment to classical philology went beyond

Heidegger's own.[6] Apart from Jaeger, the lecture course also mentions Hermann Diels, Ludwig Spengel, and Hermann Bonitz. Diels serves as the source for the interpretation of the *exoterikoi logoi*, in the sense of nonscientific discourse founded on prevailing opinions. He is also the source for the interpretation of the etymology of the fundamental concept of *entelecheia* (107, 296, 367f). Spengel contributes the conjecture of a pre-Aristotelian authorship for the *Rhetorica ad Alexandrum*, while Bonitz's *Index Aristotelicus* provides a reference for a certain use of the concept of *ousia* (113f, 345). Hence, when it comes to some of the areas, such as lexicology, etymology, and the determination of authenticity, which traditionally belong to the craft of classical philology, Heidegger is now and again quite willing to place himself under the care of recognized scholars.

For the rest of it, however, so exclusively does Aristotle's text govern Heidegger's interpretation that Luther's principle of *sola scriptura* seems to find application here: Aristotle *sui ipsius interpres*. Heidegger makes it clear immediately, in the very first hour of the lecture, that his approach to Aristotle will be concept-centered, and that to this end it will also be text-centered and reading-centered: the goal is "the understanding of *some fundamental concepts of Aristotelian philosophy*," and this understanding is to be gained "by way of the study of the *text* of the Aristotelian treatises," which in turn is intended to "bring the *reading* of philosophers somewhat more into practice" (3, 5). According to the formulation in the manuscript, this way of gaining understanding is at the same time hearing-centered: the course should yield instructions for "*listening* to what Aristotle has to say" (333). It may be inferred that in these notions of reading and listening are asserted two separate principles of textual interpretation, which Heidegger, somewhat in passing, makes mention of during the course: (1) *As reader*, the interpreter must base interpretation on the actual text. That is, the reader must show that that upon which it is based "stands in the text itself and is not . . . fabricated," that it "has its ground" in the text (216, 237). (2) *As listener*, the interpreter must go beyond the text standing before him to what is genuinely said and meant therein, such that interpretation in this sense "is nothing else than emphasizing what is not there" (66). That these principles do not, in Heidegger's view, contradict each other, but rather coincide in the concrete activity of interpretation, is made plain by the fact that both play an equal part in his interpretation of the Aristotelian concept of *zoē* as being-in-the-world.[7]

It obviously belongs to the notion of text-centeredness that the original Greek wording be cited extensively. As such, Heidegger relied on the then-current scholarly editions, complete with critical apparatus. To be sure, it is not possible to know whether he looked at different editions of the same text in order to make judgments about their worth, but by no means does he ever simply accept uncritically the publisher's preferred version. He carefully takes into account the critical apparatus, either throwing out conjectures he regards as unnecessary, or else inserting his own conjectures based on expectations drawn from corresponding texts (295). As a rule, Heidegger never cites from the German translations, but rather gives his own translation or paraphrase. A comparison of Heidegger's own manuscript with student notes reveals that these translations were generally formulated at the podium during the lecture. Often, they contained individual Greek concepts, or even entire sentence parts, which were left untranslated and were elaborated with additional commentary. Hence accusations that Heidegger arrogantly ignored the German translations of Aristotle that were then available, or that his translations were marked by an excessive freedom and looseness, quite simply fail to do him justice. Indeed, the rough and imprecise practice of translation effectively makes evident that the character of translation is in principle experimental, provisional, and always incomplete, and it thus rules out the erroneous notion that a translation could ever replace the Greek text and thereby render superfluous the necessity of reading and attending to the original. Moreover, whenever Heidegger notices a mistake of his own—or, as the case may be, has them pointed out by his attentive audience, which was astonishingly strong in Greek—he takes quite deliberate pains to set things aright, that is, to show that the interpretation entailed by his translation has done no violence to the text (222, 226f). With respect to the range of texts used, Heidegger occupies a middle ground between a fickle leaping to and fro between every text in the Aristotelian corpus and an immanent preoccupation with a single text. Guided by his initial question concerning the rootedness or autochthony of conceptuality (*Bodenständigkeit der Begrifflichkeit*), he follows a pattern of taking up a sizable segment of interrelated texts and thoroughly attending to them before following the thread to another segment of similar scale that either advances the interpretation already under way, or else prepares for another interpretation that seems called for on the basis of what has preceded it. In this way the context receives attention on both the micro- and the macrolevel: on the microlevel to the point of a precise analysis of the construction of single chapters,[8] on the macrolevel in the form of going beyond not only single texts, but also the various groups of texts, insofar as this is suggested by the internal relations of the texts.[9]

This way of dealing with the texts is motivated and guided by the concept-centeredness of the lecture: it is the concepts that demand such a deep immersion in the Greek milieu in which they took shape, and it is precisely the concepts that determine the contexts. In accordance with the insight that technical terms are rarely neologisms, but rather are much more typically formed out of common or familiar words through discrete measures of semantic shift,[10] Heidegger repeatedly gives close attention to the prephilosophical and nonphilosophical, that is, natural, language usage of the Greeks, most emphatically in the case of the fundamental concept of ousia (12). The reflection on the event of *metapherein*, "transference," which is explicitly raised by Aristotle himself, moves along the same lines. In such transference, a meaning is borrowed from the "first and primordial" addressing of something and is transferred to a new way of addressing a thing—a process whereby the borrowed meaning lets itself be seen exactly as such (83). Heidegger takes into account this event of meaning transference whenever it lends itself to the investigation of the "first and primordial" meaning of a word. Thus he is able to make the translation of the word *soma* as "body" more precise by pointing out that corporeality in this case does not mean stuffness (*Stofflichkeit*) or materiality (*Materialität*), but rather that strange obtrusiveness of a being that can be detected in later usage, when *to son soma*, as well as *su* and soma, could mean "slave" or "prisoner" (28, 347). Particularly when translating fundamental concepts, Heidegger exhibits even less confidence in the standard German translations than he does when translating contextually related material. If fundamental concepts tend to remain untranslated—both in Heidegger's translations of Aristotle into German as well as in the course of his interpretive remarks—those common German translations that do appear are either, as with soma, given more precise meanings, or else they are explicitly rejected and replaced by something that comes nearer to the meaning favored by Heidegger. An instructive example is *hekaston*: "This is not 'each' [*jedes*] or even 'single' and 'individual.' Such translations stray from the correct path. *Hekas* means 'distant,' and so hekaston means 'what in each case obtains' [*Jeweiliges*] insofar as I linger with it and thereby see it from a certain distance" (32). Here we find a reason for Heidegger's negative regard for the available translations: not only do they inadequately reproduce what is meant, but they virtually block the path that leads to understanding insofar as they cling to thinking with an excessive familiarity and do not expose it to that element of the strange that is proper to every originary concept formation. It is precisely this goal—namely, to expose thinking to the element of the strange—that is served by the suggested translation "what in each case obtains," insofar as it is bound up with the demand to hear this word from out of a lingering and the distance that can be taken up in such a lingering—that is, to hear it in a new way. Other examples include *telos*—not "goal" (*Ziel*) or "purpose" (*Zweck*), but "end" (*Ende*) in the sense of completion[11]; ousia—not "essence" (*Wesen*), but "existence" (Dasein) in the sense of being available (25, 40); *aisthēsis*—not "sensation" (*Empfindung*), but "attending to" (*Vernehmen*) the world in the sense of having-it-there (52); and *energeia*—not "reality" (*Wirklichkeit*), but "being-at-work" (*Im-Werke-Sein*) in the sense of a distinctive "how" of being (*ausgezeichneten Wie des*

Seins).[12] As the last example shows, Heidegger is more than willing to employ etymological discussions in connection with the translation and interpretation of basic concepts. This turns out to be all but necessary in the case of the Aristotelian neologism entelecheia, the meaning of which, according to Diels, is derived from the components *enteles* and *echein*. It is characteristic of Heidegger's relation to the philologist that, on the one hand, he does not shy away from even the most minute details of linguistics, and yet that, on the other hand, he will readily depart from his translation and substitute one of his own: "'Possession of completeness' [*Besitz der Vollkommenheit*]—this does not convey the meaning that is ontologically fundamental: 'holding-itself-in-completion' [*Sich-im-Fertigsein-Halten*]."[13]

On the basis of the preceding observations, one may now give the following answer to the question posed at the outset: in this lecture course Heidegger may be said to engage in philology in a rigorously academic sense, insofar as he does not work in the company of a single philosopher, but does in fact enlist the aid of a number of philologists—some of whom have, through the application of genuinely philological methods, reached conclusions that are relevant for Heidegger's own interpretation and have, in a manner that is generally characteristic of philology, placed the original text and its concepts at the center of their concerns. At the same time, however, it is clear that Heidegger has not entirely become a classical philologist. In a negative sense, this means that he fails to take into account the research literature to any extensive degree, nor does he apply consistently and self-sufficiently the specialized philological methods that were then current, methods pertaining to the general principle of remaining close to the text. In a positive sense, this means that his conceptual discussions, which are carried out in close connection with the concrete texts—so strenuously does Heidegger reject the aim of reconstructing a philosophical system—actually turn out to order these concepts, by virtue of the guiding question of the autochthony of conceptuality, into a systematic whole that exceeds the horizon of classical philology.

II. Philology, Hermeneutic Phenomenology, and Rhetoric

What is remarkable about this is that Heidegger explicitly rejects the title of philosophy in favor of philology even for this region that exceeds the horizon of classical philology. As already indicated, Heidegger's aim of distinguishing his project from Werner Jaeger's study of the development of Aristotle's philosophical system would naturally have played a role in his rejection of the designations of philosophy and the history of philosophy. But Heidegger himself provides a few more indications. At one point, somewhat in passing, he remarks to his students "that it would perhaps be a good idea if philosophers would resolve to consider what it actually means to speak to others" (169f). This statement, directed critically at Heidegger's philosophical colleagues, attests to their lack of conscious reflection on the fundamental conditions of the very thing that they themselves, as teachers, were practicing in the auditorium. Is the discourse of teaching simply a matter of moving the listeners to a specific conclusion, or is it rather a question of making a thing evident in its substantive character (*Sachcharakter*)? And what does this imply with regard to the disposition required of the speaker, the listeners, and the discourse itself? Inasmuch as Heidegger is addressing those individuals, referred to generally as "the philosophers," who no longer concern themselves with the questions dealt with by Aristotle, philosophy becomes a synonym for the lack of self-understanding that now prevails in research and teaching concerning its own discourse. Along the same lines, there is the remark that philosophy today is "in better shape [than philology], provided that it maintains the fundamental presupposition that things could not be better" [es sei alles in bester Ordnung].[14] That is to say, as the context shows: philosophy maintains the illusory fundamental presupposition that it does not itself stand under any presuppositions of which it must become conscious in order to conduct research and to teach in the bright light of clear self-understanding; it divests itself of any claim such presuppositions might make; it regards itself as presuppositionless and as having an ultimate foundation (*letztbegründend*). We can accordingly assume that the philology which Heidegger mobilizes against philosophy would be the attempt to conduct one's research and teaching precisely while confronting the claim made by the presuppositions involved in such practices, and while seeking to understand the fundamental conditions of one's own discourse.

This assumption is confirmed by what is explicitly stated concerning philology in the introduction to the course. According to Heidegger, it is precisely the philological intent of the lecture that "by nature" entails certain presuppositions.[15] The first of the six presuppositions enumerated there—namely, that in view of the philological intent of the lecture it is Aristotle alone whose discourse is relevant—is already telling: philology is obviously not just a particular way of access to Aristotle, a mere method to be applied to an object—Aristotle—selected in advance; it is instead a fundamental matter of concern in its own right. Admittedly, such a concern lends itself especially well to a lecture course on Aristotle, since his writings deal extensively with the question, so neglected by later philosophers, of the fundamental conditions of discourse. But if the philologist is to allow Aristotle to say something, a couple of things are involved. On the one hand, as the second presupposition makes clear, the philologist must not regard himself as so far advanced that he has nothing more to learn. On the other hand, as the sixth presupposition states, the philologist must attribute to the historical past in general, to which Aristotle belongs, a saying power that reaches the philologist himself. That is, Heidegger's concept of philology involves the following: the researcher and teacher must always recognize that, on his own, he can never achieve an adequate reflection concerning what is said but remains dependent for that on an impulse from tradition, and that the essential impulse can only come from Aristotle. The third, fourth, and fifth of the presuppositions enumerated by Heidegger concern the particular status of the discourse called for by the adoption, so urgently needed, of such a conception of philology. Conceptual discourse is not simply the appropriate medium for definition and communication, it is the substance of all scientific research; and yet this scientific research is not simply an external and more or less incidental circumstance of life, but rather a possibility of existence for which human beings must choose and decide, and indeed, in a certain contrast to religious existence, it is that possibility in which human existence takes up a position with regard to its own interpretation that is centered solely upon itself. Hence to Heidegger's concept of philology belongs further the following: as the reflection of research and teaching upon its own discourse, a reflection that relies on an impulse originating with Aristotle, philology deals with itself as a science, and thereby with the distinctive possibility of human existence that seeks to come to an understanding of itself without recourse to divine revelation—that is, philology is the existentially-ontologically grounded directive of scientific research. Heidegger's lecture is accordingly directed to students in every department, challenging them not so much to philosophize or to take up the study of Aristotle, but rather to turn to their own, freely chosen disciplines and "to become *aware*" of the conceptuality found there, "to really *grasp* it and to pursue it in such a way that the *activity* of conceptual *research* comes to *life*."[16] And this, let it be said, not in the sense of a scientific propaedeutic that must be completed before science proper can begin, but rather in the sense of a task that, in connection with the objects of study, is always to be undertaken anew.[17]

With this, we have gained a clue to a more precise understanding of the definition of philology as "passion for the knowledge of that which has been expressed and of its self-expression," which at first had seemed rather cryptic and idiosyncratic.[18] Obviously this definition takes its orientation from the two elements, both rooted in Greek, that comprise "philo-logy," according to which philology is a *philia* of logos, a "love of speaking." When Heidegger explicates this "love" as a "passion for knowledge," he thereby gives precedence to a theoretical conception as opposed to a practical one (which would have been equally plausible): it is not a matter of the practical exercise of speech, but rather of its theoretical cognition (*Erkenntnis*). However, such theoretical cognition does not, as might be supposed, stand in contrast to the practical exercise of speech by virtue of its indifference toward its object. Instead, like the practical exercise of speech, it too remains carried along by "passion." In this connection we should think of Aristotle's notion of *pathos*—which Heidegger, let it be noted, translates in his lecture course as "attunement" (*Befindlichkeit*), and which is thereby designated as the historical impulse for Heidegger's own existential-ontological thematization of the attunement of Dasein (4, 120, 168). Just as, with Aristotle, theory represents a state of being composed (*Gefasstsein*) against the pathos of fear, namely the fear that what is constantly there (*das Immerseiende*) could perhaps one day cease to be (289f), so likewise existential ontology takes science, as a possibility of existence grasped by Dasein, to be an attuned understanding disposed by moods—just like all other possibilities of existence. For the philologist, the question of the cognition of speech (*Erkennen des Sprechens*) is a matter of the philologist's attuned and comprehending being-in-the-world (*befindlich-verstehendes In-der-Welt-sein*). In his definition of philology, Heidegger unfolds speech as the duality "of that which has been expressed and of its self-expression" [des Ausgesprochenen und des Sichaussprechens]. In this way, he indicates the structural multiplicity displayed by the Aristotelian concept of logos. To wit: (1) *Legein*, "speaking" in the sense of accessing, that is, in the sense of an approach to something, addressing it and showing it forth—this speaking about something is essentially both speaking with and to others, or again, the ability to listen to such speaking and expressing of oneself (*Sich-selbst-Aussprechen*), that is, self-expression (*Sichaussprechen*). (2) *Legomenon*, "the spoken," "that which has been expressed" (*Ausgesprochenes*) in the sense of an answer, that is, what is shown forth by the being that was addressed (*von dem angesprochenen Seienden*); (3) Legein and at the same time legomenon, "speaking" and "that which has been expressed" in the sense of something that just pops into one's head and comes out, something that I don't really do and that therefore no longer really belongs to me, but rather has become generally available public property (17, 19f, 104f, 123f, 212, 216f, 276f, 304, 341, 358).

The task of philological knowledge is to separate the logos into its multiple structural moments. However, the fact that philology, as revealed by our first approach to what Heidegger means by this word, aims in particular at conceptual speaking in scientific research and teaching means that this conceptual speaking should be situated in the structural whole of human speaking and made transparent in its genesis from that speaking. Philology tries to show what makes up the conceptuality of concepts as distinct from nonconceptual speaking, as well as how this conceptuality is rooted in speaking as the fundamental attunement of the being of human beings, and thereby in Dasein itself as the being of human beings. For this purpose it investigates the everyday self-expression of human beings with others concerning whatever contributes to the end of its concerns—which is where the average understanding, in which Dasein comports itself as just anyone (*als Man*), can find expression (55f, 63f). But because logos in the third sense, the sense of something that just pops into one's head and comes out—in short, idle chatter—comes to prominence, so that the genuine meaning is ever more obscured, this means that the possibility of the concept first appears in the possibility one has of disregarding everyday concerns and of appropriating the genuine meaning in an original way, as a countermove against idle chatter (217, 276f). Let it also be said, however, that the concept can also and immediately sink back again into idle chatter and thereby betray what was originally appropriated from it,[19] so that, on the conceptual level, philology must delimit authentically conceptual speaking from that which is inauthentic.

How then does the project, sketched above, of an existential-ontological philology that exceeds the horizon of classical philology, stand in relation to the still more comprehensive project of a hermeneutic phenomenology, which Heidegger had pursued since the War Emergency Semester of 1919, and which finally wound up being systematically drafted in *Sein und Zeit*, published in 1927? Heidegger mentions phenomenology only sparingly in the lectures on Aristotle, and then, characteristically, only in the form of an allusion to what is Aristotelian in phenomenology and what is phenomenological in Aristotle. In one place there is even a kind of criticism of phenomenology, when Heidegger asserts the superiority of an Aristotelian insight over a claim of phenomenology (199, 237, 254). Talk of hermeneutics, by contrast, seems to be on the rise: in preference to logic and ontology, it is considered to be the more appropriate title for the thematization of Dasein, and, in the sense of the interpretation of concrete Dasein, it is designated as the topic of Aristotle's *Rhetoric*.[20] Above all, however, hermeneutics is present as a matter of fact in that Heidegger distinguishes as the three moments of conceptuality the *concrete fundamental experience*, the *guiding claim*, and the *prevailing intelligibility*, and he accounts for their possibility in Dasein by means of distinguishing *fore-having*, *fore-sight*, and *fore-grasping* as the three moments of the interpretedness of Dasein. The concrete fundamental experience, as the experience of a being in its primary appearance that forms the basis of the entire further process of concept formation and thus presents the object in advance, is possible by means of fore-having, in which the attuned Dasein already in a certain way has there before itself the world and the beings that belong to the world. The guiding claim, as the addressing of beings in accord with a sense of being that gives guidance in a more or less inexplicit manner, is possible by means of fore-seeing, in which the understanding Dasein, in its dealings in the world and with the beings that belong to the world, always already looks toward a particular sense of being. The prevailing intelligibility, as the conceptual explication that in each case suffices to provide an acceptable standard of knowledge and evidence, is possible by means of fore-grasping, in which Dasein always already grasps the determinations of beings in a dominating way and renders them distinguishable (13f, 270f, 338f, 354f). As hermeneutical, phenomenology seeks access to the things themselves from the starting point of the interpretedness of Dasein. Indeed, it does so in such a manner that, by means of the explicit appropriation of its fore-having, fore-seeing, and fore-grasping, it throws into relief—along with the interpretedness that is always governing in a historical Dasein—the distortions through which Dasein conceals the things. However, to the extent that the current prevalence of a form of interpretedness, along with the distortions inherent in it, is actually carried by the logos that, as everyday idle talk, or even as inauthentic conceptual talk, governs all interpretations of Dasein in an ever greater distance from things,[21] to such an extent philology—in the sense of the thematization of the authentic conceptual speech that takes shape as a countermovement against such idle talk—is disclosed as a necessary element of hermeneutic phenomenology: it is the element with which hermeneutic phenomenology takes into account the leading function of speech in the dominance of the interpretedness of Dasein.

Some of what Heidegger says about Aristotle's *Rhetoric* makes it clear that in certain respects, he sees this conception of a hermeneutic-phenomenological philology prefigured there: the *Rhetoric* attests to a primordial viewing of speech, the phenomena of which are surveyed and distinguished in terms of the basic possibilities Dasein has of speaking-with-one-another (*Miteinandersprechen*)—the result being an interpretation of concrete Dasein as being-with-one-another (*Miteinandersein*).[22] There are, however, two respects in which the concerns of philology cannot be equated with those of rhetoric. In the first place, philology—even if passionate—remains a theoretical cognition of speech, whereas rhetoric, as treated by Aristotle, represents the practical possibility of seeing what speaks for the subject matter for whoever is resolved to convince others of something (114f). Only insofar as Aristotle's *Rhetoric*, in the sense of the treatment of rhetoric as a practical possibility, maintains a theoretical character throughout its general reflection on the fundamental conditions and possibilities of discourse (a reflection that is carried out for the sake of this treatment)—only to this extent can Aristotle's *Rhetoric* be regarded as a predecessor to Heideggerian philology. In the second place, philology has to do primarily with the conceptual speech of scientific research and teaching, whereas rhetoric, by contrast, deals primarily with the everyday speaking-with-one-another that Dasein directs toward the regulation of its everyday being-with-one-another. To be sure, this everyday speaking-with-one-another is made thematic in philology as well, to the extent that it needs to disclose idle talk as the negative impulse with respect to the development of conceptual speech, but it exceeds the scope of rhetoric at least in the direction of that which Aristotle himself delimits from rhetoric as dialectic.[23] It is precisely in connection with dialectic that Heidegger, at the beginning of the course, explains how he proposes to deal philologically with philosophy: "*Dialektikē* has, to be sure, its seriousness (the same that has been lost by every philosophy that has become sophistry). But this is only the seriousness of an attempt at seeing what could ultimately be meant (by the concepts). In this sense we are dealing with philosophy" (7).

Notes

1. Martin Heidegger, *Grundbegriffe der aristotelischen Philosophie: Marburger Vorlesung Sommersemester 1924*, Gesamtausgabe, vol. 18, ed. Mark Michalski (Frankfurt: Klostermann, 2002), 4, 333. Henceforth all page references not otherwise specified are to this text.

2. German words in parentheses or brackets have been inserted by the translator. –*Trans.*

3. Hans-Georg Gadamer, *Philosophische Lehrjahre* (Frankfurt: Klostermann, 1977), 14ff.

4. Quoted in Jean Grondin, *Hans-Georg Gadamer: Eine Biographie* (Tübingen: Mohr Siebeck, 1999), 139.

5. 4, 333. Cf. Werner Jaeger, *Aristoteles: Grundlegung einer Geschichte seiner Entwicklung* (Berlin: Weidman, 1923).

6. Hans-Georg Gadamer, *Sechs Briefe an Martin Heidegger aus der Marburger Zeit* (Marburg: Jahresgabe der Martin-Heidegger-Gesellschaft, 1999), 14f. Hans-Georg Gadamer, "Werner Jaeger, Aristoteles" (review), in *Gesammelte Werke,* vol. 5: *Griechische Philosophie I* (Tübingen: Mohr Siebeck, 1985), 286f.

7. Heidegger admits that one might initially hold the opinion that this interpretation is "read into" Aristotle (66), and hence he later attempts with great vigor to establish its validity on the basis of a text out of *De partibus animalium* (234f).

8. As in the case of *Metaphysics* 5.16 on *teleion* (83f), *Rhetoric* 2.5 on *phobos* (249f), and *Physics* 3.1–3, with its three approaches to the definition of *kinēsis* (287f, 316, 323f).

9. Thus the consideration of *agathon* in *Nicomachean Ethics* 1.1–6 is interrupted by a consideration of teleion in *Metaphysics* 5.16 precisely where teleion

shows itself as a criterion for agathon in the sense of a *telos di hauto* (80f). As far as the different text groups are concerned, the predominant ones are, to be sure, those that are in a broad sense ethical and ontological, but the logical texts of the *Topics* (152f) and the natural science texts, in particular *De partibus animalium* (208f), also receive a look.

10. 23. On the application of this distinction of the two possibilities of the formation of terminology in Heidegger's own concept formation, compare this author's essay, "Terminologische Neubildungen beim frühen Heidegger," in *Heidegger Studies* 18 (2002): 181–191.

11. 39. Later, Heidegger adds, "The translation of telos by 'purpose' or 'goal' obviously has some basis, and is not simply taken out of thin air. The question is whether these translations are primary, and whether one is permitted, at this level of the investigation into being, to mix up primary and derivative meanings" (82). "Purpose and goal are founded on telos as end as the primordial meaning" (85).

12. "If our expression 'reality' [Wirklichkeit] were not so well worn, it would be an excellent translation" (70)—doubtless because, just as energeia refers back to *ergon*, "work" (43), so the German word for "work," *Werk,* is hidden in the word for "reality," Wirklichkeit. Here one sees that, for Heidegger, the over-familiarity of a word can be the decisive criterion for rejecting a translation.

13. 368. Cf. also 296. Further recourse to etymology is found in connection with the suffix *–de* (302) and *kategoria* (303).

14. 6. Cf. the formulation in the manuscript: "*Philosophy*, by contrast, especially today, does not need [the presuppositions], because it maintains the fundamental presupposition that things could not be better" (334).

15. 5, 333f.

16. 14, 339.

17. "The precondition of being-able-to-be-attentive is that one *stands in the matter*. Hence it is not the case that you can just spend a semester speculating about concepts while saying to yourself: Well, first I have to know what philology is, then I can begin. Such a person will never reach the beginning, because he will never get to know what philology is" (339).

18. 333. This is the wording in the manuscript. In the text taken from student notes (4), the ending words "and of self-expression" are missing.

19. "This [that the logos bears within itself as idle chatter the possibility of distortion (*Verstellen*)] refers not only to the everyday . . . but directly concerns in a much sharper degree the interpretation of Dasein that would make research and philosophy into explicit tasks of Dasein. It can happen that certain *logoi* once expressed, precisely in times when research is young and lively, take on such a prominence that for a long time they make inaccessible the very beings they intend" (276f).

20. 110 and 337. On the use of the adjective "hermeneutic," cf. 270, 351, 380f, 403.

21. "The *being of this dominance* lies in logos" (358). "The dominance of the interpretedness has the logos. The logos is the *authentic bearer* of interpretedness" (276).

22. "But the logos is seen in a primordial way by the Greeks. Today, we have only a primitive impression [*Vorstellung*] of speech—if we have one at all. The concrete instance of the primordiality of seeing is the entire *Rhetoric*" (61). "*The* Rhetoric *is nothing else than the interpretation of concrete Dasein, the hermeneutic of Dasein itself*" (110). "How can we obtain from Aristotle himself an impression of the fact that, and the manner in which, being-spoken [*Sprechendsein*] became for the Greeks the fundamental phenomenon of their Dasein? We are in a fortunate position insofar as we have a *Rhetoric* of Aristotle, which surveys the phenomena that are given in speech" (113). "It is better for us that we have Aristotle's *Rhetoric* than it would be if we had a philosophy of language. In the *Rhetoric* we have before us something that deals with speech as a fundamental mode of being understood as the being-together of human beings themselves" (117). "We can take the *Rhetoric* as a concrete guiding thread insofar as it is nothing else than the *interpretation of Dasein with respect to the basic possibilities of speaking with one another*" (139).

23. Cf. the investigation of *paradeigma* and *enthymēma*, on the one hand, and of *epagōge* and *syllogismos*, on the other, as parallel forms of speech dealt with respectively by rhetoric and dialectic (127f).

4

Michael J. Hyde

A Matter of the Heart: Epideictic Rhetoric and Heidegger's Call of Conscience

Recalling what it was like to listen to Heidegger lecture on Aristotle in the early 1920s in Freiburg and Marburg, Hans Georg-Gadamer writes, "Today no one would doubt that the fundamental intention which guided Heidegger in his engrossment with Aristotle was critical and de(con)structive. . . . Heidegger brought superb powers of phenomenological intuition . . . to his interpretations and, in so doing, freed the original text . . . thoroughly and effectively from the overlay of the scholastic tradition and from the miserable, distorted picture that critical philosophy of the period had of Aristotle."[1] Gadamer goes on to relate how he first experienced his teacher's critical and deconstructive talents during a 1923 seminar on Aristotle's *Nicomachean Ethics*. The specific topic was Aristotle's appreciation of *phronēsis* (practical wisdom) and how this type of knowledge, although it "admits of no reference to a final objectivity in the sense of science," nevertheless is crucial for understanding what Heidegger was after: "the most original experience of *Dasein*." According to Gadamer, "This violent appropriation of the Aristotelian text [by Heidegger] for use with his own questions reminds one of how the call of the conscience in *Being and Time* is what first makes the 'Dasein in human beings' visible in its ontological and temporal event-structure."[2]

The violence being referred to here must, of course, be understood in a specific "philosophical" manner—one recommended by Heidegger when he speaks of how his phenomenological and hermeneutical investigation of human being has "the character of *doing violence*" to its subject matter. The violence of hermeneutic phenomenology, according to Heidegger, is the result of its commitment to exposing the "complacency" and "tranquillized obviousness" of everyday interpretations that cover up and leave unspoken essential aspects of whatever these interpretations claim to be about.[3] Indeed, Heidegger's way of doing philosophy is "critical and de(con)structive"; it is meant to "interrupt" the routines and habits of common sense and common practice such that they may be perceived for what they are and how they operate to hide the "truth" of things and circumstances that, for whatever reason, warrant more respectful attention and acknowledgment. Moreover, the result of this interruption is also meant to be emotional, inciting the specific feelings of "anxiety" and "joy."[4] Gadamer is thus right to point out a similarity between Heidegger's violent ways and what is described in *Being and Time* as the ontological disposition of the "call of conscience" [*Ruf des Gewissens*]; for this specific call, as will be discussed in greater detail later, is heard first and foremost as an "interruption" that comes from the temporal structure of human existence and inspires an emotional response that summons our attention to the ways in which we have become conditioned to relate to our environment and to all those things and others who share this habitat with us. Hence, one might describe Heidegger's violent appropriation of the Aristotelian text as an act of conscience whereby Heidegger called his students' attention to the thinking of an ancient Greek whose understanding and appreciation of a host of matters (for example, phronēsis) had become lost in the prejudices of the scholastic tradition. Heidegger advocates violence as a way of getting at the heart, and thus the truth, of the matter at hand.

This way of being toward a text is also at work when Heidegger first lectures in 1924 on the worth of Aristotle's *Rhetoric* and then later declares, "Contrary to the traditional [scholastic] orientation, according to which rhetoric is conceived as the kind of thing we 'learn in school,' this work of Aristotle must be taken as the first systematic hermeneutic of the everydayness of Being with one another" (BT 178).[5] Indeed, as rhetorical scholars have long made clear, with his *Rhetoric* (and such related works as the *Nicomachean Ethics* and the *Politics*, for example), Aristotle instructs us on the importance of developing our rhetorical competence such that we might maintain and improve the sociopolitical workings and well-being of our communal existence. The genuine function of such competence extends beyond mere persuasion to include the development of judgment (*krisis*) and practical wisdom (phronēsis). Rhetorical competence lends itself to collaborative deliberation and reflective inquiry (including the self-deliberations of individuals). In the rhetorical situation an audience is not set at a distance. Rather, it is acknowledged, engaged, and called into the space of practical concerns as the orator works to establish an emotional connection with the audience and its immediate concerns and interests. For Aristotle, knowing how to stir the soul rhetorically is essential because existential questions concerning the livelihood of a community are not usually decided with the equations of demonstration or the syllogisms of dialectic. Existence is a gamble based on probabilities, and the emotional outlook of the hoi polloi influences their judgment at the time the bet is placed. If rhetoric is to perform its most worthy function of trying to move people toward "the good," it must cast a concerned and knowing eye on the emotional character of those whom it wishes to move. A moving of the passions is a sine qua non of persuasion; truth alone is not sufficient to guide the thoughtful actions of human beings.[6]

Heidegger sees in Aristotle's *Rhetoric* not only an answer to Plato's call in the *Phaedrus* for an intellectual assessment of emotion and its relationship to the disclosing of truth, but also the beginnings of a basic ontological interpretation of the affective life that had yet to be significantly advanced since Aristotle. Heidegger takes up this task in his 1924 lecture course and especially in *Being and Time* (1927), where he provides an analysis of the emotional disposition of everyday life ("publicness") that would eventually inspire philosophical and rhetorical literature dedicated in part to emphasizing and further clarifying rhetoric's ontological status.[7] With this literature Heidegger is recognized for providing valuable assistance in extending an understanding of the scope and function of rhetoric. Here also, however, Heidegger is criticized for what remains absent or confused in this assistance. In what follows I continue this twofold way of responding to Heidegger's reading of Aristotle's *Rhetoric*.

My discussion centers around a topic that most definitely caught Heidegger's eye: Aristotle's analysis of the emotions (*pathē*) and how they should be used by the orator to establish a communal bond or "identification" with an audience. Although some of what I have to say about the matter will not be new to those who are well acquainted with the literature on Heidegger's thinking on rhetoric, I do hope that my discussion will enable readers to see how Heidegger's appropriation of the Aristotelian text offers insights that not only commend the orator's art but also call into question certain of Heidegger's intellectual endeavors that begin taking recognizable form in the early 1930s. Heidegger sounded a call of conscience to his students as they read Aristotle's *Rhetoric* and related works. I also intend to sound such a call, and with a bit of violence, too. This violence takes form as I discuss certain aspects of the relationship between emotion and rhetoric and the special role that the rhetorical syllogism or enthymeme assumes in this relationship. Appreciating what Aristotle and Heidegger have to say about the enthymeme allows one to make a connection between this topic and the call of conscience. With this connection in mind, I will argue that the call of conscience operates as a primordial form of rhetorical (that is, *epideictic*) discourse. My violence reaches its peak when considering this last point and its moral implications.

I. Emotion and Rhetoric

Plato argues in his *Gorgias*, *Phaedrus*, and *Sophist* that rhetoric caters to its audience's emotional impulses, inhibits people from developing an intelligence (*noēsis*) based on a rational knowledge (*epistēmē*) of reality, and thereby encourages the members of the *polis* to become the greatest of all sophists. In the *Phaedrus*, however, one also finds the admission that the practice of rhetoric may indeed serve the truth. Socrates' personification of rhetoric speaks to this point: "Why do you extraordinary people talk such nonsense? I never insist on ignorance of the truth on the part of one who would learn to speak; on the contrary, if my advice goes for anything, it is that he should only resort to me after he has come into possession of truth; what I do however pride myself on is that without my aid knowledge of what is true will get a man no nearer to mastering the art of persuasion."[8]

With Aristotle this point receives further emphasis as he clarifies two fundamental and related issues: (1) The emotional character of human beings plays an important role in their development; it constitutes a person's spirited potential for coming to judge what is true, just, and virtuous. (2) Rhetoric, conceived as the "art of persuasion," is a faculty or power (*dynamis*) in its nascent state, a potential for acting and doing; when actualized in discourse, this potential not only excites (*emovere*) people to take an interest in the truth but encourages them to act in accordance with this truth. "Rhetoric," in other words, "is the counterpart of Dialectic."[9]

Aristotle recognizes that emotions function primordially as vehicles for the active sensibility of human beings: an emotion serves to orient a person's consciousness toward the world in a certain way. In book 2 of the *Rhetoric*, Aristotle employs this understanding of emotion to help the orator determine how to "put his hearers . . . into the right frame of mind" (1377b24) so that their orientation toward the world is advantageous to the orator's persuasive intent. This advice is intended to promote the effective and just use of emotion and rhetoric in the polis. Heidegger restates the point this way: "The feeling of the one being addressed must be taken into account, as must the particular situation at the time and the speaker's own attunement to the issue at hand." [Es muß bei der Vorgabe anderes in Hinsicht gestellt werden, es muß Rechnung getragen werden der Stimmung derjenigen, zu denen gesprochen wird, die jeweilige Lage der Dinge und die Art and Weise, wie man selbst zur Sache steht (163).]

And "[The orator] must understand the possibilities of moods in order to rouse them and guide them in a right and just manner." [Er bedarf des Verständnisses der Möglichkeiten der Stimmung, um sie in der rechten Weise zu wecken und zu lenken.][10] Heidegger thereby affirms that there is something good about the practice of rhetoric, something that enables it to be more than a mere communicative device for the public's "idle chatter" (*Gerede*). This affirmation is worth noting because of how Heidegger can easily be read as one who holds the traditional philosophical bias against the "manipulative" nature of the orator's rhetorical competence.

For example, in his description in *Being and Time* of how the "publicness" of our everyday way of being with others defines a world of "averageness," of common sense and common praxis, Heidegger tends to emphasize its "masslike" (Plato), "crowdlike" (Kierkegaard), and "herdlike" (Nietzsche) propensity to bring about a mindless conformity in its adherents: "In this averageness with which [publicness] prescribes what can and may be ventured, it keeps watch over everything exceptional that thrusts itself to the fore. Every kind of priority gets noiselessly suppressed. Overnight, everything that is primordial gets glossed over as something that has long been well known. Everything gained by a struggle becomes just something to be manipulated" (BT 165).

Perhaps anyone who has ever become dismayed at the thought and action of some collectivity may not find Heidegger's assessments to be off the mark. But such assessments of publicness define only a part (albeit a large one) of what Heidegger is telling us about the everydayness of our being-with-others. For he also admits that publicness "belongs to Dasein's positive constitution" (BT 167). That is, owing to the traditions, customs, rules, and norms that inform its way of being, publicness provides a sense of order to what would otherwise be a state of chaos and confusion. In his much-acclaimed reading of Heidegger's *Being and Time*, Hubert Dreyfus emphasizes this very point when he notes that, for Heidegger, "the source of the intelligibility of the world is the average public practices through which alone there can be any understanding at all."[11] Although such practices and the rhetoric that informs them can and oftentimes do provide a breeding ground for the evils of conformism, they nevertheless also provide the necessary background for coming to terms with who we are first and foremost as social beings and for determining whether or not our extant ways of seeing, interpreting, and becoming involved with things and with others might be changed for the better. Heidegger's positive take on the workings of this entire process is suggested when he notes how the understanding constituting the received opinion (*doxa*) of a given public "reveals authentic being-with-one-another in the world" [Die *doxa* ist die eigentliche Entdecktheit des Miteinanderseins-in-der-Welt (149)].

For Aristotle, such a genuine enhancement of public opinion requires, among other things, that the orator modify the lived and attuned space of others by making present to them what the orator has reason to believe is true, just, and virtuous. The practice of rhetoric operates in the immediacy of the present; it seeks thought and action in the pragmatic world of the here and now. Rhetoric calls upon emotion in order to facilitate this pragmatic endeavor—an endeavor that makes possible a perceptual restructuring of a person's existential temporality and spatiality. Heidegger recognizes the importance of this endeavor when he emphasizes that the emotional workings of rhetorical speech, unlike the purely "exhibiting" (*Aufzeigen*) function of dialectic, are committed to the everyday world of practice and know-how wherein the "taking care of things" (*Besorgen*) is worked out and accomplished and where rhetorical speech functions to exhort people to an active krisis or decision (122f). What Heidegger does not explore in any detailed way, however, is how rhetoric and emotion work together to modify the lived and attuned space of others. Some of what Aristotle has to say about the matter is worth noting, especially given my earlier stated intention to do violence to Heidegger's own violent reading of Aristotle.

Consider, for example, Aristotle's analysis of anger. He describes this emotion in personal terms. He does not mention the possibility of anger at an object, often the result of frustration. He implies that personal anger is more forceful in rhetoric than anger at an object when he notes that the impulse is to "a conspicuous revenge for a conspicuous slight" received from someone close to us in some way (*Rhetoric* 1378a32–34).[12] Such a slight causes anger and its attending pain. The pain involved remains as a privation in one's everyday existence until the slight is forgotten or redressed when one begins to envision and plot some form of revenge. According to Aristotle, revenge adds pleasure to the pain of anger, for "the angry man is aiming at what he can attain, and the belief that you will attain your aim is pleasant" (*Rhetoric* 1378b3–5). This expectation of revenge, wherein one's anger is now attended by pleasure, reveals an important temporal dimension associated with the experience of anger. The pleasure of anger emerges as people project themselves into the future—into another place in time and into another role—to visualize how their anger can be appeased. While imagining the act of revenge, the future becomes the present in an existential way; it becomes immediate, a place to be here and now. But as the presence of the future recedes into the past, and as one's expectations are fulfilled, relaxed, or forgotten, anger loses its intensity and its ability to move the listener. The object of anger becomes remote. Aristotle notes, "When time has passed . . . anger is no longer fresh, for time puts an end to anger" and converts it to calm (*Rhetoric* 1380b5). Because orators seek to transform anger into calm as often as they seek to transform calm into anger, they need to understand how to move their hearers away from the circumstances that are now provoking the anger and thus away from the present of future revenge. Clearly, for the orator who is dealing with anger in order to excite or calm it, time is of the essence.

Anger modifies time by making present the "not yet" of some imagined future. At the same time, however, anger also modifies the lived space of our everyday being-with-others. Aristotle offers further insight into the workings of this modification as he discusses how anger and fear are interrelated by way of physiological and psychological pain that manifests itself when a person is slighted by another who has some acknowledged power over the person and who thereby has the ability to affect the person's survival or self-respect. According to Aristotle, the pain involved is a "terrible thing"; it poses an immediate danger to the person's well-being. There can no longer be an imagined safe distance between the person and those who stand before the person in a vividly powerful way. The person's fear of these circumstances forces the realization that what was heretofore perceived to be remote (a potential threat) is actually close at hand (*Rhetoric* 1382a30, 1382b20, 1383a15–20). Thus, the person would become not only angry with those who created such a situation through their slighting behavior, but fearful of the threat that can accompany this behavior. In its interrelationship with fear, anger modifies the lived space of our everyday being-with-others.

Aristotle's discussion of this phenomenon within the context of anger's relationship to fear is elucidated further when he discusses pity. He notes, "Speaking generally, anything causes us to feel fear that when it happens to, or threatens, others causes us to feel pity" (*Rhetoric* 1382b26). From this statement one can conclude (although Aristotle does not do so explicitly) that anger also can be directly related to pity. For example, if individual A perceives individual B to be slighting individual C, and if A can identify with C's circumstances, then A not only would pity C due to A's own fear of such circumstances happening to A but would be incited to experience anger toward B. The key to understanding this interrelationship between anger, fear, and pity lies in A's identification with C's circumstances.[13] This identification, this lack of remoteness between A and C, marks a modification in the interpersonal dynamics of A's lived space—a modification that brings C's threatening circumstances close to A. What is now brought close to A's personal existence gains a dimension of immediacy, a presence that is not without a past and future. "We feel pity," writes Aristotle, "whenever we are in the condition of remembering that similar misfortunes have happened to us or ours, or expecting them to happen in the future" (*Rhetoric* 1386a1–3). Like the fear that can incite it, and like the anger that can then come about, pity is evoked in terms of time and space (*Rhetoric* 1385b15–34, 1386b5–10).

The reader familiar with Aristotle's analysis of the pathē in the *Rhetoric* undoubtedly is aware that the discussion of this analysis so far has not adhered strictly to Aristotle's three step procedure for investigating each emotion.[14] Rather, I have been reading Aristotle in a way that, as Heidegger would have it, recognizes how the *Rhetoric* offers a "systematic hermeneutic of the everydayness of Being with one another," whereby one is instructed on how emotion and rhetoric have a fundamental role to play in our communal existence. Heidegger, I think it is fair to say, continues and extends the teachings of his philosophical ancestor when, in *Being and Time*, he shows how the temporal and spatial workings of fear are to be distinguished from the more "primordial" temporal and spatial workings of anxiety.[15] Aristotle has nothing to say about this most "dreadful" of emotions; rather, he offers instead what Heidegger admittedly chose to omit in his assessment: a more in-depth analysis of "the ways in which [the pathē] are interconnected in their foundations" (BT 178). Yet, having gained some appreciation of the matter with the above discussion, we are in a better position to understand how far we can go with Heidegger in forming a positive assessment of the scope and function of rhetoric. The related topics that I now wish to consider in advancing this assessment are the enthymeme, the call of conscience, and what I take to be the fundamental epideictic nature of this call.

II. The Enthymeme

In book 1 of the *Rhetoric*, Aristotle explains that "the enthymeme is a syllogism" (1356b3), a form of deductive reasoning that, like dialectic, is not constructed "out of any haphazard material, such as the fancies of crazy people, but out of materials that call for discussion . . . [and] debate" (1357a35–39). The enthymeme thus serves rhetoric in performing its "duty": "to deal with such matters as we deliberate upon without arts or systems to guide us, in the hearing of persons ['untrained thinkers'] who cannot take in at a glance a complicated argument, or follow a long chain of reasoning" (1357a1–4). Hence, in dealing "with what is in the main contingent . . . the enthymeme must consist of few propositions, fewer often than those which make up the normal syllogism. For if any of these propositions is a familiar fact, there is no need even to mention it; the hearer adds it himself" (1357a15–20). The enthymeme thus functions to invite an audience to become interested and thus active in a reasoning process initiated by a speaker or writer. This invitation is intended to put the orator's audience "into the right frame of mind" (1377b24) so that, as noted earlier, their emotional orientation toward the world is advantageous to the orator's persuasive intent. Enthymematic reasoning is assisted by the workings of the pathē or emotions. Hence, Aristotle's treatment of the matter in book 2 of the *Rhetoric* where, as detailed above, he explores how emotions work to incite and direct the interests of an audience and, in so doing, modify its temporal and spatial orientation toward a given subject matter.

In book 3, however, a contradiction arises with what is being suggested here when Aristotle notes that you should "avoid the enthymeme form when you are trying to rouse feeling; for it will either kill the feeling or will itself fall flat: all simultaneous motions tend to cancel each other either completely or partially" (1418a11–14). This contradiction may be the result of Aristotle's tendency to associate the enthymeme not just with the rousing of feeling (*enthymeisthai*: taking something to heart) that is meant to lead to the formation of common concern, judgment, and action, but also with the more theoretical and intellectual process of simply "giving consideration" (also enthymeisthai) to some designated topic.[16] With Heidegger's ontological and hermeneutical appreciation of the matter, however, the contradiction need not arise; for as he shows in his lecture course (122f, 146f) and then in much greater detail in *Being and Time* (e.g., 95–107), any "purely theoretical assessment" of some subject matter is "derivative" of one's more practical, everyday, and emotional involvement with things and with others. Heidegger thus acknowledges rhetoric's enthymematic function as being rooted first and foremost in what book 2 of the *Rhetoric* is all about: the emotional fabric of a person's existence, or what Heidegger designates as the "ground and soil of the *logos*" (*den Boden des* logos *selbst* [169]) that nourishes and is nourished by the everyday rhetorical practices of communal existence (Being-with-others). Here, according to Heidegger, the primary function of the enthymeme is associated with engaging others in the process of "taking something to heart" (*sich etwas zu Herzen nehmen* [128]) so that they might be moved to thoughtful action. Recalling once again one of Heidegger's key observations about rhetoric offered in *Being and Time*, it thus makes perfect sense to say that the orator who wishes to be as effective as possible in initiating and directing this process "must [therefore] understand the possibilities of moods in order to rouse them and guide them in a right and just manner."

According to P. Christopher Smith, Heidegger's ontological and hermeneutical appreciation of the enthymeme serves to "radically redirect" Aristotle's assessment of the matter, at least as this assessment allows for an ambiguous reading of enthymeisthai.[17] As noted at the beginning of this essay, one might also associate this move on Heidegger's part with what Gadamer describes as his teacher's "violent appropriation of the Aristotelian text," whereby Heidegger sounds a "call of conscience" to those whose reading of the *Rhetoric* remains misdirected by the prejudices of the scholastic tradition and its simplistic reading of the text. Since

1969, philosophers of rhetoric and rhetorical theorists and critics have certainly been aroused by this call: the heart of the matter for rhetoric is the matter of the heart, the seat of the pathē, for the art's primary function is to attract and direct the interests of others by having them open their hearts (and thereby establish emotional attachments) to a speaker or writer and to what the speaker has to say about some matter of concern.[18] I believe, however, that one can still go further than what has been said so far about this matter in heeding Heidegger's call to advance an ontological appreciation of the orator's art. I develop this suggestion below by discussing how the call of conscience operates ontologically as a primordial and emotional form of epideictic rhetoric and how an understanding of these concerns, in turn, directs one back to certain practical and moral teachings that Aristotle offers those who would use rhetoric for the good of the community.

III. The Call of Conscience

Heidegger is correct: the orator "must understand the possibilities of moods [the pathē] in order to rouse them and guide them in a right and just way." This is how the orator enhances the chance that the audience will take an interest in what is being said so that they, too, may have a say in the matter. Without the formation of such a common interest in the matter in question, collaborative deliberation is all but impossible. Aristotle speaks to the importance of such deliberation when, for example, he talks about the role played by "the Many" in public policy debate:

> There is this to be said for the Many. Each of them by himself may not be of a good quality; but when they all come together it is possible that they may surpass—collectively and as a body, although not individually—the quality of the few best. . . . When there are many [who contribute to the process of deliberation], each can bring his share of goodness and moral prudence; and when all meet together the people may thus become something in the nature of a single person, who—as he has many feet, many hands, and many senses—may also have many qualities of character and intelligence.[19]

The instrument of collaborative deliberation is rhetoric informed and guided by moral prudence or practical wisdom (phronēsis). Such wisdom, notes Aristotle, "is concerned with things human and things about which it is possible to deliberate; for we say this is above all the work of the man of practical wisdom, to deliberate well. . . . The man who is without qualification good at deliberating is the man who is capable of aiming in accordance with calculation at the best for man of things obtainable by action."[20] Rhetoric, phronēsis, and collaborative deliberation go hand in hand. The root of phronēsis is *phren*, the "heart." Collaborative deliberation is a "knowing together" (Gr. *syn-eidesis*; Lat. *con-scientia*). This "togetherness" of knowing presupposes the workings of emotion, which, as should now be clear, have an essential role to play in calling on and bringing together the interests of others. Perhaps, then, it would be fair to say that as rhetoric performs its enthymematic function of speaking to the heart so as to encourage collaborative deliberation, judgment, and action, it essentially is sounding a call of conscience that can inspire the formation of practical wisdom. Although Heidegger never stated the matter exactly this way, he was heard to say when lecturing on Aristotle's *Nicomachean Ethics* that "phronēsis is *Gewissen* [Conscience] set in motion which makes an action transparent [*durchsichtig*]."[21] A more nuanced assessment of what I take to be the meaning of this claim will be helpful.

Possessing the discernment of practical wisdom—which, for Aristotle, would certainly include knowing how to arouse the pathē in a right and just manner—the orator is better prepared to assume the ethical responsibility that comes with one's rhetorical use of speech to announce, justify, and defend one's worldview regarding a given matter. For Heidegger, this and all other employments of speech are rooted in an ontological phenomenon that reveals itself in the temporality of human existence: the call of conscience (*Ruf des Gewissens*). This call comes forth originally in the way in which our temporal and spatial existence (Dasein's Being-in-the-world) confronts us with a fundamental challenge calling for a response: we are creatures who are always caught up in the play of time, always on the way toward understanding what can or will be in our lives but is not yet, and thus always confronted with the task of trying to make sense of and to do something with our lives. Human being is its own evocation and provocation: it calls for the responsiveness of concerned (emotionally attuned) thought and action, for that which enables us, even in the most distressful situations, to take charge of our lives as we assume the responsibility of affirming our freedom through resolute choice and thereby become personally involved in the creation of a meaningful existence. This is how systems of morality come into being in the first place. The language of morality is the language of responsiveness and responsibility.

Notice, however, that the call of conscience is always already operating before the specific ethical prescriptions and prohibitions of this language are created by human beings. The call of conscience is not a human invention; we did not create the ontological (temporal/spatial) structure of existence—the way it opens us to the contingency of the future and thereby, within this openness, gives us a place to be toward all that stands before us. The call of conscience is human existence disclosing itself to the one who is living it and who can and must respond to its challenge.[22] In both his early and later philosophy, Heidegger understands this specific act of disclosure as a primordial "saying" (*Sage*) of language whereby the temporal event structure of human being shows itself. Here, at this ontological level of existence, language is not understood first and foremost as a capacity for communication but rather as the original and silent manifestation, the showing (*Aufzeigen*), of what is.[23] Hence, following Heidegger it can be said that the call of conscience is the original saying of human being whereby it shows its challenging nature—the way it constantly and silently calls for concerned thought and action: "The call dispenses with any kind of utterance. It does not put itself into words at all. . . . *Conscience discourses solely and constantly in the mode of keeping silent*" (BT 318).

Heidegger speaks to us of a discourse, a voice, that is more original than anything he or anyone else has to say about it.[24] He provides a description of what he is doing when he notes, "To speak means to say, which means to show and to let [something] be seen. It means to communicate and, correspondingly, to listen, to submit oneself to a claim addressed to oneself and to comply and respond to it."[25] Conscience calls and Heidegger, listening attentively, phenomenologically, responds with a discourse meant to communicate to us the ontological workings of this call, its logos, its way of saying and showing itself to that particular being (Dasein) who has the linguistic ability to put into words the call's disclosive workings. Listening to a bit more of what Heidegger has to say about the phenomenon and how it makes itself known in our everyday lives will bring us back to the related topics of emotion, rhetoric, and the enthymeme.

Heidegger emphasizes that when heard in the context of our everyday way of being with things and with others, the call of conscience makes itself known as an "abrupt arousal" that interrupts our conditioned and typical involvements with our surroundings, especially as these involvements admit little more than a complacent and conformist allegiance to those values, standards, and conventions that govern and normalize the perceptions, thoughts, and practices of our everyday existence (BT 316).[26] Although such an existence certainly has its rewards in that it caters to our communal need of inhabiting a world of common sense and common practice, it also can prove to be quite a dangerous thing in that, as noted above, it provides the breeding ground for the evils of conformism. For Heidegger, conformism defines an inauthentic state of our Being-with-others because it operates to relieve us from the burden of explicitly dealing with a challenge that is known for inciting the emotion of anxiety and that is disclosed by the call of conscience: the personal challenge of assuming the ethical responsibility of affirming our freedom through resolute choice.

Heidegger makes much of the *anxiety of conscience* (BT 342), for the two phenomena go hand in hand. The experience of anxiety signals a significant loss of meaning and stability in our lives. It arises when our daily progress is impeded, if not shattered to its very core, by occurrences (for example, a serious illness) that disrupt our accustomed routines and relationships with things and with others and that thereby expose us to the contingency and uncertainty inherent in our temporal existence. Anxiety focuses on this uncertainty. That is what makes the emotion so disquieting, dreadful, and distinctive. In anxiety we remain open to how the future orientation of existence works to call into question the orderliness of our everyday habits of living. Anxiety thus attunes us most directly to the deconstructive dimension of our temporal existence; it concentrates our attention on the way in which human being makes an issue of itself every second, minute, and hour of the day. In anxiety, that in the face of which we are anxious is not merely the presence of some ontic occurrence raising havoc in our lives, but rather is that primordial condition of existence—the temporal openness of our Being—which makes itself known by way of such an occurrence. This ever-present condition is the true source of anxiety. For example, we may feel anxious when suddenly stricken by a serious illness, but the experience of this emotion is possible only if we care enough about what is to become of our existence now that it is no longer what it used to be and perhaps may never be again. In anxiety, we stand face to face with the not yet of the future and thus with the uncertainty that accompanies this dimension of existence that is always ahead of itself. Or, as Heidegger would have it, "Anxiety makes manifest in Dasein its Being towards its ownmost potentiality-for-Being," a potentiality "which it always is" and that is spoken of directly with the saying of the call of conscience (BT 232, 317–35).

With his analysis of the anxiety of conscience, Heidegger continues to provide a way for advancing an Aristotelian understanding of the scope and function of human emotion. For if, as Heidegger maintains, such an understanding requires one to recognize how the emotional fabric of human existence constitutes the "ground and soil of the logos," then it follows (in accordance with Heidegger's assessment of the anxiety of conscience) that this ground and soil runs as deep as does a specific call that lies at the heart of human being. As I now hope to show, this way of thinking about emotion and its relationship to the call of conscience also enables one to advance one's understanding of the ontological status of rhetoric.

IV. Epideictic Discourse

As I have detailed elsewhere in a study of the moral discourse of the euthanasia debate, rhetoric is quite capable of reaching down to the heart of human being in order to create anxiety in others and to show them, with the employment of additional emotions, how to heal its wounds. In the euthanasia debate, rhetoric is both a deconstructive and reconstructive force as it sounds calls of conscience intended to help people come to terms with such issues as the sanctity of life and one's right to die a dignified death.[27] Taken together, these calls mark out a domain of discourse comprising the three major divisions of rhetoric—political, forensic, and epideictic—that Aristotle identifies and analyses in book 1 of the *Rhetoric*. Yet it is the epideictic rhetoric of the euthanasia debate that is the most existentially elucidating and instructive for appreciating the debate's bottom line: what it means to live the good life and to die the good death. A brief explanation of why this is so will help me make a point that is central to the purpose of this chapter.

The noted classicist E. M. Cope tells us that compared to political and forensic rhetoric, epideictic is the "demonstrative, showy, ostentatious, declamatory kind: so called because speeches of this sort are composed for 'show' or 'exhibition' . . . and their [primary] object is to display the orator's powers, and to amuse an audience."[28] Aristotle's understanding of the matter, however, is not so limited, for he tells us that epideictic discourse (*epi-deixis*: to disclose, evoke, display, or show forth) is also employed in narratives to "praise or attack" a person who is deemed "worthy of honour or the reverse" (*Rhetoric* 1358b27–28): "Praise is the expression in words of the eminence of a man's good qualities. . . . To praise a man is in one respect akin to urging a course of action" (*Rhetoric* 1367b26–39). Praise, in other words, can be made to function in an enthymematic way. And this is how epideictic discourse is oftentimes used in the euthanasia debate: to construct narratives that tell the personal stories of patients, family members, and medical personnel who have firsthand experience of the wide range of emotions that inform the debate and who, in telling their stories of pain and suffering, joy and relief, survival and demise, enable listeners and readers to join with the speakers/writers in taking to heart the reality of life and death. These stories praise people for their courage to face death, their compassion toward others, and their moral stamina. In these stories, too, one learns about people whose actions are blameworthy because they lack such virtues and, as a result, make it more difficult for patients to enact their right to die, as well as their right to life.

Hence, with the euthanasia debate one is exposed to what I believe Aristotle takes to be the genuine power and function of epideictic rhetoric: how it unfolds as a beholding and a showing-forth (epideixis) of what is and as a competence for acknowledging others whom the orator desires to instruct as he or she gains and maintains their interests. What shows forth most clearly in the epideictic rhetoric of the debate are accounts of people hearing the call of conscience as illness or accident reek havoc in their lives and whose responses to the call offer concrete and stark illustrations of human beings struggling to meet the fundamental challenge of existence: assuming the ethical responsibility of affirming one's freedom through resolute choice. Perhaps, then, it would be fair to say that in the euthanasia debate, calls of conscience are announced through a rhetoric given over to displaying or showing-forth the ontological basis of these calls, which, as discussed above, is itself a disclosive saying of the temporal and spatial structure of human existence. Or to put it another way: in the euthanasia debate one finds epideictic rhetoric revealing what might be termed the most original epideictic event there is to be witnessed and taken to heart: the call of conscience.

Of course, one cannot make this claim by simply appealing to Aristotle, for the essential connection here is that between the call of conscience and epideictic rhetoric, and it is Heidegger, not Aristotle, who directs us toward an ontological understanding of the first of these two phenomena. Aristotle, however, speaks of the second phenomenon in a more robust way than what Heidegger admits when he associates the category of epideictic speech with a eulogy, "*eine Lobrede*" (125). What I am suggesting about the epideictic nature of the call of conscience thus requires one to move back and forth between the two philosophers in order to grasp a point that neither of them explicitly admits in his teachings. Heidegger certainly helps us to see the ontological potential of his ancestor's thinking on rhetoric and related matters, especially as he emphasizes throughout his lecture course on Aristotle (e.g., 104, 123, 169) how rhetoric (like the call of conscience) demands a hearing from those whom the orator would move with his discourse.[29] Still his violent appropriation of the Aristotelian text is not violent enough when it comes to revealing how the saying of the call of conscience has something fundamentally rhetorical about it: conscience calls; it appeals to us most forcefully by way of an emotion (anxiety) that transforms time and space, opens us to the openness of our own existence, and thereby challenges us to think and act for the purpose of creating a meaningful existence that perhaps marks an improvement in our self-understanding and in our communal being-with-others. The call of conscience, which lies at the heart of human being, is a showing-forth (epideixis) of this heart, a rhetorical revelation par excellence, whereby a call for concerned thought and decisive action is announced.

I recognize, of course, that in making this point I may be accused of being too violent in my appropriation of the Heideggerian text. Neither in his 1924 lecture course nor in *Being and Time* does Heidegger ever attempt to relate the call of conscience and epideictic discourse. He describes the call not as a rhetorical interruption, but merely as an interruption that, at one and the same time, calls one's existence into question and beckons one toward taking a needed course of action. In his later works Heidegger continues to think of this primordial temporal process as a way of attending to the "call of Being itself"—a call that is not a human creation and does not come from God nor from a cosmic ground. "Being," claims Heidegger, "is farther than all beings and is yet nearer to man than every being, be it a rock, a beast, a work of art, a machine, be it an angel or God. Being is the nearest. Yet the near remains farthest from man"—at least, according to Heidegger, until man learns to "dwell poetically," to remain open to the call of Being so that its saying can be heard over the chatter (*Gerede*) of daily existence and then brought into the language of mortal speech, whereby the truth of some matter can be declared and, at a moment's notice, defended.[30]

Such chatter, as admitted earlier, certainly constitutes a form of rhetorical praxis that, from Socrates to Heidegger (and beyond), has been criticized and condemned by philosophy. But rhetoric, as Aristotle and Heidegger's reading of Aristotle make clear, is not only chatter; rather, it is also a form of discourse that works hand in hand with emotion in order to promote collaborative deliberation, to encourage others to take matters to heart, and to guide their thinking and behavior "in a right and just way" (*in der rechten Weise*). Rhetoric's epideictic function helps to ensure that a showing-forth of truth will take place in this process. Rhetoric thereby shows itself to be especially responsive to the call of conscience which, like this art, calls for concerned thought and action with its showing-forth of truth. When in his later philosophy Heidegger speaks of the call of Being rather than the call of conscience, he associates this call with the original bringing-forth (*poiēsis*) of the truth of what is to our attention.[31] One may ask, however: What is the difference between epideixis and poiesis, between the rhetorical act of showing-forth the truth and the poetical act of bringing-forth the truth? Heidegger, as far as I know, never considers this question as he moves from a concern with rhetoric in his early philosophy to a concern with poetry in his later philosophy. What I have suggested above regarding the epideictic and thus rhetorical nature of the call of conscience is certainly meant to question this omission—one that when articulated grants rhetoric an ontological status that Heidegger appears not to have noticed in his violent appropriation of Aristotle's *Rhetoric*.

V. Conclusion: Where Art Thou, Rhetoric?

One can only wonder what, if anything, would have changed in Heidegger's work if he had taken notice of just how far rhetoric can be traced back into the heart of human being. Perhaps, for example, he would have demonstrated a more heartfelt response to the showing-forth of death that came with the Nazi regime in the 1930s and 1940s and that he eventually acknowledged in 1949 when he noted simply, "Agriculture is today a motorized food industry, in essence the same as the manufacture of corpses in gas chambers and extermination camps, the same as the blockade and starvation of countries, the same as the manufacture of atomic bombs."[32] The moral and rhetorical inappropriateness of this claim is obvious. For the particular showing-forth of death in question here calls for witnesses who can speak the truth of the horror that faces them by using words in such a way that the resulting rhetoric becomes itself a showing-forth of what is—an epideictic event that is moving enough to have its witnesses realize how dreadful the consequences can be when people know not how to take to heart the presence and cries of others who would have us never forget what was done to them. In the Old Testament one reads, "I will give them a heart to know Me, that I am the Lord" (Jeremiah 24:7). The gift here is that of conscience: the capacity to remain open to and be awed and instructed by the happenings and mysteries of life.[33] Where was Heidegger's conscience as he spoke about the call of Being and poetry at a time when a most competently created work of epideictic rhetoric was desperately needed in order to instruct the thinking and actions of others who lived on during and after the Holocaust? Remember, when heard, the call of conscience calls for the active involvement of the speaker in the rhetorical situation.[34]

I began this chapter with insights drawn from Hans-Georg Gadamer's recollection of how Heidegger's reading of certain works of Aristotle defined a "violent appropriation" of these works. Another insight offered by Gadamer speaks to the problem I have with Heidegger's decision to omit in his later philosophy a respectful concern with the goodness, the right and just ways, and the showing-forth capacity of the orator's art: "What man needs is not just the persistent posing of ultimate questions [for example, the meaning and truth of Being], but the sense of what is feasible, what is possible, what is correct, here and now. The philosopher, of all people, must, I think, be aware of the tension between what he claims to achieve and the reality in which he finds himself."[35]

This insight harkens back to the rhetorical, moral, and political teachings of Cicero and, hence, to the beginnings of civic republicanism and its democratic spirit. Commenting on the cultural and educational influence exerted by Socrates' and Plato's critical assessment of the orator's art, Cicero accused it of bringing about "the undoubtedly absurd and unprofitable and reprehensible severance between the tongue and the brain, leading to our having one set of professors to teach us to think and another to teach us to speak."[36] Although made by one who was certainly committed to the theory and practice of rhetoric, this accusation was not intended as a mere put-down of philosophy. Like Socrates, Plato, and Aristotle before him, Cicero held firmly to the belief that "if we bestow fluency of speech on persons devoid of... [the] virtues [of integrity and supreme wisdom], we shall not have made orators of them but shall have put weapons into the hands of madmen."[37] Hence, Cicero insisted that "philosophy is essential to a full copious and impressive discussion and exposition of the subjects which so often come up in speeches and are usually treated meagerly, whether they concern religion, death, piety, patriotism, good and evil, virtues and vices, duty, pain, pleasure, or mental disturbances and errors."[38]

But Cicero also insisted that "we are not born for ourselves alone," that "our country claims a share of our being," and that if we intend "to contribute to the general good," we must not disparage and retreat from the politics of public life, but instead use "our skill, our industry, and our talents to cement human society more closely together, man to man."[39] The obligation stated here speaks to the importance of rhetoric. Philosophy is essential for the education of the orator, but it is the "art of eloquence" (*oratio*) practiced by this advocate of the *vita activa* that instructs one on how to equip (*ornare*) knowledge of a subject in such a way that it can assume a publicly accessible form, and function effectively in the social and political arena. The severance between the tongue and the brain is an impediment to this civic-minded, persuasive, and moral endeavor. For the good of the community, philosophy and rhetoric must work together. Cicero—who admitted that "whatever ability I possess as an orator comes, not from the workshops of the rhetoricians, but from the spacious grounds of the Academy"[40]—would have it no other way. Conscience calls. Cicero heard it. And his interpretation was clear: "To be drawn by study away from active life is contrary to moral duty."[41] No wonder Cicero felt obliged to offer counsel in the ways of rhetoric. For "what function is so kingly, so worthy of the free, so generous, as to bring help to the suppliant, to raise up those who are cast down, to bestow security, to set free from peril, to maintain men in their civil rights? . . . The wise control of the complete orator is that which chiefly upholds not only his own dignity, but the safety of countless individuals and of the entire State."[42]

Aristotle never put the matter exactly this way. Nor did Heidegger, although his reading of Aristotle's *Rhetoric* is not incommensurate with such an understanding of the orator's art—an art whose essential truth is found happening with the call of conscience that lies at the heart of our being and whose saying opens us to the future. The Nazis corrupted this art, for their brand of rhetoric made it impossible to encourage, by way of what Heidegger describes in *Being and Time* (159) as "considerateness" (*Rücksicht*) and "forbearance" (*Nachsicht*), an open, truthful, and thus authentic response from non-Arian Others.[43] With what it shows forth, the call of conscience calls for what it itself is: an openness to the future, to uncertainty, to otherness, and thus to the ever-present possibility that what one believes to be right now may be wrong later.

Perhaps Heidegger became disillusioned with rhetoric as he heard the rants of Nazi ideologues and watched the masses, the public, respond like cattle. Perhaps he thereby thought that his most authentic course of action was to remain true to the ways of poetic thinking. This nonrhetorical option, however, is not without its problems. For example, when caught up in the midst of life's contingencies, of sociopolitical happenings that can bring us to our knees and perhaps send us to our graves, can we afford merely to sit back and wait and see what Being has in store for us? When the sufferings of others provoke us to hear the call of conscience, is it enough to release ourselves from the practical and ethical matters at hand so that we may properly stay attuned to the call of Being? Are there not times when the right and just thing to do is at least to speak up in a willful and deliberative way, to acknowledge and reach out to others, and thus to communicate and struggle with them? In *Being and Time*, Heidegger makes mention of this rhetorical process as having an important role to play in the building of authentic community.[44] The claim finds support in Aristotle's teachings, and even more so in the works of those like Cicero who emphasize the essential relationship that exists between rhetoric and democracy. Heidegger, as is well known, was skeptical about the worth of this specific political institution in today's technological age.[45] Perhaps this skeptism, too, played a role in his failure to acknowledge the full ontological status and worth of the orator's art.

Whatever the reason, however, the fact remains: as Heidegger developed his philosophy, a sincere concern for the truth and goodness of rhetoric disappeared from view. Throughout the history of Western philosophy, such a disappearance has never been a healthy sign for rhetoric. Following the later Heidegger's directives for thinking about the call of Being and how such poetic thought constitutes the highest form of action,[46] rhetoricians are likely to get nervous and perhaps a little annoyed. They might even recall Cicero's critique of philosophy in *De oratore* when he spoke about how this profession's calling too easily encourages the "absurd and unprofitable and reprehensible severance between the tongue and the brain." The critique is well worth remembering when journeying on Heidegger's path of thought that leads away from rhetoric and the call of conscience and toward poetry and the call of Being.

NOTES

1. Hans-Georg Gadamer, *Heidegger's Ways*, trans. John W. Stanley (Albany: State University of New York Press, 1994), 31–2.

2. Ibid., 33.

3. Martin Heidegger, *Being and Time*, trans. John Macquarrie and Edward Robinson (New York: Harper & Row, 1962), 359. Further references to this work (hereafter BT) will be cited in the text.

4. Ibid., 358. For a more detailed discussion of this point, see my *The Call of Conscience: Heidegger and Levinas, Rhetoric and the Euthanasia Debate* (Columbia: The University of South Carolina Press, 2001), especially chapters 1 and 2.

5. For Heidegger's discussion of how Plato prepares the ground for Aristotle's assessment of rhetoric, see his *Plato's Sophist*, trans. Richard Rojcewicz and Andre Schuwer (Bloomington: Indiana University Press, 1997), 214–44.

6. The literature on Aristotle's *Rhetoric* is quite extensive. For two recent and excellent works on the topic that offer a sense of the history of this literature, see Thomas B. Farrell, *The Norms of Rhetorical Culture* (New Haven: Yale University Press, 1993); and Eugene Garver, *Aristotle's* Rhetoric: *An Art of Character* (Chicago: University of Chicago Press, 1994). Heidegger touches on all of the points mentioned here in *Grundbegriffe der aristotelischen Philosophie: Marburger Vorlesung Sommersemester 1924*, Gesamtausgabe, vol. 18, ed. Mark Michalski (Frankfurt: Klostermann, 2002). More will be said about this lecture course throughout this chapter, noted with internal citations. Special thanks are due to Susanne Nitsch, who provided invaluable assistance in helping to translate certain material from the lecture course.

7. For a recent collection of essays wherein a substantial amount of this literature is referenced, see Walter Jost and Michael J. Hyde, eds., *Rhetoric and Hermeneutics in Our Time* (New Haven: Yale University Press, 1997).

8. Plato, *Phaedrus* 260d-e, trans. R. Hackford, in *Plato: The Collected Dialogues*, ed. Edith Hamilton and Huntington Cairns (Princeton: Princeton University Press, 1973).

9. Aristotle, *Rhetoric* 1354a1, trans. W. R. Roberts (New York: Modern Library Series, Random House, 1954). Further references to this work (hereafter *Rhetoric*) will be cited in the text.

10. Martin Heidegger, *Sein und Zeit* (Tübingen: Niemeyer, 1979), 138–39. Macquarrie and Robinson translate "in der rechten Weise" as "aright" (BT 178). As indicated above, however, a less condensed translation is possible: "in a right and just manner." The German *recht* can bespeak the moral sense being emphasized here, as when, for example, one says, "Es ist nicht recht von dir" (It's wrong or unfair of you). Moreover, if one is to credit Heidegger's gloss of the *Rhetoric* in *Being and Time* as being right, just, and fair, then my suggested translation

should be seen as appropriate since, for Aristotle, rhetoric certainly has a moral role to play in the workings of the polis.

11. Hubert L. Dreyfus, *Being-in-the-World: A Commentary on Heidegger's* Being and Time, *Division 1* (Cambridge: MIT Press, 1991), 155.

12. What is being noted here about Aristotle's analysis of anger was originally presented in a more extended form in Michael J. Hyde and Craig R. Smith, "Aristotle and Heidegger on Emotion and Rhetoric: Questions of Time and Space," in *The Critical Turn: Rhetoric and Philosophy in Postmodern Discourse*, ed. Ian Angus and Lenore Langsdorf (Carbondale: Southern Illinois University Press, 1993), 68–99.

13. Aristotle alludes to the importance of identification in *Rhetoric* 1386a1–3. Kenneth Burke makes much of the phenomenon throughout his theory of rhetoric. See, for example, his *A Rhetoric of Motives* (Berkeley: University of California Press, 1969), 19–29, 43–46.

14. Aristotle specifies the procedure using anger as his model: "Take, for example, the emotion of anger: here we must discover (1) what the state of mind of angry people is, (2) who the people are with whom they usually get angry, and (3) on what grounds they get angry with them. It is not enough to know one or even two of these points; unless we know all three, we shall be unable to arouse anger in any one" (*Rhetoric* 1378a22–28).

15. BT 179–182, 228–235. More will be said about Heidegger's assessment of anxiety, especially its relationship to the call of conscience, later in this chapter.

16 For an excellent discussion of this point, see P. Christopher Smith, *The Hermeneutics of Original Argument: Demonstration, Dialectic, Rhetoric* (Evanston: Northwestern University Press, 1998), 27–29.

17. Smith, *Hermeneutics of Original Argument*, 27.

18. Henry W. Johnstone Jr. was one of the first philosophers of rhetoric to introduce Heidegger's thinking to rhetorical scholars in the late 1960s and early 1970s. For a collection of his essays where he incorporates Heidegger into some of his work, see his *Validity and Rhetoric in Philosophical Argument: An Outlook in Transition* (University Park: Dialogue Press, 1978), esp. 62–76.

19. Aristotle, *The Politics of Aristotle*, trans. Ernest Barker (New York: Oxford University Press, 1979), 1281b1–6.

20. Aristotle, *Nicomachean Ethics*, trans. W. D. Ross, revised by J. O. Urmson, in *The Complete Works of Aristotle* (revised Oxford translation), vol. 2, ed. Jonathan Barnes (Princeton: Princeton University Press, 1984), 1141b8–11.

21. Quoted in Jacques Taminiaux, *Heidegger and the Project of Fundamental Ontology*, trans. and ed. Michael Gendre (Albany: State University of New York Press, 1992), 141. Taminiaux consulted the manuscripts of Heidegger's lecture courses on *The Sophist*, on *Philebus* (winter semester 1924–25) and, *The Basic*

Concepts of Ancient Philosophy (SS 1926). Taminiaux does not identify the specific manuscript from which the quotation is taken. Also see Hans-Georg Gadamer, *Philosophical Hermeneutics*, trans. and ed. David E. Linge (Berkeley: University of California Press, 1976), 201, where Gadamer, recalling Heidegger's 1923 seminar on Aristotle's *Nicomachean Ethics*, also notes how Heidegger related phronēsis with conscience.

22. For a detailed discussion and critical assessment of Heidegger's theory of the call of conscience, see my *Call of Conscience*.

23. BT 49–58, 314, 310–325; also see, for example, Martin Heidegger, *On the Way to Language*, trans. Peter D. Hertz (New York: Harper & Row, 1971), 57–136. In this and other later works, Heidegger speaks of the "call of Being" rather than the "call of conscience."

24. Commenting on this point, Francoise Dastur writes, "Here there is no metaphor for Heidegger but, on the contrary, a genuine experience of what voice is. This is because it is not essential that discourse be phonetically articulated to be language (*Sprache*), and because voice (*Stimme*) does not in German have the purely vocal sense of the Greek *phonē*, but rather a juridical sense, that of giving one's judgment by a vote. This is why Heidegger emphasizes that 'the 'voice' is taken rather as a 'giving-to-understand' (BT 316). Thus there can be a silent voice, which does not speak, as a pure phenomenon of comprehension, a pure phenomenon of meaning, just in the same way there can be an understanding, which is not reduced to simple acoustic perception." See Francoise Dastur, "The Call of Conscience: The Most Intimate Alterity," in Francois Raffoul and David Pettigrew, eds., *Heidegger and Practical Philosophy* (Albany: State University of New York Press, 2002), 94.

25. Martin Heidegger, *Zollikon Seminars: Protocols-Conversations-Letters*, trans. Franz Mayr and Richard Askay, ed. Medard Boss (Evanston: Northwestern University Press, 2001), 215.

26. For an extended discussion of how the interruption of the call of conscience takes place, see my *Call of Conscience*, 46–50. Here I show how Heidegger's analysis of the matter must be complemented with his earlier assessment (BT, 102–107) of how human awareness arises out of everyday human activity.

27. See my *Call of Conscience*, part 2.

28. E. M. Cope, *An Introduction to Aristotle's* Rhetoric (London: Macmillan, 1867), 121. In his reading of Heidegger's interpretation of Aristotle's *Rhetoric*, Smith also speaks of epideictic as "show-off" rhetoric "—panegyric—in which not so much the subject matter is to be judged as is the 'ability' of the speaker" (*Hermeneutics of Original Argument*, 23).

29. Nancy Struever makes much of the topic of hearing in her contribution to this volume. In writing about Heidegger's lecture course, Theodore Kisiel notes, "Almost perversely, Heidegger's interest in rhetoric gravitates toward [hear-

ing], in which speaking has its end. For speaking finds its completion in the communication, in being received or accepted by the auditor who undergoes or 'suffers' the speech. A seemingly marginal topic, the 'suffering' and resulting 'passion' (pathos) of the listener is made central." Theodore Kisiel, *The Genesis of Heidegger's* Being and Time (Berkeley: University of California Press, 1993), 296–97. In fact, as Walter Jost and I have argued elsewhere, this gravitation to hearing retrieves Gorgias's invaluable contribution to the history and theory of rhetoric and hermeneutics, whereby he stresses how rhetorical invention is a power that one receives, chiefly by listening and hearing rather than by speaking. At the same time, however, this gravitation to hearing risks losing the active involvement of the speaker in the rhetorical situation. See Jost and Hyde, *Rhetoric and Hermeneutics in Our Time*, xv–xvi. In concluding this chapter, I will have more to say about the social and political consequences of this risk, especially as they pertain to Heidegger.

30. Martin Heidegger, "Letter on Humanism," trans. Frank A. Capuzzi in collaboration with J. Glenn Gray, in *Basic Writings*, ed. David Farrell Krell (New York: Harper & Row, 1977), 210.

31. See, for example, Martin Heidegger, *The Question Concerning Technology and Other Essays*, trans. William Lovitt (New York: Harper & Row, 1977), 10–11; Martin Heidegger, *Poetry, Language, Thought*, trans. Albert Hofstadter (New York: Harper & Row, 1971), 62–74.

32. Quoted in Richard Wolin, *The Politics of Being: The Political Thought of Martin Heidegger* (New York: Columbia University Press, 1990), 168.

33. For an extended discussion of this point, see the introduction to my *Call of Conscience*.

34. The point I am making here hearkens back to observations included in note 29 above.

35. Hans-Georg Gadamer, *Truth and Method*, trans. Joel Weinsheimer and Donald G. Marshall, 2nd rev. ed. (New York: Crossroad, 1991), xxxviii.

36. Cicero, *De oratore*, trans. H. Rackham (Cambridge: Harvard University Press, 1942), 3.16.61.

37. Ibid., 3.14.55.

38. Cicero, *Orator*, trans. H. M. Hubbell (Cambridge: Harvard University Press, 1962), 33.118.

39. Cicero, *De officiis*, trans. Walter Miller (Cambridge: Harvard University Press, 1913), 1.7.22.

40. Cicero, *Orator* 3.12.

41. Cicero, *De officiis* 1.6.19.

42. Cicero, *De oratore* 1.8.32.

43. For an expanded discussion of Heidegger's notions of "considerateness" and "forbearance" and how they play a role in the rhetorical construction of authentic community, see my *Call of Conscience*, 57–64.

44. "Only in communicating and struggling [with others] does the power of destiny become free" (BT, 436).

45. For an excellent examination of the topic, see Michael Zimmerman, *Heidegger's Confrontation with Modernity: Technology, Politics, Art* (Bloomington: Indiana University Press, 1990).

46. See, for example, Martín Heidegger, *What is Called Thinking*, trans. J. Glenn Gray (New York: Harper & Row, 1968), 113–147; Martin Heidegger, "Letter on Humanism," 193–242.

5

NANCY S. STRUEVER

Alltäglichkeit, Timefulness, in the Heideggerian Program

> Rhetorik ist nichts anderes als die Auslegung des konkreten Daseins, die Hermeneutik des Dasein selbst.
>
> —Heidegger, SS 1924

> Rhetorik [ist] . . . die erste systematische Hermeneutik der Alltäglichkeit des Miteinanderseins
>
> —Heidegger, *Sein und Zeit*

I. THE PLACE OF RHETORIC IN THE ARISTOTELIAN PROGRAM: LIFE AND TIMES

The lectures of the summer semester of 1924, "Grundbegriffe der aristotelischen Philosophie," represent an extraordinary opportunity for the historian of rhetoric. What is notable in the beginning lectures is Heidegger's perspicacity in reading the *Rhetoric* as a mode of inquiry, as, indeed, giving us a life science, an account of our defining life capacities. His ingenious strategy, I would argue, is to use the *Rhetoric* to gloss the *Grundbegriffe*.[1] The power of rhetoric, and of the *Rhetoric*, lies in the explanation and control of the premises, issues, and tactics of Hellenic political discourse, and Heidegger's strategy is to take the basic concepts—"being," "good," virtue," "happiness," "end," "potency/act"—back to these issues and tactics. Heidegger claims that "the Greeks lived in oratory" [daß die Griechen in der Rede lebten (108)], in the assemblies and courts, and in the oratory of the games (110, 122, 136, 162), a claim that requires us to embrace the rhetorical account of the discourse, *Miteinanderreden*, that reveals Hellenic political life, *Miteinandersein* (127, 134, cf. 56). The crucial step is to insist that life is not something "wild, and deep, and mystical" (21), but a plenum of capacities and actions best exposed, it seems, by rhetoric. Human life is defined by possession of language (*logon echon*), it is a life fulfilled by the use of language, *zoē praktikē meta logon* (105). Since speech is addressed to another, the use of language entails that the basic character of *Dasein* is essentially political; the focus is on the "Grundcharakter des Dasein als *zōon politikon*" (104, cf. 45-46, 63).

Thus Heidegger's contention: rhetoric is not a pure formal discipline, a *technē* for manipulating discourse, but exists wholly inside politics. ("Die Rhetorik ist keine auf sich selbst gestellte *technē*, sondern steht innerhalb der *politikē*" [134].) Rhetoric gives an account of the *polis* as the "potentiality of being of human life, the authentic life." [Im Sein des Menschen selbst liegt die Grundmöglichkeit des Seins-in-der-*polis*. Im Sein-in-der-*polis* sieht Aristoteles das eigentliche Leben des Menschen (46).] Also rhetoric, in action, construes political life, constitutes community, *koinōnia* (49); rhetoric claims to *be* politics (136). And there is no gap between nature and culture in its work: "Die Begriffe vom Sein-in-der-*polis* haben ihre Grundlagen in den Naturbegriffen" (241). In the lectures of July 3 and 4 (207-219) we find, then, Heidegger's zealous intrication of the biological texts such as the *Parts of Animals* and the *Motion of Animals* with the *Rhetoric* in his discussion of the passions as life capacity. And in the final lectures of July, he uses the *Rhetoric*'s account of political life as movement to gloss the *Physics*, with its account of nature as the principle of motion and change, *archē kinēseōs kai metabolēs* (200b12, GA 18, 284), with its intrication of *dynamis, entelechia,* and *energeia* (195). At all points, I shall argue, Heidegger's investigation of life confronts and deals with issues of time. Heidegger's rhetoric studies language as it lives in *Alltäglichkeit* (62). Alltäglichkeit is the vital time dimension of Dasein.

1. Heidegger's Account of the Nature of Rhetorical Inquiry: Rhetoric as Life Science

> Daß wir die aristotelische "Rhetorik" haben, ist besser, als wenn wir eine Sprachphilosophie hätten.
>
> —Heidegger, SS 1924

What is the place of Heidegger's definition in the twentieth-century revival of rhetoric, and how does his sense of time help define this place? Pierre Aubenque has claimed that the *Rhetoric* delivers a fully rhetorized psychology, with the elements already organized in topics for use in argument.[2] Just so, at all points, Heidegger intricates the life capacities—passions (*pathē*), desire (*orexis*), choice (*prohairesis*), habit (*hexis*), and cares (*Besorgen*)—with the basic strategic concerns of rhetoric: belief (*pistis*), opinion (*doxa*), shared opinion (*endoxa*), commonplaces (*topoi*), and rhetorical argument (*enthymeme*). Thus, for example, enthymeme etymologically discloses its roots in *thymos*, "affective desire," "heart" (128).

Heidegger's careful, even cautious working through of the key terms is vital to the innovatory moments in his account. Thus his lectures on doxa (136–158) are crucial for the account of politics to be derived from discourse. The assertion that the rhetor's purpose is to push Dasein into doxa is essential to the understanding of a continuous pragmatic engagement with time, Alltäglichkeit (136). Heidegger understands the Aristotelian relation between pistis and doxa (from *De anima* 428a 20–21: one can't hold an opinion without belief; here belief is, perhaps, the psychological state of holding an opinion). He employs as well the equivocation of pisteis, both as means or proofs, and as ends—beliefs or convictions. Then, *pisteuein* is doxa coming to speech; pistis is not pure belief, but that which speaks *for* a thing to win belief (118). The doxa and endoxa furnish the topoi as both maxims and as principles of argument, which in turn act as premises, *protaseis* in the enthymeme (133–134); they also are the energizing conclusions arrived at, held. Any proposition, any argument functioning within the political domain functions for belief, very like C. S. Peirce's belief as "energized knowledge"; functions, in short, as *Jasagen*, affirmation (137). Heidegger claims doxa is the way we *have* life in time, not a *Wissen*, science: "Die *doxa* ist die Weise, in der wir das Leben in seiner Alltäglichkeit da haben" (138).[3]

Note the implication of discursive action in Heidegger's definition of doxa as *Orientierung*, with orientation as a kind of refocusing task. Heidegger grasps, then, the source of rhetoric's strength is its concern with articulation, *Aussagen*, the speaking-out, the speaking-to, speaking-for, in the community (109–136). Being-with-one-another demands less internal acquiescence or silent rejection than specific, timely articulations of the current state of endoxa in the speaking-hearing community. Rhetoric needs Aubenque's rhetorized psychology, which is not enclosed in a timeless, theoretical domain; Aristotle's definitions of the passions, for example, are sentences to be employed in political negotiation.

Like Klaus Dockhorn, Heidegger sees rhetoric not as a tradition of teaching manuals, but as a formation, indeed, the second, alternate formation to philosophy in the classical period. Dockhorn claimed that of Aristotle's three kinds of proof—*ethos, pathos,* and *logos*—which pertain respectively to speaker, audience, and text, the proofs ethos and pathos exhaust the category of the "commonsense," the intersubjectively shared communal beliefs contained in the *koinoi topoi*.[4] For Heidegger, ethos and pathos constitute speech, *legein* (165), and legein is the "Grundbestimmung des Daseins selbst in der konkreten Weise seines Seins in seiner Alltäglichkeit" (114). Aristotle's *Rhetoric* is a compendium of early Greek endoxa (45), that is to say, a comprehensive list of historically shared beliefs. Thus Heidegger follows Aristotle carefully in devoting so much space and time to the discussion of ethos and pathos. He recognizes the accounts of ethos and pathos as valuable descriptions of Hellenic assumptions; the endoxa embed the constructs prominent in the history of Greek philosophy, the constructs that furnished the topic of these lectures; the rhetorically revised list will thus revise this history. Thus Heidegger on the history of philosophy. Now compare Michel Meyer on the history of rhetoric. Meyer thematizes this history as simply a succession of shifts in dominance in the relations of the three complementary concerns of ethos, pathos, and logos.[5] Heidegger certainly does not bog down in the purely technical consideration of the peculiarly rhetorical as opposed to dialectical instruments. This is, of course, a standard way of denigrating rhetoric in the ordinary confrontations of rhetoric and philosophy. For Heidegger rhetoric is not a technē, the inauthentic definition (114), but a potentiality for theorizing, a *dynamis tou theoresai* (1355b26, GA 18, 122). It is a potential, with all its peculiar time-fraughtness, not an energeia, an actuality. It is not a complete Wissen; it does not give all information—in spite of all those manuals (113-114)! It thus describes the radical incompleteness, the unending, timeridden task of politics. And just so, Michel Meyer has argued the "problematological" nature of rhetoric, claiming that it flourishes in the lack of system, or failure of systemic thought. Meyer has defined politics as in constant motion, as the process of negotiating differences and distances through discursive interventions. Politics as the task of negotiation presumes no end to differences, or alterations, no end to the need to link the shared beliefs of the community to an indefinite range of particular cases, no end to politics, in short.[6] All the Aristotelian stipulations of legein as *pithanon* (116), or rhetoric as defense/attack as opposed to dialectic as test, maintenance of argument (1354a3–11), mark rhetoric as irrevocably timebound.

2. Rhetoric and Politics: Time and Motion Studies

If life, then motion, *kinēsis* (286). If motion, then time. If the basic concern of life studies is movement, *Sein-als-Bewegtsein* (286), then the primary strategies of rhetoric must deal with time. The lectures devoted to pathos can be seen as a long meditation on 1378a19–21: "The emotions are all those feelings that so change men as to affect their judgements [*kriseis*] and that are also attended by pain and pleasure." Again,

Heidegger grasps the emphasis on change, and therefore time. In his account of Aristotelian psychology, kinēsis gives the authentic Da-Charakter to Dasein, the vital place-time of Being (287). Thus, the ontological significance of the passions lies in our capacity for change, the *Veränderlichkeit* of Being. Passion itself is both motion and a cause of motions; it is a capacity for altering: *veränderliche Beschaffenheit* (167).[7] Of Aristotle's notion that passions alter judgements, Heidegger observes that this is where passions intrude on logos—here *articulated* judgements, although frequently translated by historians of philosophy as "reason" (248). But passions are not Wissen, static knowledge, but *Befindlichkeiten*, dispositions (232). Most importantly, passions are dispositions oriented on others' dispositions that define our in-the-worldness (178): "Das *eidos* der *pathē* ist ein Sichverhalten zu anderen Menschen, ein In-der-Welt-Sein" (207). The rhetor, as politician, must become oriented to the hearer's dispositions (121, 250) in order to do his work, *ergon*, which is to bring Dasein into doxa, make us "take to heart" an opinion. Thus logos functions only in a Dasein defined as a lively practice of doxa, and of cares, and of passions.

Heidegger's account of Aristotle's rhetoric, then, describes a radically timeful practice of changes, alterations designed to take account of past, present, and future in the respective genres of judicial, epideictic, and deliberative oratory. Thus in lectures July 14 and 15 (246–261) Heidegger claims that Aristotle's account of the passion of fear, *phobos,* reveals Greek genius, a genius that in particular possesses great sensitivity to temporal dimensions of affect. Heidegger points out that pathos is "already there" (246) as *Boden*, "ground" (262). Yet Aristotle defined fear as "a pain or disturbance due to a mental picture [*phantasmata*] of some destructive or painful evil in the future" (1382a21–22). Fear becomes present to us not by direct experience, *aisthēsis*, but through our imagination, *phantasia*; fancies replace sensations as stimulus (250–251). Note the discursive mode: existence is an announcement, and it is announced through signs, *semēia*, not facts; the semēia furnish the Da-Charakter of fear (103). And Heidegger notes the peculiar tense, voice, and mode of fear: the tense is future, the voice is subjunctive, the mode is the possible. It is still not really here and it might *not* happen; yet it still has an intimacy, or nearness: "ein Nicht-Dasein im Sichnähern zu sein" (253). And Heidegger is much taken by Aristotle's grasp of the capacity of fear to inaugurate and stimulate political-rhetorical action: "fear sets us thinking what could be done," or "fear makes us deliberators," *phobos bouleutikous poiei*. It is a balance of hope and fear that makes the hearer a political actor, articulating choice: *kaitoi oudeis bouleuetai peri tōn anelpistōn* (1383a6–8, GA 18, 259-260). Thus fear as belief (pistis), a basic articulation in play in politics, as well as fear as pathos, disposition, is essential to rhetorical analysis and crucial to settling affairs. The political domain is one of labile balances, fantasies of the future (fantasies that also structure memory), subjunctive formulations—radical tinkerings with time.

3. Time is of the Essence: Heidegger's Formulation of Alltäglichkeit

Heidegger's fascination with time fits with his revisionary account of the staple Hellenic philosophical terms such as *ousia*, as being or essence, and, indeed, time becomes the essence, metaphorically speaking, of the SS 1924 project. Heidegger contrasts the philosophic obsession with the search for timeless truths, for eternal certainties, *aei on* (140) with rhetoric's concern for *Zeitlichkeit*, the timely, the timeful. Rhetoric handles, discloses the "Miteinandersprechen im Sinne des alltäglichen Miteinanderredens" (155), not some pure, monologic, theoretical usage. Because of its interest in Aussagen, articulation, speaking-out to someone, rhetoric develops an account of life in its dailiness, its timefulness, its radical specificity of time, its care for tense: "Being itself as care and care-full speech is *timely*; it cares for the *still not-at-hand*, speaks about the *already-appeared*, investigates that which is *now with us*." ["Das Sein in sich selbst als Besorgen und besorgendes Sprechen ist *zeitlich*, besorgt das *noch-nicht-Vorhandene*, spricht über das *schon-Geschehene*, betrachtet das *Jetzt-Daseiende*" (131).] This, of course, is a Heideggerian explication or justification of the three rhetorical genres: the deliberative, which deals with future policies; the judicial, which deals with past justice or injustice; and the epideictic, which secures the shared values of the present. While the genres seem to separate time and task, the orator actually integrates them. There are necessary connections of deliberation, judgement, and praise as speech acts in politics; the emphasis is on the intrication, simultaneity of generic issues and political issues, interests in actual performances, and timely intrusions. Smith argues that Aristotle seems to claim that deliberations are only about time; thus Smith cites the *Rhetoric* (1356a4–6): to take counsel is to deal with "what appears susceptible of being either way . . . for no one deliberates about what is incapable of having been otherwise, or being otherwise in the future, or being otherwise now."[8] With the naming of the three genre tenses—"having been," "being in the future," "being now"—Aristotle is, in effect, underscoring that deliberation is timeful, and that tenses imply modalities (cf. 125). Time, in short, places.

The classical rhetorical shift in interest is toward people living in concrete situations (im eigentlichen *kairos*) as investigative object (59). *Kairos* is in Hellenic treatises the primary canon of the rhetorically valuable. Kairos is both measure of time, the moment, and the response to the moment, the appropriate strategy, *to prepon*, and in Latin, what is fitting, *quod decet*, for dealing with the radical contingency of practical life. Thus, the force and breadth of the rhetorical interest in time affects Heidegger's notion of the other major investigational interests of the Greeks. The June 27 and 30 lectures (183–199) give an account of the basic concepts of the *Nichomachean Ethics*, but the peculiar and revisionary perspective is that of time and timedness, timefulness of action and decision, and the source of this perspective is Aristotle's *Rhetoric*.

Kairos is the character of Besorgen, the indispensable—and rarely translated into Greek—term of Heidegger's account of the Aristotelian Grundbegriffe (140). Kairos, in Heidegger's account, qualifies the hegemony of needful care, Besorgen, the careful prudential strategies, *phronēsis* (183), in the domain of interactive practices, *praxis* (180): "Die Handlung selbst hat ihr *telos* im *kairos*" (189). Thus, when Heidegger claims that ethics needs *chronos*, but "Die Zeitcharakter der *ēthikē* liegt in *pollakis*," frequency, and not *Dauer*, "duration" (194), he not only reorients the ethical project away from a consideration of timeless foundational values, but radically affirms the operational value of rhetoric's canon of kairos.

Thus, the equation of the most frequently invoked term in reading Aristotelian ethics, the "mean," *meson*, with kairos—"Die *meson* für die *praxis* ist der *kairos*" (144)—is, in effect, a sharp commentary on the virtue of prudence.[9] Heidegger finds it significant that Aristotle shifts the construct of meson from medicine to ethics (185); health as meson becomes meson as kairos, and appropriateness is moral health. Meson, as the mean, *Mitte*, had been constantly evoked as absolute norm in the tradition of Aristotelian philosophy; there it is a value to be described geometrically, arithmetically, that is to say, exactly described (185). But Heidegger focuses on the Aristotelian distinction between Mitte as object and Mitte as agent's capacity, *meson pros hemas*, and here Mitte is integrated with kairos, and it is not to be arrived at in a geometrical mode. Rather meson is *Jeweiligkeit* (temporal particularity—"particular while") in respect to the agent, for Dasein is ever *jeweiliges* (respective) Dasein (201).

In the same lectures Heidegger gives a timely reading of Aristotle's hexis, "habit." Hexis is the Grundbestimmung of *aretē* (185), basic to the definition of virtue, excellence. Here Heidegger is most ingenious in deploying the basic Aristotelian concepts of dynamis, entelechia, and energeia to represent the movements of potency and actualization in life phenomena, in the phases of morality. That hexis is a dynamis, *Gefaßtsein* (185), a potential for having, is crucial for Aristotelian ethics. Habit is not pure duration, but is timebound, acquired and lost. Habit is also the "*energeia*, das eigentliche Da, das Gegenwärtigsein des Habenden und des Gehabten"; it is the presencing, contemporizing of having (174–175), and, in particular, the having of *hekaston*, specific pathē as dispositions (192).

Habit is recurring response to socially constituted opinions, or; is a specific having, or holding of constitutive dispositions. As dynamis, it is a potentiality forming, therefore, a very thick texture of predispositions to choice. In one of many etymological strategies, Heidegger asserts that passions transpire, they are life modes of active and passive, for passions are not simply enduring, undergoing, suffering, *pathēsis,* but also an active making, *poiēsis,* a fulfillment, energeia (192, cf. 325). Hexis helps us grasp the being of pathē; hexis is "ein Wie des *pathos*" (184), and the movement, or lack of movement, from potency to act describes a basic dimension of moral agency.

And, just as the connection kairos/meson, the relation of hexis/pathe¯ reveals the rhetorical gloss. Heidegger concentrates not on timeless virtues but on the potentiality of Dasein to reorient in changing discursive circumstances. The mean is grounded in an *Orientiertsein* (187). Rhetoric handles orientations as transfers, interactions of speaker and hearer; the mean is effect and effecting. Note the qualifications: the dunamis in each *mesotēs* is for each moment, *Augenblick* (188); we are not dealing with routine, but a *Freihalten*, a "freeholding" (190). If the time dimension of ēthikē is *pollakis,* the habits are products of "*öfter Durchmachens,*" frequently transpiring, or undergoing (191). Alltäglichkeit becomes the primary qualification of ethical life in its ineluctable particularity: "Öfter ist gerade dasjenige, was die Zeitlichkeit des Daseins charakterisiert" (191).

Heidegger's concern is with iterability, with repetitiveness as challenge in political life. Timefulness pervades rhetorical argument structure as well. The elements of argument are timeful—the shared beliefs, which make up the premises, are revisable, have a *Revisionsfähigkeit,* as opposed to the *epistēmē* which is not revisable (138). The passions of the hearer, the *sich-befindet* (262) as *orientiert* are occasions of revisions. And Heidegger notes Aristotle's grasp of the timely virtue of the enthymeme, the foreshortened rhetorical argument, for the audience "takes more to heart" short chains of argument, not elaborate demonstrations (133). Oratory requires the continuous, unremitting effort in connecting the doxa, endoxa, and topoi (commonplaces of commonsense) in the premises with particular cases, with, indeed, an indefinite range of specific occasions: political as well as physical occasions (*Physics*, 201b27-202a9; GA 18, 317–318). The invocation in argument of the indefinite, the boundless, *apeiron* (292), a revisability, undermine philosophical arguments devoted to maintaining stability, eternity, and duration. Any philosophical theory of depth or abstraction is late, derived, only applied to the originary overt, surface occasions of politics. Thus Heidegger implies our foundationalist accounts of Greek ethics are late, extraneous applications of the Grundbegriffe. There is nothing fundamental or early about foundationalist projects; the life phenomena described in rhetoric's timeliness do not stand under theoretical axioms (132). In fact, it is dailiness that destroys theoretical complacency as a boast of isolation from time.[10]

The antimentalist concerns of Heidegger's rhetorical psychology are thus of a piece with his antifoundationalist moments. For continuous motion implies continuous impurity. Heidegger notes carefully Aristotle's attribution of the passions to the whole person, not just to the soul (122, 192, 197). The formula *Seele* as ousia specifies the *Sein eines Lebenden*, both notes and relegates Aristotle's entification (30), and seems to correspond to Heidegger's later rejection of the model of mind as a "cabinet of consciousness," an enclosed, autonomous intellectual functioning.[11] In Aristotle's life science the concern is the whole living being, the human life. Indeed, one of the benefits for Heidegger of the rhetorical account is its inclusive psychology, a continuum of contiguous, interactive life faculties and actions (194-219). "Mind is not at all pure." [Das *noein* des Menschen ist kein reines (202).] It is dependent upon imagination, among other faculties, and imagination is, of course, dependent upon bodily sensation; imagination is the Boden of *noein* (199).[12] Thus impurity supports Alltäglichkeit, timefulness, as hermeneutical focus; impurity prejudices pure duration.

4. Alltäglichkeit as Qualification of Miteinandersein

In the SS 1924 program, temporality corrodes foundationalism, and Alltäglichkeit is the catalytic agent of temporality. In the definition of rhetoric in *Being and Time* Alltäglichkeit is the primary qualification of Miteinandersein. Rhetorical interests thus must support equal and heavy emphasis on temporality and interaction. Alltäglichkeit defines everydayness not as "ordinary" but as "timefulness," the timely character of practical life: it designates the continuous, if intermittent, repetitious demands of daily life, its iterability. "Miteinandersein" stipulates as primitive, ineluctable, living-with-one-another. Man is not self-sufficient (96); life, any life, is there (da) for another being (241). And Heidegger finds a basic account of this interpersonality in Aristotle's chapters on the passions. Here there is an illuminating similarity to an early modern strategy of rediscovery of rhetoric as politics. Like Hobbes before him, Heidegger defines the passions as intrinsically social, interpersonal, rather than simply physiological ("ein Sichverhalten zu anderen Menschen" [207]).[13] Paul Dumouchel—perhaps he would cite the Heidegger text as well if he were aware of it—claims the originality of Hobbes in recognizing that to attribute an emotion to a person is a performative, a political deed, not a description of an internal state of a subject.[14] For Dumouchel, "the emotions are social in the sense that they are not the means, but the *being* of human living together. The fact that we have an affective life, is not the cause, it *is* the fact that we are not completely independent of one another." [Le fait que nous ayons une vie affective, plutôt que cause, *est* le fait que nous ne sommes pas des *êtres* complètement indépendents les uns des autres.][15] And Meyer insists on Aristotle's insight—and this repeats Hobbes as well—that passions are our reactions to our representations and to the presentations of us by others.[16] Just so, Heidegger was much impressed by Aristotle's account of the fearsome men, the *phoberoi*, those who create fear, as a telling account of both the relations of one city, polis, to another as well as of the relations of individuals within the polis. The phoberoi define a whole bearing of Miteinandersein; indeed, they are "most characteristic" of the polis. Heidegger admired the subtlety of Aristotle in claiming that the gentle, *praoi*, and the ironic, *eirōnes,* as uncertain, and unstable are more to be feared than the obviously dangerous (256-263). But this intriguing discussion of passion as function must be related at all points to Heidegger's recovery of Aristotle's insight that fear is inextricably engaged with the future tense and subjunctive voice, with the *noch nicht da*. At no point does the Heideggerian discussion wander far from the considerations of demands of time.

Consider the politics of hearing. The obdurately timeful domain of discourse is reception. To speak is to address a hearer, the hearer defines the speaker's task: "Das Sprechen sein *telos* hat beim 'Hörer,' beim *akroatēs*" (123). Or another formulation: "Das *akouein*, 'Hören,' ist die eigentliche *aisthesis*" (104)—the hegemonous perception? Hearer relations writ large are politics. Heidegger's close attention to the phenomenology of hearing explores temporality as qualifying response, and focuses on living-with-one-another as it transpires. Heidegger has an acute sense of rhetoric's intense commitment to the priority of hearing over speaking; notice his frequent uses of the *Rhetoric* as offering analysis of the different possibilities of *Sich-befinden* of the hearer (169). Of course, very early in the *Rhetoric* Aristotle insists on the primacy of the hearer in determining the rhetorical telos (1358b1). The repetitive, meticulous accounts of hearer activity in SS 1924 raise the issue of hearer responsibility. And similarly, Barbara Cassin has illumined the passage in *Metaphysics* 1006a24–26 on dialectic (here this takes in all dialogic argument), where Aristotle stresses that the responsibility for the success of an argument rests with the listener, *hypomenon,* rather than with the speaker or demonstrator, *apodeiknys*.[17] In no sense does this Aristotelian account of the listener give us a sense of a monologic, timeless address, univocally constraining a single, necessitated response (the inadequate philosophical model); rather, Heidegger's rhetorical model deploys politics as changes, alterations in hearing. Heidegger perhaps responds to more of the *Rhetoric* text than he cites in his characterization of rhetoric as hermeneutic.[18]

When Heidegger claims that the *Rhetoric* gives us the Greek endoxa—interactively generated opinions (45)—he proffers another way of defining the rhetorical pragmatic focus on audience capacity, and the Greek genius for pragmatics. Thus the perspicacity of Heidegger's recovery of the *Rhetoric*, for the *Rhetoric* brilliantly summarizes the Greek ingenuity in giving a very thick account of the essentially conflicted *listeners*, the divided responsibilities and demands of the audience, relentlessly time bound, embedded in specific problematics of context. In just this way, Greek dramatic texts supply evidence for Greek ingenuity. In, for example, the *Acharnians*, Aristophanes dramatically represents the audience as pulled both by the ties of democratic citizenship and by investigative (philosophical?) loyalties, responding to both communal conviction and to the individual truths of philosophical formation, as hearing both as a citizen and as a member of a theater audience, with its topical, place-oriented isolation. Just so, in this particular lecture series Heidegger attempts to recover a Greek rhetoric as an explanatory mode for hearing, for the *Rhetoric* describes the process of formation and reception of endoxa. Since it is the case that "das *legein* [ist] die Grundbestimmung des Daseins selbst in der konkrete Weise seines Seins in seiner Alltäglichkeit" (114), and that rhetoric is "die Auslegung des konkreten Daseins, die Hermeneutik des Daseins selbst" (110), rhetoric thus focuses properly on all the discursive possibilities subsisting in the "Alltäglichkeit des Daseins" (114). Therefore, a prime value of the rhetorical program is timefulness.

II. Meditations on Time

1. *Making a Place for Rhetoric in the History of Inquiry*

> Es gilt nicht Neues zu sagen, sondern das zu sagen, was die Alten schon meinten.
>
> —Heidegger, SS 1924

Aristotle's *Rhetoric* is for Heidegger in the SS 1924 lectures primarily a mode of investigation: he must make a place for it in the history of Greek inquiry. Heidegger's work thus involves layers of temporality: rhetoric in history illumines history. In SS 1924 he speaks with the voice of one construing a fresh, more precise intellectual history (cf. 219-221). For Heidegger, rhetoric has three important, and somewhat counterintuitive qualities: rhetoric is "better than a *Sprachphilosophie*" (117); it is not simply a purely formal verbal technē; and it exists inside politics. The combination insures that rhetoric is a most basic hermeneutic of "Dasein selbst" since the vital life capacity is discursive. Aristotle took into account a strong, pre-Platonic program not simply to be aligned with the work of the early Sophists and rhetors (108–109). What Heidegger observes is the perspicacity of the relation of Aristotle to Sophistic. Aristotle may, as Aubenque claims, both have as principal object of his work the refutation of the Sophists, and, at the same time, take over the Sophistic (Gorgian) assumption—and this is manifest in Heidegger's account of his rhetoric as the hermeneutic of Miteinandersein—that discourse is the instrument of existential relations, an assumption that denies the thesis that language simply communicates "things"—an assumption, Aubenque claims, that is the source of the Sophists' unique power. Rather, speech and rhetoric work with intentions and judgements.[19] Heidegger's assertion that rhetoric is "inside politics" is thus not the same as calling rhetoric the "handmaiden of politics"; it is an ontological position.[20] If anything, Aristotle's *Rhetoric* pushes Sophistic notions further; rhetorical dynamis contrasts with Sophistic, Heidegger claims, as it is oriented to all the possibilities of persuasion, where Sophistic is devoted to the *unbedingt*, the absolute, definite conviction: *unbedingt zu überzeugen* (115). But this defines rhetoric as research, and sophistry as morally relativist.[21]

While the relation of Aristotelian rhetoric and Sophistic presents a rather fruitful ambiguity, what is vital for Heidegger the philosopher is the relation of the *Rhetoric* to Platonic inquiry. Aristotle "corrects" Plato, and the *Rhetoric* in particular has great revisionary force. Heidegger claims there is a simple, and dysfunctional, continuity in Hellenic inquiry—the philosophers are the true Sophists (136)—but that Aristotle broke new ground, moved past Plato when he improved upon the early Greek definitions (26, 223–224). Plato "misses" Dasein (37), but Aristotle "gets Socrates right" (184); Aristotle also gives a better account of Greek doxa (140). But, alas, we have lost this originary Hellenic rhetoric presented so carefully and fully by Aristotle; rhetoric in Hellenistic and medieval times became a *school* discipline (110)—the array of pedagogical practices and school manuals that is the primary interest of the historiography of rhetoric today. In Heidegger's account rhetoric constitutes a high point in Greek inquiry, preceding loss, fulfilling, correcting past moments. True, Heidegger's careful analysis of the lengthy treatment of the passions in book 2 of the *Rhetoric* accompanies his claim for the heavy influence of rhetorical *Affektenlehre* on the Stoa (122), as well as on Christian theology from the patristic period through Thomas and Luther (177). But, Heidegger observes, only Wilhelm Dilthey has recognized this vital historical initiative.[22]

If we return to the epitaph, "What is valuable to say is only that which the Greeks earlier meant," this last sentence of the lecture notes proclaims, I would argue, the liberation of Heidegger from the standard accounts of Hellenic thought, with their deleterious effects on German philosophy. Heidegger has arrived at and presented a different sense of development, of the change through time in Hellenic inquiry. He sees that those who claim Aristotle gave a philosophic account of rhetoric, if by that they mean a Platonic one, are wrong. Aristotle's account of rhetoric reverses the philosophic emphases, discounts the motives, and corrects our modern notions of the historic presence of rhetoric.

2. *Time in and as Discipline*

The *Rhetoric* corrects as well Heideggerian inquiry, thus raising the issue of timely development in his thought. It is truly piquant that Heidegger's account of rhetoric, by purveying such an acute critique of the standard history of Greek philosophy, enables, to a certain extent, the Heideggerian philosophical innovations he will produce in *Being and Time* in 1927. While Heidegger may have thought he had effaced rhetoric in his new philosophical program of *Being and Time*, rhetoric effectively colonized his philosophy from within.

I have argued that a careful reading of the *Rhetoric* allowed Heidegger to exploit its initiatives as a powerful revisionary force in his account of Greek inquiry. But also, the rhetorical focus on Alltäglichkeit reinforces Heidegger's important effort in the exploration of time and temporality. Heidegger not only has a strong commitment to give a perspicacious account of inquiry in time, he has the strongest possible commitment to temporality as qualification and object of intellectual life. The lectures demonstrate that for Heidegger it is important to grasp how inquiry modes have changed over time. But, it is even more important to grasp that time itself furnishes the most pressing of our problems; the road to the problematic of death, thus authenticity, in *Being and Time* is through Alltäglichkeit. Heidegger is assigning in SS 1924 not simply the place of rhetoric in Aristotelian inquiry, and the place of Aristotelian rhetoric in Hellenic inquiry, but the place of Heidegger in the history of inquiry in general, a temporality Heidegger awards himself.

The important values, then, of rhetorical accounts of experience and rhetorical judgments drawn from these accounts are qualities of incarnate, interactive timefulness.[23] Rhetorical inquiry is corrective because of its temporal values, that is, time is corrective. Again, dailiness destroys theoretical complacency (130–131), and theory grows out of Alltäglichkeit (66). Heidegger cites and paraphrases Aristotle's linkage of rhetoric and dialectic: neither constitutes an epistēmē, in the usual sense of science, Wissen. For both, the modality is the possible, the topic is the probable; rhetoric as offshoot, *paraphyes*, of both dialectic and ethics, displays the practical "cares," pragmatism, that makes it the *antistrophē* of dialectic (125-130). The intervention, intrusion of rhetorical time occurs between Heidegger's simple notation that Aristotelian epistēmē deals with the timeless, *aei on* (140) and Heidegger's odd qualification in the last lecture: "Ich verstehe gar nicht den Seinscharakter der *epistēmē*, wenn ich nicht das Wovon [*pros ti*] in Betracht ziehe" (324).[24] It is not simply that rhetoric is not a science, science itself has been problematized by Heidegger's exploration of rhetorical inquiry. It is as if the rich rhetorical descriptions of political capacities and actions have destabilized for Heidegger the heavy, pervasive insistence of Aristotle and his commentators on the value and methods of scientific certainty.

Thus Heidegger's reading of the *Rhetoric* affects the balance between stable epistēmē and labile *paideia* Aubenque has described in Aristotle. Rather than absorption in a timeless truth, rhetorical discipline depends on dailiness; rhetorical practice makes public, *offenbar*, or *sichtbar* (136), the true, *Wahr*, in the verisimilar, *wahrscheinlich* (122), a seeming that by its nature cannot stand still, lose its temporal particularity. The daily speech, legein, that is its object is Grundbestimmung (an emphasis on enunciation [114]), but does not define, *horizein*, in the sense of producing the stable definitions of logic. Logos as *horismos* is not alltäglich (36), and in this defining activity the inquirer somehow steps outside of time. Heidegger thus problematizes the task of definition of concepts, the ostensible subject of SS 1924. The suppleness, not to say ingenuity of Heidegger's enterprises in unsettling definition are frequently concessions to the timeful. Unsettling are the various comparisons to medicine: rhetoric, like medicine, does not address particular individuals, Socrates or Callias, but the possibilities of (political) therapy (122); thus both disciplines invent problematic. But rhetoric, unlike medicine, does not have a domain of specific expertise, is not a technē (114); rhetoric functions outside of expertise. Further, Aristotle's insistence that the doctor must acknowledge the distance between knowledge of healing and healing itself (cf. *De anima* 433a3–6), between treatise and action, becomes Heidegger's insistence (addressing the rhetor?) that life as praxis has nothing to do with technē (183); rhetorical pragmatism is investigation, not instrument. If we characterize rhetoric as a life science, we do not assert its scientific ambitions, but call attention to its devotion to life. Again, this life not at all "wild and deep and mystical."

Observe the complexity of the relations of the disciplines: Heidegger's rhetoric exists inside politics, which deals with the authentic life. Yet while psychology is the "Lehre vom Sein des Lebenden," the politician is not simply a psychologue (101). And while the concepts of politics are rooted in nature (241), the rhetorician is not simply a physiologue (220–221), since his domain is always, usefully, limited to *Rede* (139). Then, in our definitions of disciplines, we have become anachronistic; Greek *bios* is not understandable to modern biology (74). We must set aside our modern notions of ethics and politics (64–67); we must contemporize, that is to say, update, rethink our rhetoric (123). For the implication is that when we lost Greek rhetoric, we lost Greek politics.

3. Modern Times: Specific Twentieth-Century Revisions of Time

> There is no mechanical truth in saying the past determines the future, rather than the future the past.
>
> —C.S. Peirce, "Reply to the Necessitarians"

A. Manifolds

In Blattner's account, Dasein's temporality is a "non-sequential manifold of future, present, and past," a complex simultaneity. The innovations in theory of time division 1 of *Being and Time* represent the very fundamental commitment in Heidegger's theory to a temporal manifold, rather than to a linear sequence of past, present, and future "nows." The intellectual historical question to be addressed is, to what extent do the Aristotelian rhetorical initiatives described in SS 1924 prepare us for Heidegger's definitions in *Being and Time*, and, what is the relation of these rhetorical tactics to the descriptive psychology of Dilthey's and Husserl's phenomenology in Heidegger's formation?

Rhetorical therapy disengages the theorist from idle, that is, inappropriate, speculation. Where in the contemporary philosophy of ordinary time discussions proceed, Heidegger saw, within the horizon of an "apriori, mathematical projection of nature,"[25] as opposed to this, Heidegger in SS 1924 found a very different account of temporality within the political parameters of the *Rhetoric*. A Hellenic focus on life and motion and on the interruptive demands of being-with-one-another—enhanced by rhetorical devotion to occasions of speaking-out and listening-for—enables a sense of time as simultaneous, intricated, experientially complex. According to Blattner, *our* time, Heidegger discovers, if accounted for minutely, is not at all ordinary, not at all the contentless, vapid flow of a succession of nows stipulated for our philosophy by the contemporary mathematical models.[26] Similarly, in SS 1924 Aristotle "improves on" Plato in his rhetorical account of the experience of time; the definitions produced are a Greek ontology *in nuce*, of being in motion (321).

I have argued that the rhetorical account that intricates the tasks of genres and the tenses of topics projects a temporality much closer to a manifold than to a linear sequence. The subtleties of Heidegger's temporality require, of course, far more than a rhetorical influence. Yet the motives of Heideggerian temporality cohere with the rhetorical contestation of the entification tactics of Hellenic philosophy, the depictions of being as an occurrent entity, described in a series of nows.[27] In the Heideggerian definition of tense in *Being and Time* the future is not "out there," off someplace, nor is the past.[28] The future does not equal a location, a now in a succession of things, but "coming to be" as process. What is important is what Heidegger emphasized in his account of Aristotle in SS 1924: potentiality. Aristotle's dynamis, is reformulated in *Being and Time* as a "pressing ahead into," "for the sake of which."[29] Purposiveness, readiness, and ambition are key concepts;[30] they are potentialities, capacities rather than complete, finished actualities (contrast Aristotelian energeia). And, as for the definition of the past, affectivity is central—the facticity of the past is a lingering, affect is *schon da*[31]—recall Heidegger's delight in the intricate presentation of tense in Aristotle's account of the effect of fear in SS 1924. At the same time habit, with its connotations of duration, and past presence, is described in SS 1924 as process, as a "present-ing," a *Gegenwärtigen des Habenden* (175). This is of a piece with his stipulation of the Greek focus on the present as a "making present" (192). In the *Rhetoric* and in *Being and Time,* passions, potentialities, and habits are ineluctably temporal, yet at the same time blurring, undermining the neat divisions of a flow of past, present, and future linearity. Further, there is no sense in which Heidegger's use of the Aristotelian terms in SS 1924 develop a stable pastness of the text, a philologically established dead letter. On the contrary, the aim is to use Aristotle in a temporal manifold, by means of a manifold. Perspicacity is particularized use. Unless an etymology illumines this use it is ignored, it disappears.

Further, there is a suggestive compatibility of Smith's emphasis on the "original" argument of Hellenic culture as matrix with Blattner's account of Heidegger's "originary" temporality as explanatory core. In Blattner's account, crucial is the sense of Dasein' care[32] which, as an "original" time, explains or roots our abstractions of world time, or ordinary time, just as Smith makes a claim for Heidegger's genius in focusing on the "original" argument of the Greeks as logically and chronologically prior in generating and encompassing both late modes: dialectic as dialogue on scientific matters, and logic as demonstration, *apodeixis.* The experience of time is at the heart of concern, Besorgen, in *Being and Time,* just as in SS 1924 Alltäglichkeit is the primary qualification of being-with-others as object of rhetorical research. It is the virtue of rhetoric that it discloses this structure, and, in doing so, clarifies some temporalities of Dasein. Blattner notes Dasein does not usually experience abstract, contentless moments; it confronts not nows that require later interpretation, but nows that are appropriate or inappropriate (kairos again), for choices.[33] Indeed, the tendentiousness of rhetorical kairos has a corollate in the fractiousness of care.

Alltäglichkeit, as starting point for Heidegger's meditations on time, is both ante- and anti-Platonic, a catalyst, precipitating new redescription tactics in handling life experience. It is a temporality defined in rhetoric's concentration on public oratory, Rede, as constitutive of the actions and formulae of public life (54). To be sure, Blattner points out that *Being and Time*—apolitically?—erodes Alltäglichkeit into everydayness, ordinariness, and thus must erode rhetoric.[34] Yet it is in *Being and Time* that Heidegger claims that Alltäglichkeit as timeful character of Dasein in its living-with-another defines rhetorical hermeneutic. Therefore Heidegger's fascination with the *Rhetoric* becomes, first in SS 1924, and then in *Being and Time*, a series of elaborations of the timeful as modifying care, and reception. The dispositions of the hearer in Dasein's authentic life build political life. But there is a loss of problematic: note how Heidegger, in defining in SS 1924 the three rhetorical genres, the three tasks of Aussagen, emphasizes tense as qualifying task; since the deliberative, juridical, and epideictic are simply divisions of political work, they, with their specific tense preoccupations, both share and connect political time frames. Politics requires simultaneous consideration of past, present, and future dimensions of political action and choice. In politics there is no pure present, no unmotivated future, no isolated past. It is a political manifold—public and accessible. The rhetorical interest, then, is the reverse of idealist formalism, and thus there is a strong realist aspect to Heidegger's early formulations, the reverse of the Kantian temporal idealism Blattner finds in Heidegger.[35]

B. Realism in Aristotle, Dilthey, and Husserl?

The SS 1924 lectures can be seen as glossing not only the later temporality of *Being and Time,* but the descriptive psychology of Dilthey and the phenomenological *epochē* of Husserl of Heidegger's immediate philosophical background. Recall Heidegger's claim that only Dilthey had recognized the historical importance of Classical rhetorical Affektenlehre (178). Heidegger appreciates Dilthey's historical tact; but also there is throughout the 1924 lectures a "Diltheyan" concern for time as intrusive, pervasive, qualifying life capacities and actions. Rudolf Makkreel has noted Dilthey's temporality as realist; Dilthey's time is derived from an *Innewerden*, an inner or reflective awareness, rather than from a Kantian representative consciousness, *Vorstellen*, which produces subjective time in the forms of a linear sequence of contentless nows. "Dilthey," according to Makkreel, "rejects the . . . claim that time is the ideal form of inner experience. Inner experience is not phenomenal like outer experience. Because, according to Dilthey, inner experience is real—it consists of facts of consciousness which are indubitable—time also must be real."[36]

In the collection *Dilthey and Phenomenology*, both Makkreel and David Carr link temporalities of Dilthey, Husserl, and Heidegger as an investigative initiative of importance, an initiative that rejects linearity, the very linearity that the "manifold" that Blattner describes subverts. But, once again, I would argue that Heidegger's use of Aristotle's *Rhetoric* in SS 1924 is pivotal to his development. There is, indeed, a curious temporal manifold in Heidegger's inquiry itself. The past, Aristotle's *Rhetoric*, enables Heidegger's contemporized rhetoric, and critiques as well a future in respect to Aristotle: Dilthey's hermeneutic of Heidegger's immediate past. And by using Aristotle's *Rhetoric* to gloss Aristotle, a contemporary restatement glossing a received Aristotle, Heidegger can employ the rhetorical formulae to articulate the centrality of Dasein as living-in-the-world, as well as the centrality of life experience in inquiry in his own theory, *and* in Aristotle—demonstrated in his intrication of the biological texts such as *Parts of Animals* with the *Rhetoric* in the lectures. Again, Heidegger's claim that for Aristotle life is nothing "wild or deep or mystical" evokes the tone of Dilthey's assertions that the fundamental concepts are those of life itself.[37] Dilthey, Husserl, and Heidegger focus on time for us, on a manifold of lived, not conceptualized time; recollect Heidegger's discussion of the Aristotelian mean as "for us." The *Rhetoric* in SS 1924 not only glosses Aristotle's philosophy, in its *present* historical guise, but gives a classical justification for the investigative habits of the psychological and phenomenological research of the early twentieth century of Heidegger's immediate past.

C. SS 1924 and SS 1925: "The History of the Concept of Time"

There is one more connection to be made in Heideggerian inquiry into time. In Kisiel's account of SS 1925, "The History of the Concept of Time," time is, again, the temporality of Dasein, and again, rhetoric's Alltäglichkeit offers a way into the problematic.[38] Recalling Dilthey, time is not outside, a framework for world events, but something "whirring away" inside consciousness.[39] But this is a consciousness ready to be defined as Dasein, as a manifold of co-original structures, ways of being; for example, care as a primary structure (totality), of the constitution of being of Dasein.[40] In these lectures there is a brief, but significant, intrusion of rhetoric, where Heidegger defines rhetoric as "the first part of logic, rightly understood,"[41] and there are diffuse echoes of the rhetorical formulae of SS 1924: there is the connection of language, life, and truth, since life is language capacity (the Aristotelian *zōon logon echon*); thus life capacity is political capacity, and thus discourse as social practice, Miteinanderreden, has priority over language as concept.[42] In short, there is in SS 1925 a recollection of a rhetorical politics of language, an investigational initiative that underwrites the politics of time.

4. Special Effects of the Rhetorical Connection: Politics First

It is the *use* of Aristotle's *Rhetoric* that is consequential. To give prominence to the *Rhetoric* in the Aristotelian oeuvre in a series of lectures on the Grundbegriffe is notable—surely there were not many philosophy courses in the German universities that did so. But when Heidegger uses the *Rhetoric* to elaborate or oppose the hoary philosophical usages we have derived from the major texts, he generates some specific, critical effects. Most specific is the critique of time. The quintessentially rhetorical initiative in the development of temporality is the focus on the politics of time, and thus on the reach of the construct kairos, appropriateness. Heidegger underlines the subtle contrast between two Aristotelian statements. First, ethics belongs to politics: "Die Ethik gehört in die Politik" (127). Second, rhetoric is inside politics: "Rhetorik . . . steht innerhalb der *politikē*" (134). The first statement conveys, to my mind, a Heideggerian claim for the dependency of ethics on politics. Contrary to the philosophic, or Platonic, assumption that ethics as a domain of inquiry encompasses politics, and ethical issues as originary and enduring enclose political problematic, Heidegger defines the Hellenic politics as the care of our authentic being, the Dasein im Miteinandersein (64). Politics encloses ethics. The second statement, that rhetoric is inside politics, affirms that far from being a mere technical mastery, rhetoric is the investigation of the possible political uses of technique. Rhetoric provides the hard investigative edge of political inquiry in its capacity to theorize, and give an account of the basic transactions of politics; it is intrinsic, not dependent. The basic operations of politics are described in *Rhetoric* 2: the creation, alteration, and reception of doxa, endoxa, pathē, prohairesis, pisteis, and krisis exhaust the limited repertoire of political acts. Thus the claim that rhetorical material does not stand under, or derive from theoretical axioms; insofar as rhetoric locates elemental functions specifically, it epitomizes political action, rather than supplements a general preexistent theory. Or rhetoric, in terms of Hellenic task, is prephilosophical in a strong sense. Heidegger is placing in time theoretical work; it is not useful to regard as a primordial situation an event in investigation.

The integrated political/rhetorical interests thus have as source of their competence a peculiar tact in addressing time, confronting the basic elements and operations in their temporal particularity. What philosophy attacks as rhetorical relativism is, in the Hellenic politics of SS 1924, an inquiry into *relatedness*, an extraordinary sensitivity to the constraints of time in Dasein's living-in-the-world. Political time is minute. First, meson, the mean, when defined as Jeweiligkeit, is functional, not immoral. Dasein as discursive, as absorbed, attuned ability, experiences only appropriate or inappropriate nows, the right time or the wrong time to choose to act—within its authentic domain, its Alltäglichkeit, made public by rhetoric. And Dasein engages choices socially constituted in time by the community of agents with which Dasein shares a public world: they are coordinated social practices.[43] Heidegger notes Aristotle's transfer of the concept of meson from medicine; but the extra, rhetorical interest is in the moment of listening particularity, the temporal dimension of speaking change. Second, Heidegger notes the constancy of change, alteration. The basic nature of passion as disposition is changeability, changing and being changed. And thus, as we have observed, the coherence of Heidegger's account with Meyer's account of Aristotle in his insistence that politics is not the guardian of consensus, but the constant negotiation of the differences—differences caused by the passions that can change, alter judgments. Politics, according to SS 1924, in confronting and undertaking these tasks of discursive negotiation constitutes the authentic life. Rhetoric gives us the means for and the analysis of authenticity. And there is no part of the political that does not manifest the constraints of time. In sum, a Heideggerian politics of time appears, even if briefly, in SS 1924—a politics perhaps hypothesized by Arendt in her early fascination with Heidegger.

Heidegger's special, and transitory, political effects are addressed in Stanley Fish's *The Trouble with Principle*. Fish cites Charles Taylor's claim that in response to the growing multiculturality, we are all going to need in the years to come "inspired adhoccery": "The solutions to particular problems will be found by regarding each situation of crisis as an opportunity for improvisation and not as an occasion for application of rules and principles."[44] Or, perhaps, as an occasion for the improvisation of connections between shared beliefs and particular cases—an occasion for rhetorical, topical argument, in short. Fish finds principles troubling, when it is the case that it is *locating* principles which is troubling, not easy; there is very little experience of principles. Where can one locate the thought of a moral principle? Duration is obscure; enduring moral principles are enclosed in, prejudiced by the episodes of speaking-out of the Aristotelian doxa, endoxa. What is disseminated in political discourse is not pure, rational principles, but passionate principles, or, indeed, passions, dispositions themselves. Jacqueline de Romilly's *La douceur* depicts, for example, the strength and persistence of the value of sweetness as disposition and value in the communal history of antiquity, an enduring thematic in classical politics.[45]

Fish engages the very political issues Heidegger tries to illumine by means of the Aristotelian rhetoric. The weakness of Fish's argument, indicated in his later rejection of adhoccery, is that he fails to take sufficiently into account temporality as a factor in legal and political transactions. The rhetorical perspective, ineluctably temporal, does take into account first, the importance of sensitivity to time, and second, that the difficulty lies not in proclaiming, but in confecting stable values, a difficulty Aristotle responds to in his pervasive preoccupation with relating universal to particular. Another rhetorician has noted this: Cicero, in the *De legibus*, explores the relation of law to particular cases; it is not so much that the enduring principles of Roman law must be neatly applied to, fitted to, particular cases; rather, great ingenuity must be used in particular cases so as not to damage the shared beliefs that prop, and necessarily so, the continuous identity of the Roman state in Roman law. Thus Cicero suggests the frailty, rather than solidity of the law. And just so Vico, another rhetorician, points out the timely figurative strategies, the creative fudging of language in legal fictions to convey to the populace the continuity and integrity of the grossly episodic law of the state.

The problem with the geometrical, mechanical definitions of meson, for example, is thinness or emptiness, and this is the direct result of a philosophical desire to empty life experience. But in SS 1924 rhetorical kairos as meson in practice counters meson as theory, timeless and naive. Heidegger claims that the time dimension of ethics is frequency, pollakis; frequency as quality is explained by rhetoric as punctuations, reiterations of orientations, alterations of dispositions, and intrusions of speaking on listening that both multiply and complicate the modalities of choice. The study of language as it lives in Alltäglichkeit (62) is a consideration of the experience of time, a thick texture of articulated habits, dispositions, and opinions. Thus the discussion sets aside the philosophical staples—freedom and necessity—as insufficiently fine grained, apolitical in their articulation. But to say that man is *im eigentlichen* kairos (59), that Dasein is *immer jeweiliges Dasein* (246), that the mean equals kairos as a manifold of circumstances, *Gesamtheit der Umstände* (171)—all this complicates politics enormously; it is ineradicably pessimist as perspective. Not relativist, pessimist: Heidegger gives us all those subtle accounts of the possibilities of hearer-activity that constitute politics; what is wholly lacking is any suggestion of stable political solutions. This rhetorical pessimism, a strong critique of the naively optimist theory that Heidegger confronts in the standard accounts of Aristotle, attracts him, and changes his mind.

5. *Conclusion: The Uses of the Quarrel of Rhetoric and Philosophy*

The *Rhetoric*, then, does three things for Heidegger: it recaptures the original Greek argument in all its incarnate, patho-logical complexity, the matrix of all further conceptual and methodological development; it expresses the Hellenic endoxa, and thus serves as an intellectual history; and, most crucially, it furnishes a way into, an analysis for, the account of life as authentic, the political life. What many philosophers stipulate as a weakness must be redescribed as a strength. The philosopher may see in rhetoric an amoral fixation on discursive persuasion with no sense of timeless truths. But rhetoric's analytic strength lies in its limitation to discursive action and capacity. The rhetorical focus on Aussagen, speaking-out, and on listening as timebound social practice pointed to a range and quality of discursive experience that philosophy had not simply regarded as of little interest, but actively distrusted. It is precisely this focus on the ineradicably timely actions of speaking and listening that is effaced by our theoretical fascination with textuality and its supposed transcendence, its undecidability as immortality—a fascination that is self-gratulatory, perhaps. Its strength is its self-limitation to acts of articulation: it rejects the odd premise that there are "unarticulated thoughts" of a "cabinet of consciousness" —that apolitical piece of furniture. That rhetoric is inside politics, and not an autonomous formal technē, ensures its integrity as an investigative capacity, giving an account of constitutive acts. Further, if Blattner is correct that Alltäglichkeit is later eroded by the philosophical program of *Being and Time*, and slides into everydayness, ordinariness, and inauthenticity, in the 1924 lectures the extraordinary emphasis on Hellenic political rhetoric as originary matrix is at the same time an emphasis on Alltäglichkeit as timeful, or the solvent of eternity, the mode of eroding the timeless. Timeful politics, whose concepts are in nature, substantiate Heidegger's use of the *Physics* to express an ontology of oscillation between and transformation of potency and act, dunamis and energeia, rather than an ontology of stable entities, universal, beyond time and off stage, beyond living space and time. This, I would argue, is of crucial interest for *Being and Time*. And Blattner asserts that, even later, Heidegger had absolutely no interest in eternity.[46]

The use of the *Rhetoric* is ambitious: there is a reversal of the priorities of the history of philosophy. In SS 1924 Heidegger is using the *Rhetoric* not simply to gloss the Aristotelian Grundbegriffe, but to force a radical revision of our notion of Aristotle's place in Hellenic inquiry. Thus, for example, a very minor tactic of definition, with rhetorical overtones, pointing to a *telos kata ton kairon* (140), glosses Heidegger's very large claim that there is nothing teleological about Aristotle: "Aristoteles hatte keine 'teleologische' Weltanschauung" (82). Further, Heidegger, perhaps not self-consciously, is using Aristotle's rhetorical revisions as a model or prototype for his own revisions. It is a little alarming to see how intricated the Aristotelian and Heideggerian programs are in SS 1924—it is very difficult to separate his admiring account from his own revisionary ambitions. Most certainly, the later relation between Heidegger's philosophy and his politics is a troubling one. My claim is simply that rhetorical hermeneutics enabled him to give lucid, deft accounts of basic political elements in SS 1924.

Kisiel claims that SS 1924 offers us an "embarrassment of riches." Certainly it is a felicitous moment in Heidegger's development, with the felicity, perhaps, explaining its effacement in later political philosophical moments. What is truly embarrassing is that it remains, arguably, the best twentieth-century reading of Aristotle's *Rhetoric*. The rhetoric presented reorients, comments on our Platonic temptations of philosophy. It has critical force in the review of philosophical investigation. It leaves intact the statements of philosophical assumptions, goals, and values but represents them in a typically rhetorical fashion, that is to say, in a fluctuating mass of changes, changeability, ironies, negotiations of differences, and perversities. SS 1924 is an episode in the quarrel of rhetoric and philosophy transpiring entirely within the work of a single thinker, as a stage in the development of his own thought. And the primary issue at stake is time, and the inadequacy of the available philosophical language to account for time. And while one intellectual historical question is the relation of the meditations on time of SS 1924 to the powerful amplifications of temporality in *Being and Time*, another issue is the relative thinness of the development of these notions of political time in either Heidegger's subsequent work or in twentieth century philosophy in general. Is it the case that our political philosophy is difficult because it is insufficiently rhetorical?

Notes

1. P. Christopher Smith, in his *Hermeneutics of Original Argument: Demonstration, Dialectic, Rhetoric* (Evanston: Northwestern University Press, 1998), may claim that rhetoric, in its control of the early, all-encompassing Hellenic discursive practice, has such a critical competence as gloss. Unless otherwise noted, in-text citations refer to Martin Heidegger, *Grundbegriffe der aristotelischen Philosophie: Marburger Vorlesung Sommersemester 1924*, Gesamtausgabe, vol. 18, ed. Mark Michalski (Frankfurt: Klostermann, 2002), hereafter cited as GA 18.

2. Pierre Aubenque, "Logos et pathos: Pour une définition dialectique des passions," in *Corps et âme: sur le* De anima *d'Aristote,* ed. Cristina Viano (Paris: Vrin, 1996), 37–49. See as well *Le problème de l'être chez Aristote,* where Aubenque calls rhetoric a "practical anthropology" (Paris: Presses universitaire de France, 1994), 261–62.

3. There are, I would argue, illuminating parallels between the Modernist philosophical revisionisms of Peirce's pragmatism and Heidegger's rhetorical revisionism of SS 1924: both diagnose similar dysfunctions in philosophical lan-

guage. See, in particular, Peirce's "Fixation of Beliefs," and "How to Make Our Ideas Clear," in *Writings*, vol. 3 (Bloomington: Indiana University Press, 1985).

4. Klaus Dockhorn, review of Gadamer's *Wahrheit und Methode*, 1st ed., in *Göttingische Gelehrte Anzeigen* 218 (1966): 169–206.

5. Michel Meyer, ed., *Historie de la rhétorique des grecs à nos jours* (Paris: Librairie Générale Française, 1999).

6. Meyer, "Postface," in *Aristote: Rhétorique; des passions* (Paris: Éditions Rivages, 1989).

7. Or, even more strongly, "*Pathos* eine Bestimmung des Seienden mit dem Charakter der Veränderlichkeit" (195). Then, pathos is also defined as a kind of hexis (habit), which adds another time dimension (183).

8. Smith, *Hermeneutics of Original Argument*, 214.

9. Compare the highly rhetorical account of meson in *Nichomachean Ethics* 1106a26f.

10. Theodore Kisiel, *The Genesis of Heidegger's* Being and Time (Berkeley: University of California Press, 1993), 490. In his glossary entry for "Alltäglichkeit" he notes Heidegger's earlier focus on "the surface existence of an accentuated accent of life" in WS 1919–20, and on the "overtly temporal" sense of life in SS 1924 (274–275); Aristotle's *Rhetoric* simply gives Heidegger a different terminology and argument for surface overtness.

11. William Blattner, *Heidegger's Temporal Idealism* (Cambridge: Cambridge University Press, 1999), 47 fn.

12. Cf. *De anima* 403a3-10. Heidegger seems to disregard the passages in the *De anima* (408b20f, 413b25f, 429b, 430a16) on the eternity, purity, and separability of the mind as an Aristotelian lapse.

13. We have, of course, Leo Strauss on Hobbes's utilisation of Aristotle's *Rhetoric*: *The Political Philosophy of Hobbes; Its Basis and Genesis,* trans. E. Sinclair (Chicago: University of Chicago Press, 1984), reprint of Oxford edition of 1936, esp c.3. But we should also note that Heidegger was a close reader of Dilthey, and Dilthey's account of Hobbes emphasizes his psychological perspicacity: *Weltanschauung und Analyse des Menschen seit Renaissance und Reformation,* in *Gesammelte Schriften* (Stuttgart: Teubner, 1960), vol. 2, 360–390.

14. Dumouchel, *Émotions: Essai sur le corps et le social* (Paris: Synthélabo, 1995), 87. GA 18, 46–47: passions are not states of the individual soul but qualifications of life-in-the world.

15. Ibid., 92.

16. Meyer, "Postface," in *Aristote: Rhétorique; des passions*, 136.

17. B. Cassin and M. Narcy, *La Décision du sens; Le livre gamma de la metaphysique d'Aristote* (Paris: Vrin, 1989), 185f.

18. Besides the passage on short chains of argument (1357a3–4), there are, for example, 1356a14–20, 1395b5–7, and 1357a15–17, which deal with the effects on the hearer.

19. Aubenque, *Le problème de l'être chez Aristote*, 94–95, 104.

20. Ibid., 118.

21. Heidegger distinguishes between Rhetoric and Sophistic in their connection to politics and ethics. Note the odd historical observation: "Die Sophistik ist der Erweis für den Tatbestand, daß die Griechen der Sprache verfallen sind, die Nietzsche einmal die 'sprechbarste aller Sprachen' nannte" (109).

22. There is a very long list of patristic and scholastic authors influenced by rhetorical theory of the passions. The reference to Dilthey's *Weltanschauung und Analyse* indicates, I feel, a possible source for some of Heidegger's psychological readings of the *Rhetoric* (178).

23. See Smith's chapter, "Embodied Argument as Patho/Logical" in *Hermeneutics of Original Argument*, on incarnation as motif in Aristotle, 217–90; contrast Blattner, *Heidegger's Temporal Idealism*, on the temporal vacuity of Heidegger's discourse, 121–22.

24. Again I would suggest that Peirce's pragmatism illumines the placement as well as the essential temporality of science of Heidegger. See his "Reply to the Necessitarians," *Monist* 3 (1893): 526–570.

25. Blattner, *Temporal Idealism*, 123, 127, 129.

26. Ibid., 127.

27. Ibid., 106.

28. Ibid., 107. Cf. Louis Mink, "On the Writing and Rewriting of History," in *Historical Understanding*, ed. Brian Fay, Eugene Golob, and Richard Vann (Ithaca: Cornell University Press, 1987), 93: "We also know, that the past is not *there* at all. Events don't withdraw from the present to the past as an actor withdraws from the stage to the wings."

29. Blattner, *Temporal Idealism*, 109.

30. Ibid.,107.

31. Ibid., 112.

32. Ibid., 92, 120, 127–128.

33. Ibid., 132.

34. Ibid., 62.

35. Ibid., 229.

36. Rudolf Makkreel, "The Overcoming of Linear Time," in *Dilthey and Phenomenology*, ed. Rudolf Makkreel and John Scanlon (Washington: University

Press of America, 1987), 142. The other pertinent articles are David Carr, "The Future Perfect: Temporality and Priority in Husserl, Heidegger and Dilthey," 125f, and Frithjof Rodi, "Dilthey's Concept of Structure in the Context of 19th-century Science and Philosophy," 107f.

37. Rodi, "Dilthey's Concept of Structure," 114–115. Still, Dilthey did not approve of "biologism," Darwinism, etc.: "The material passes over the boundaries of the knowable."

38. Martin Heidegger, *History of the Concept of Time: Prolegomena,* trans. Theodore Kisiel (Bloomington: Indiana University Press, 1985), 321, 156.

39. Ibid., 319.

40. Ibid., 156: "The *cogito sum* of Descartes, to the extent that it is explicated, is directed precisely toward the determination of the *cogito,* and the *cogitare,* and leaves out the *sum.*" Dasein is not, then, a Cartesian subject, "a subject that only incidentally provides itself with a world," 305.

41. Ibid., 264.

42. Ibid., 264–265.

43. Blattner, *Temporal Idealism,* 67, 73, 131–133.

44. Stanley Fish, "Boutique Multiculturality," in *The Trouble with Principle* (Cambridge: Harvard University Press, 1999), 63. Fish is careful to note that he does not endorse adhoccery, 65.

45. It is de Romilly's rhetorical intelligence that allows her to depict the persistence of the value of "sweetness" as disposition in antiquity. *La douceur dans la pensée grecque* (Paris: Les Belles Lettres, 1979).

46. Blattner, *Temporal Idealism,* 266.

6

Theodore Kisiel

Rhetorical Protopolitics in Heidegger and Arendt

The year 1923 was a particularly bad one, an *annus terribilis*, for postwar Germany, in which the full punitive effects of the Versailles Treaty came to catastrophic fruition in the Weimar Republic. Heidegger's rhetorical-phenomenological concept of the political takes shape against the historical backdrop of a viciously internescine party politics turned more rabid in its rhetoric by the increasingly rampant inflation brought on by the Weimar parliamentary government's fiscal policies to fund the general strike in the Ruhr industrial region after its occupation by French army units. It is out of this political and economic turmoil that the Munich-based Nazi party, led by its chief rhetorician Adolf Hitler, first came to national prominence, as it decided to translate its talk into action by way of a putsch. The ensuing trial for treason served only to place Hitler indelibly in the national spotlight, and beyond.

Far from coincidentally, Heidegger at this time was busy developing his hermeneutical and protopractical ontology of *Dasein* by way of a wholesale confrontation of the phenomenological and practical Aristotle. Aristotle's several definitions of man are being interpreted in close conjunction with his practical works, including his *Rhetoric* and *Politics*. The three Aristotelian definitions of the living being called "human" are in fact understood as equally primordial: a living being that has *and is had by* speech (*logon echein* understood as middle voiced); a political life (*zōon politikon*) that expresses itself by speaking in and for community in concert with others; and a practical being-in-the-world whose action is pervaded by speech. The human being both occupies the world and is occupied by it, practically, politically, and most basically, discursively. The understanding human being in its practical and political world accordingly has hearing—responsiveness to speech—as its most fundamental mode of perception.

In SS 1924, Heidegger will make clear how deeply the Greek definition of the human being as *zōon logon echon* is itself rooted in the self-interpretation of Greek Da-sein as a being-with-one-another in the *polis,* by suggesting its approximate equivalent in the crisis year of 1923: the modern human being, and German Dasein in particular, is the living being who reads the newspapers.[1] The animal possessed by speech is through and through political and rhetorical, gregarious and loquacious. But the rhetorical locus now shifts from the predominant orality of the ancient Greek polis to the predominant textuality of the modern pulp media reporting speeches from far and wide to post-WWI German Dasein, a textuality which in its own way is just as transient as the oral speech soon to be transmitted by radio, and governed by the vicissitudes of place and time. But it is precisely this dimension of context-dependent temporality that attracts Heidegger to the problem of political rhetoric and to the need to situate it in his temporal ontology of the unique human situation, of Da-sein both as situated "I" and situated "we" in their varying historical contexts. It is this search for ontological language to formally articulate the existential temporality of the crisis situation of speech, the Da-sein of the orators and the Da-sein of their auditors, that motivates Heidegger's gloss of Aristotle's *Rhetoric* a year later.

The overt confrontation of the matter of rhetoric, more specifically, the Greek text of Aristotle's *Rhetoric*, occurs in two occasional pieces in the Heideggerian opus. The first is a talk whose full title was: "Dasein und Wahrsein nach Aristoteles (Interpretation von Buch 6 der Nikomachischen Ethik)" that Heidegger gave repeatedly in a lecture tour through the Rhine-Ruhr valley, in the first week of December, 1924. The second is the lecture course of Summer Semester 1924 entitled: "Grundbegriffe der aristotelischen Philosophie" (in Karl Löwith's transcript entitled "Aristoteles: Rhetorik II").

Although the references to politics in these two pieces are typically brief, usually by way of allusions to the model Greek polis, it nevertheless becomes clear that Aristotle's *Rhetoric*, "the first systematic hermeneutics of the everydayness of being-with-one-another,"[2] depicts a speech community, a being-with that is equiprimordially a speaking-with, whose fundamental *telos* is a coming to an understanding agreement (*Verständigung*) with one another, *hermeneia*, communication and the accord that it brings in the public sphere. It is by way of this fundamental speaking-with-one-another that a rudimentary protopolitics begins to take shape and to seek its site in Heidegger's emerging fundamental ontology (45f, 122f, 241). In view of the close proximity, indeed the "equiprimordiality," of rhetoric and politics in a Greek loquacity that places a primacy on the political, what is being situated ontologically is in fact a rhetorical politics and political rhetoric of an everydayness in its moments of crisis. For the early Heidegger, the more ontological Greek *Urtext* of political philosophy is Aristotle's *Rhetoric* and not Plato's *Republic*, which will play a different role on a later, more fateful occasion of his development of a more metontological concept of the political. At this early stage of Heidegger's political development, the *ethos* of Greek civic discourse is held up as a paradigm in counterpoint to the violence-prone, propaganda-ridden speech community of the party politics practiced in the Weimar Republic, and each will serve as a phenomenological example contributing to the formal ontological structure of the historical "interpretedness" of the "everydayness of being-with-one-another." This interpretedness or "spokenness," the present perfect apriori (SZ 85: that is, "already *having been* interpreted" by a particular tradition of "usage") of the discursive space called the everyday world of publicity, determines the temporally particular ethos of the middle-voiced milieu from which the rhetorical politics of a time takes its cues.

I. 1923–24: "Being-here and Being-true According to Aristotle"

The text of this "Ruhr-Rede" was initially drafted at the end of 1923, still near the peak of the Ruhr crisis, and is still marked by the militant and territorial rhetoric of this dramatic year.[3] But it was not delivered in its final form until the end of 1924 in several cities of the Rhine-Ruhr valley, most notably in Cologne with Max Scheler as host. In its structure and movement, the text resembles the well-known later talk marking the turn to the later Heidegger, "On the Essence of Truth" (1930–43). The uniqueness of the 1924 talk is however its quick dispatch of judgment in the usual sense of a declarative (apophantic) statement, traditionally the locus of truth as correspondence through the scientific demonstration that "lets something be seen" as it is, in order to get to the more practical and *crucial* kinds of judgment (*krinein*) at issue or in abeyance in everyday speech situations. And the everyday speech situation quickly takes us to the public space of the polis, which will soon be identified with the veritable "clearing of be-ing" that is disclosive of a linguistically developed people, of Greek Da-sein, of German Da-sein (so already in SS 1924).

The everyday speech situation generates practical judgments that are far more varied and richer than the incipient theoretical judgment of declarative sentences. Its prejudicative possibilities, not always reducible to mere preludes to judgment, include requests, wishes, questions, imperatives, exclamatories, pregnant pauses, and other such punctuations, none of which are immediately subject to the hyperjudgment: true or false. Or better, they point to a much more original, comprehensive, and tacit sense of what it means to be true. On the ordinary everyday level, *logos* does not mean judgment, concept, or even reason, but simply speech, which includes every form of discursivity and articulation, even the nonverbal kinds, in actions that "speak louder than words" (for example, passive versus active resistance, or a general strike). The basic aim of everyday natural discourse, speaking to and with one another, accordingly listening to one another, is not knowledge but understanding, hermeneia, simply put: getting along together, living in accord, the understanding (*Verständigung*) of concord. The investigation of this spectrum of phenomena of speaking to one another belongs to rhetoric, which, as the study of logos in its very first fundaments, could also be called the very first logic. The speech in question is public, not private; its judgments are not scientific but practical; its discursivity is not just linguistic but extends to the nonverbal articulations of action and of passion; its truth does not reside in the clear and distinct logic of statements, but in the chiaroscuro logos of *doxa*, the partial truth of prejudgments and opinions.

Understood as the hermeneutics of everyday life of the Greek polis, classical rhetoric has classified three peak moments of discourse, which have generated three genres of civic speech making. Heidegger's matter-of-fact summary of the three clearly bore immediate relevance to the German polis of 1923-24. For his Ruhr audience had repeatedly been, and continued to be, addressed by all three forms of public discourse over the course of the previous two years of crisis:

1. The properly political speech seeks to persuade or dissuade a popular assembly or deliberative body toward a certain decision or resolution of a crisis, say, in matters of war and peace. The speaker does not seek to educate his audience about a state of affairs, but wishes rather to talk his audience into a certain mood which will bring it in tune with the speaker's own opinions and convictions on the present condition of the state (*Lage des Staates*) and counsel on its future course of action. (Germany at this time continued to be inundated by propaganda from factions both right and left about the "November betrayal" of the 1918 armistice and the call to overthrow the "November criminals" of a Weimar Republic inept in its handling of a continuing series of state crises brought on by the generally hated Versailles Treaty.)

2. The judicial speech before a court of law in prosecution or defense is addressed to the audience of a judge or jury. (On trial for treason for his instigation of the Munich putsch, Adolf Hitler had in the past year successfully made the entire nation the audience and jury of the speech in his own defence. Having dictated the rhetorically charged *Mein Kampf* during the brief incarceration following sentencing, he was about to be released back into German public life before Christmas of 1924.)

3. The festive speech, Heidegger notes, was first designed to celebrate the victors of the Olympic games, thus also applicable to the Germany of 1924. It is intended to bring the auditor into the presence (*Gegenwart*) of something admirable and noble. But the epideictic speech may involve either praise or censure, designed to create the moods of either admiration or outrage of our folk heroes and their actions (like Benedict Arnold or the police spies who betrayed Albert Leo Schlageter to the French authorities occupying the Ruhr region. The epideictic speech thus had recurring relevance to the Ruhr at the time of the first anniversary of Schlageter's execution in Düsseldorf, and each year thereafter.)

On the tenth anniversary of Schlageter's execution on May 26, 1923, by a French firing squad, Rector Heidegger would himself give his first political speech for the new Nazi regime, in honor and praise of Schlageter, the day before his more widely publicized rectoral address of May 1933. Heidegger had clearly learned his lessons in political rhetoric quite well from Aristotle's *Rhetoric*, as well as attuned himself to the ethos of the time, as he attempts to inspire the Freiburg student body into the presence of Schlageter's final "noble" moment of death for the Fatherland:

> We commemorate the Freiburg student who as a young German hero a decade ago died the hardest and greatest of deaths. In his honor, we wish to remember this death for a moment so that from this death we may understand our own life. Standing defenseless before the French rifles . . . Schlageter died the hardest death. . . . Whence this hardness of will to withstand the hardest? Whence this clarity of heart to set the greatest and the farthest before the soul? Freiburg student! German student! Learn and know this as you, in your walks and marches, tread the mountains, woods, and vales of the Black Forest, the homeland of this hero: Primeval rock, granite, are these mountains in the midst of which the young peasant boy grew up. They have in their very duration created the hardness of our wills.[4]

The Heidegger of 1924 does not say this, but Schlageter's example of witness and death speaks directly to the titular theme of his talk: being-here itself as being-true, the truth of a life that comes from the resolute authenticity of Da-sein. In *Being and Time*, Heidegger will concede that the existential-ontological ideal of authenticity is founded upon his own *ontic-existentiell* ideal of a pantheon of heroes determined by his German ethos. Heidegger's epideictic speech for this native son of the Black Forest thus highlights Schlageter's virtue of being "true" (*treu*, "constant," "faithful," "loyal" [SZ 385, 391]) to the native roots of his homeland. Virtually from the start, the Nazi movement accepted Schlageter as the perfect specimen of the "new man," whose deeds were glorified in song and story as much as Horst Wessel's would be from 1930. In his speech, "On the Origin of the Artwork," in 1936, Heidegger will identify "essential sacrifice" as one way in which truth happens, along with the artwork and the "state-founding deed." By way of further exemplification in this context, an earlier unpublished version identifies the "people-saving death" as still another form that the "happening of truth" assumes in historical context.

From his concrete rehearsal of the three speech situations, all broadly regarded as political speaking-with-one-another, Heidegger now summarizes the elements of Aristotelian civic rhetoric that would become important for his own protopractical ontology in the making, to begin with, for his ontology of everydayness:

1. Deliberation over a future course of action, judgment of a past action, reliving the presence of a praiseworthy action: the simple temporality of the three genres of speeches of the Greek polis spell out, punctuate, and define the rhythms of its public life, of political everydayness in crisis.

2. These speeches have as their telos not the communication of expertise on the everyday matters at issue, but rather the auditors themselves, aiming to win the audience over to a view of things by way of forming a receptive disposition or mood, which sometimes involves transforming another prevalent mood, typically apathy. The *pathos* of the listener is therefore the most basic of the three classical means of persuasion and opinion formation, the three *pisteis*, the trusts that inspire confidence in the credibility of the speaker and his speech. In addition to the pathos in which the hearer is placed (or "thrown," as Heidegger will soon put it), the confidences include the ethos of the speaker and the *deiknynai* of the speech itself (logos).

3. Over the ethos of the speaker, Heidegger will have precious little to say in this Greek talk on truth, since he is more concerned with the concealment of truth that comes from rhetoric and its more malicious cousin, sophistry. We must wait for SS 1924 for a bit more precision. Let me at least summarize what he does say on this ethical dimension of the speech situation, since it does suggest that ethos is not just character, let alone moral character, but is to include both where the speaker is coming from and in particular how he projects himself out of this thrownness: "His entire existence speaks along with what he speaks for," demonstrating whether he is trustworthy as a person, familiar with his subject matter, well-disposed toward his audience. The speaker, in short, must throw himself into his speech with the full expanse and meaning of his existence. Heidegger's language recalls his later depiction of what it means for authentic Da-sein to be truly "there" in its situation, as an already thrown project that is equiprimordially discursive in both its throw and projection. In fact, Heidegger will soon translate ethos, in the language of *Being*

and Time, as the action of resoluteness receptive to the call of conscience, the call of the situation. (In the later Heidegger, ethos will be the usage of the situation itself which we accept as our abode and standard of dwelling.)

4. The kind of demonstration (deiknynai, "showing," "pointing out") in the everyday speech situation is not a matter of logical proof or scientific procedures. They are instead enthymemes, the abbreviated syllogisms of rhetoric, literally curt speech that goes directly "to the heart" (*en-thymos*): striking examples, memorable punch lines (what are currently called "sound bites"), emotionally charged but pithy tales ("November betrayal"), narrative arguments that hit home quickly and powerfully. Opinion formation is sometimes opinion creation, giving currency to a new view which however is never out of keeping with the prevalent and average public opinion (doxa). The public speaker draws upon the way one on the average thinks about things, upon popular prejudices and suspicions, from which are selected the seldom-stated major premises that found the speaker's abbreviated but striking conclusions about how things look and what seems to be the case (doxa). For the thinking of the crowd (*hoi polloi,* "the many") is shortwinded, having absolutely no interest in the lengthy process of getting at the things themselves. The Greeks, who loved to talk, had a strong sense of this most immediate phenomenon of speech, of being with one another in common gossip, chatter, and idle talk. The human being even for Aristotle is first of all not the rational animal but rather the living being dwelling in ordinary language and idle talk, who has neither the time nor the inclination to speak primordially about the things themselves. Socrates and Plato in particular took arms against this dimension of the prevalence of idle talk, which Heidegger here identifies as one of the inescapable concealments of truth, the concealment of and by opinions in which daily life on the average first of all and most of the time operates. But Aristotle the rhetorician had a much greater appreciation of the doxa of his native language, its folk wisdom (for example, the *gnomen* [maxims and proverbs] of *Rhetoric* 2.20–22), and so its partial truth when properly authenticated by a native orator who uncovers it in appropriate speech situations that aim at the preservation and advancement of the polis.[5] His common front with Socrates and Plato was rather against sophistic phrasemongering, which deliberately perpetuates and exploits idle talk to self-advantage. Through the preponderant use of the catchphrase and cliché, through the glib polish of concepts, the pseudophilosophical sophist takes originally disclosed matters of the philosopher and puts them forward in the guise of obvious matter-of-fact self-evidence, parading his pseudoknowledge as a familiar possession that is in no need of being returned time and again back to its original sources, in a constant interrogation of its authentically original concealment, its mystery.

Thus, in his very first listing of the three modes of concealment, Heidegger attributes two of them directly to the language of rhetoric. Correlatively, the three modes of becoming true, of "trueing," the process of wresting matters out of concealment, are:

1. The disclosure that brings beings to the fore by way of the initial and immediate opinions commonly held about them, since such everyday views do contain a partial glimpse and measure of insight into the being of these beings.

2. Pressing into those unfamiliar original domains of being that have hitherto never been revealed at all, about which we are still totally ignorant.

3. The struggle against chatter and idle talk, which gives itself out to be knowledgeable and disclosive of the way things are. The struggle (*Kampf*) comes in tearing off the disguises of the concealing catchphrase and cliché, thereby exposing not only the underlying being of things but also the forces of concealment that militate against such discovery.

This very first listing of truth's concealments and unconcealments thus enlists not only the philosopher but also the rhetorician-statesman into the gigantic struggle *(Titanenkampf, gigantomachia)* of wresting truth from its concealment, which always begins with the struggle of tearing away the disguises of the concealing catchphrase, the surface cliché, the sound bites of popular jargon, in order to expose the more telling enthymeme befitting the particular speech situation of a native people, more in keeping with the ethos (custom, usage) of its folk wisdom.

One cannot help wondering how Heidegger, professor at a state university and so a civil servant of the state, might have applied this threefold structure of truthful exposition drawn from the Greek Dasein, admittedly involving a measure of interpretive violence, to the then-current German Dasein, to the trying events of the day and the crucial affairs of state that his country was undergoing in the crisis years of 1923–24. As Heidegger clearly states at the beginning of this talk as well as at the end of it, in response to a question from Max Scheler, his goal is to transform the ontology of constant presence inherited from the Greeks into a radical ontology of history and the temporal human world, "which not for one moment has the sense of cultivating any sort of antiquarian interest."

One might say at this point in the talk that it was the inherently practical nature of life that was to found Heidegger's temporal ontology, were it not for the fact that the practical is normally understood in contrast to, and thus in terms of, the theoretical. For this reason, it is better to speak of a "protopractical" understanding that Heidegger wishes to draw upon, a know-how of what it means for us to be with others among things in the world that comes simply and directly from already having lived and acted in the arena of the world. In short, it is the know-how that comes simply from the primal action of be-ing, here focusing on simply being-with-one-another and the protopractical politics to which its rhetoric gives rise.

This is important to keep in mind as we take our orientation for such an ontology, as Heidegger himself has done since 1922, from the five excellent habits of being-true according to Aristotle's *Nicomachean Ethics*, book 6, now rehearsed for his Ruhr audience. Two of these ontological habits are theoretical, two practical, and a fifth, *nous*, governs and guides these four, which accordingly are called the dia-noetic virtues. As a virtue, each is a habit (*hexis*) of excellence (*aretē*), something that is had by us, or better, like language, a habit that has us, *echein*, determining how we have and hold ourselves, behave, "be-have." Only the supreme habit of nous, direct contemplative seeing of being, is regarded by Aristotle as beyond language. This will change with Heidegger, who will replace eternal nous by a temporal clearing comprehending being by way of the ecstatic unity of Da-sein's contextualized, and thus finite, temporality. In the terms of Greek ontology, it is a shift in focus from the being that always is (*aei on*) to that which can also be otherwise (*endechomenon allos echein*), the being that manifests itself in the vicissitudes of history and thus displays an ever-changing context, *je nach dem*.

The excellent habits of being-true oriented to "beings that can be otherwise" are pretheoretical practical excellences, the *technē* of *poiēsis*, knowing how to get around in one's occupation with producing things, and the *phronēsis* of *praxis*, circumspective insight into human actions, the ethicopolitical virtue. Such circumspective insight at its most authentic always begins with one's own self-referential actions in the resolute response to the call of conscience, the demands of the practical situation, and then accommodates one's own self-referential action to the actions of others by becoming the conscience for others, being for the other by "leaping ahead and liberating" that significant other (SZ 122, 298). Such a liberation movement is the seed of an authentic politics in Heidegger, which of course can only be sustained by an authentic rhetoric, by a language that transcends the everyday in the direction of the lifetime considerations of fate and destiny, once again the language of politics at its best—and religion. Since these two pretheoretical and therefore protopractical dispositions of being-true constitute the respective ontological paradigms of the two published divisions of *Being and Time*, and the more theoretical habits of trueing are now to be derived from these two ways of coping with historically varying contexts, "je nach dem," it is clear that the science (*epistēmē*) that Heidegger is after no longer has as its objects merely the traditionally static ones of constant presence, but in particular the ec-static ones of past self-finding and future projection. Aristotle himself once identified such sciences of the past and the future, calling them "mantic" divining and prophesying, the stuff of religion—

and politics. The comprehensive theoretical virtue, the authentic understanding of philosophy, *sophia*, in turn would now become the comprehensive temporal science of the ever unique human situation. This unique temporal clearing (*Lichtung*), the nous-surrogate that would provide the temporal standards (ethos) of the customs and traditions for human dwelling in its productive activity (division 1) and its properly human actions (division 2) would have been the topic of the unwritten third division of *Being and Time.* The temporal science of the ever-unique human situation, which is "in each case mine (ours)," with each human being or generation allotted its own time, must accordingly develop those peculiarly temporal universals sensitive not only to the distributive "each" (*jede*) but also to its varying temporal contexts, "je nach dem." Such novel universals adaptable to the changing situations of history might therefore be called *jeweilige Universalia*, the temporally particularizing universals. After all, Aristotle had already observed that "being is not a genus," cannot be reduced to the indifferent commonality of a generic universal, of the All or Everyone.

II. SS 1924: Ground Concepts of Aristotelian Philosophy

The basic aim of the course is to understand some of Aristotle's ground concepts in their native growth out of the native soil from which they sprang and continue to stand (*Bodenständigkeit*). That native soil was the Greek language. A glance at the lexicon of *Metaphysics* 5 shows that Aristotle developed some of the most basic terms of his philosophy by way of a refinement of ordinary everyday Greek, the doxa of its language. The most important of the thirty concepts that Aristotle lists in his lexicon is the eighth, *ousia*, one of Aristotle's words for "being." It is a word which since Parmenides, as Heidegger had just discovered in a major revolution and caesura in his own thought, meant "constant presence" for the Greek titans, Aristotle included. More specifically, in the native soil of the Greek language, the word *ousia* finds its practical roots in the domestic domain of household goods, property (*Habe*, having), and real estate (*Anwesen*), which in the German tellingly also means "presence." In placing ousia first in his philological analysis, Heidegger is here inaugurating his own lifelong project of replacing it, of displacing the ousiological elements of "being as having" and habit operative in the Greek fixation on the real estate of an eternal, everlasting world. He wants instead to translate these ousiological insights of Greek Da-sein into the kairological language of a German Da-sein that never possesses itself but is always dispossessed, thrown into the world temporarily, in this temporal situation never constant and static but ever ec-static, that is, underway in its project toward life, and death.

Heidegger goes to Aristotle's practical philosophy to draw out the native soil and natural growth of Aristotle's insights into nonstatic temporal being, "that which also can be otherwise." The life that repeatedly encounters changeable being proves to be the practical and political life of the living being possessive of speech.

Since life always means being in a world, this means that the human being both occupies the world and is occupied by it practically, politically, and most basically, discursively. Understanding human being in its practical and political world accordingly has hearing, *akouein*, responsiveness to speech, as its most fundamental mode of perception (44). Aristotle's emphasis here on the primacy of hearing in understanding is striking, inasmuch as the model theoretical life will for him, by contrast, have the direct intellectual seeing of knowing, nous, as its most fundamental form of perception. This nous is accordingly *aneu logou*—without speech, speechless, beyond language.

Our analysis of SS 1924 here will be confined to highlighting some of the rhetorical-political categories that arise in this survey of Aristotle's ground concepts.

III. The Public Generic Anyone

Speech has the basic function of making a world manifest to one another and, in that communicative sharing, at once manifesting one's being-with-one-another in mutual accord and active concert, which accordingly is the locus of the political. What speech first makes manifest politically is that I am one-among-many, the Anyone, *das Man*, in an *average* concrete being-with-one-another. This is not an ontic fact but an ontological how-of-being. The true bearer of the peculiar universal of averageness called the Anyone is our language (64). The domineering prevalence of the Anyone properly resides in language, in the prevalence of the self-evident "what one says" first and foremost that the Greeks called doxa, opinion (73), the usually tacit major premises of rhetoric. It at once points to the possibility of forms of being-with-one-another authentically by way of a more developed being-in the polis (64), that of *hoi aristoi*, the few who excel. As many readers of *Being and Time,* like Pierre Bourdieu, have long suspected, das Man, hoi polloi, "the many" understood not as a loose sum of individuals but as a public kind of power of apathy and indifference built into the repeatability of language, is the baseline category or existential of Heidegger's properly political ontology. And since political being-with is speaking-with, communication, sharing this public linguistic world with the other, a *Mit-Teilung*, the anonymous impersonal Anyone is likewise a starting category that defines an extreme limit of levelling, that of least common denominator with regard to how one in general or on average is (64), in what might be called Heidegger's "rhetorical ontology,"[6] since language itself is the proper locus and modus operandi of the Anyone. This rhetorical-political realm of language that circumscribes the self-evidence of public opinion (73) also provides the basis for the universal validity so indispensable for agreement in the objective sciences (64).

But what many readers (Bourdieu, Marcuse, Arendt) of the political-rhetorical ontology of *Being and Time* have not noticed is that Heidegger also formally outlines a path out of the levelling impersonal anonymity of the masses whereby a "being-with-one-another in the same world . . . in *communication* and in *struggle* (Kampf)" (SZ 384, my emphasis of these two rhetorical dimensions) finds its way to an authentic grouping by actualizing the historical uniqueness and self-identity of its community. In the levelling of its essentially general state (SZ 300), the Anyone itself is not historical, just as the masses are rootless, homeless, and stateless, stripped of all uniqueness and credentials of historical identity. The everyday Dasein is infinitely scattered in the average with-world and in the multiplicity of the surrounding world (SZ 129, 389). The groupings of the Anyone are endlessly dispersed and manifold—businesses, circles, classes, professional associations, political parties, bowling clubs, robber bands—"such that no one stands with anyone else and no community stands with any other in the rooted unity of essential action. We are all servants of slogans, adherents to a program, but none is the custodian of the inner greatness of Dasein and its necessities. . . . The mystery is lacking in our Dasein. . . ."[7] The authentic grouping of being-with-one-another can never arise "from the ambiguous and jealous conspiracies and the garrulous factions of clans in the Anyone. . . . Authentic with-one-another first arises from the authentic self-being of resolute openness" (SZ 298). The passage to authentic coexistence "in the rooted unity of essential action" proves to be a historical rite of passage to a concerted historical action in first finding that one's own unique fate is inextricably rooted in the historical destiny of a unique historical people acting in community: "The fateful historical happening of unique Dasein as being-in-the-world is thereby a co-happening which is defined as destiny. This is how we define the happening of a community, of a people. . . . The power of destiny first becomes free in communication and in struggle. The fateful destiny of Dasein in and with its 'generation' constitutes the full authentic historical happening of Dasein" (SZ 384f).

IV. The Political Life as Historical

One way of exposing the essential historicity of the political life even in Aristotle, of capturing the historical characters of that model life in *medias rei publicae*, is by contrasting it in its distinction from the life of pleasure on its one side and the theoretical life on its "higher" side: *bios apolaustikos, bios politikos, bios theoretikos*. These three options of model lives all offer their unique reward (good or telos) to the individuals who lead them. (But a focus on the personal goals of the statesman or politician should always keep in mind, in counterbalance, the communal goals of a polis, that of a being-with-one-another in the world set upon fulfilling communal cares and practical concerns that range from economic distribution of functions and of wealth to social peace within the commonweal, all of which tend telically toward the closure of communal self-sufficiency. The public discussion, in its orientation toward communal goals, seeks therefore to discriminate the useful from the inexpedient, the fitting from the improper, the just from the unjust. The propriety of these distinguishing judgments vis-à-vis an ever-fluid historical situation is the measure of the prudent statesman and public speaker.)

The goal of the individual political life, in contrast to the narrow self-satisfaction of the life of pleasure, is *timē*, honor, or *endoxon*, a good reputation, a recognition amplified in and by the doxa of shining in the splendor and glory of public esteem, like Schlageter through his death and Heidegger through his commitment to the Nazi cause. Dependent as it is on the public opinion of the many, it is just as temporal and temporary as the temporally particular situations (*kairos*) that our politician-rhetor must address and judge in the crisis of krinein, discriminating judgment. Of the three life-styles that Aristotle examines, only the political life manifests the full temporality of the unique human situation in its momentous decision that is the ultimate focus of Heidegger's own protopractical ontology of historical being, of that being "which can also be otherwise." The constancy of presence achieved by the life of theoretical contemplation is matched in its constancy at the other extreme by the constant state of well-being that comes from just being alive that Aristotle identifies as the very background as well as telos of the life of pleasure, and calls a natural and normal settled state of *catastasis*. That is why pleasure as a ground stasis of well-being is ultimately not a pathos, like the ek-stasis of fear that charges the speech situation of deliberations over war and peace. For emotions move and thus make for history; pathos by Aristotle's lexical definition is intrinsically upsetting and peace disturbing, even revolutionary in its historical impact. Only the political life in Aristotle's scheme takes a look, in its measured Greek way, at the full tumult of life in motion that Heidegger was witnessing as a matter of course in postwar Germany and wished to make central in his own temporal ontology. No pain, no history. Instead of a steady state of seeing that is theoretical contemplation, Heidegger takes us squarely to its historical genesis in the aporetic shock that startles its interrogation and initiates the movement of search and research, the movement of human history.

V. Equiprimordial Modes of Persuasion and Trust (Truth)

Heidegger finds the same historical qualities in Aristotle's book on rhetoric, where the genres of speeches explored involve cases of ordinary speech exponentialized by crisis down to their most incipient interrogative moments. Aristotle's *Rhetoric* is for Heidegger accordingly a hermeneutics of everydayness in crisis, of being with one another in an everydayness that has been radically disturbed and thus exposed, in its structures, for ready ontological examination. Greek Dasein, understood as a public life of human speech, is being translated into the analytic of Da-sein, understood as a situated being in historical transit subject to abrupt transition, *metabolē*. To complete the circle of translating from Greek to German Da-sein, Heidegger at times reads his own hermeneutic emphasis and sense of Dasein back into the Dasein of the politician-rhetor and Greek audience confronting their particular situation of "that which also can be otherwise." Greek rhetoric's three modes of persuasion—pathos, ethos, and logos—that structure the speech situation thereby become close kin to the three modes of "being-in" and disclosedness of the human situation: disposedness, understanding, and discursivity. The exploration of this equiprimordial trio of the truth and trust in Heidegger's rhetorical ontology of SS 1924 will conclude our necessarily brief summary of the rich lode of ontological insight incorporated in that lecture course.

If hearing belongs properly to the auditor, it is also a component of the rhetor first having to size up the critical speech situation in which all in common find themselves (104). The skilled rhetor is at once *phronimos*, a statesman whose keen responsiveness to the crisis situation generates prudent counsel appropriate to the common situation of action. The rhetor demonstrates his mettle by demonstrating phronēsis (practical wisdom, prudence) or resolute openness to the demands exacted by the situation of action, which in one formula in *Being and Time* is characterized as the capacity to listen to (heed, hear) the call of (communal) conscience. Being able to hear is the other side of speech, in a way of being possessed by speech. One allows something to be said to oneself by the authentic Other functioning as the conscience of the community. In practical life, one first listens not so much to learn as to receive some directive for concrete practical concern, to heed it. This is the most rudimentary type of understanding, found on the level of *orexis*, the life of desire, care, and concern.

And care is deeply ensconced in the life of pathos, mood. The cultivation of the appropriate mood of the auditor by the skilled speaker, so that the attentive listener will then speak with the speaker by speaking after him or her (*Nachreden*) in contagious attunement, suggests that speech finds its deepest roots in mood (177). Discourse is not only rational, but impassioned, or better, passional in its rationality. We need only add the third mode of persuasion to complete the speech situation at its roots. As Heidegger puts it, "ethos and pathos are constitutive of *legein* itself" (165). There is an equiprimordiality, convertibility, thus interchangeability of the basic terms of conviction, trust, and confidence that define the speech situation, ethos, logos (first as doxa, *enthymēma*), and pathos.

This also entails an interchangeability of the roles of speaker and auditor: the speaker is first auditor to oneself (one's "conscience"), while the auditor already speaks simply by auditing. As Heidegger puts it in *Being and Time*, attuned silence may well be the most authentic form of speaking. The not-yet-speech of hearing, the receptive tension of listening to speech becomes the receptivity of the discoverer to the never-before-said about the world, a self-receptivity of listening to oneself speak and being-spoken-to, or in more Christian terms, of listening to the silent call of one's own conscience. After all, Aristotle himself suggested this direction into the not-yet-logos of ignorance and silence in his analysis of the practical speech situation as an appeal to the passions and the call to future action, to the unspoken dimensions of the human psyche, the *alogon* of orexis (desire, care) which in its responsiveness to the logos is itself a kind of speech (105). This relation becomes important in translating the counseling dianoetic virtues into the actional ethical virtues that the speaker, armed only with the power of words, must incite.

What then does the speaker as speaker bring to the speech situation? *To ethos* is the general bearing of the person, how one presents oneself, the figure one cuts. In the Aristotelian context, it is usually translated as the "character" of the speaker, judged to be appropriate or not in this speech situation of judgment and action, persuasive or not by and for the audience. One listens as much to the ethos as to the words of the speaker. This bearing and demeanor, comportment and attitude, this behaving, this manner of holding oneself in the world with and toward others is *to ethos* (68, 165). As a demeanor, it might be described as being or at least appearing to be "savvy, solid, and politic," where the speaker is seen to display "good sense, goodness, and good will."[8] As a way of comporting oneself to the world it bears on the question of where one stands and what one stands for, the conviction of a person with regard to polity and policy. In the deliberative speech, the speaker projects a deliberate choice, or better, prechoice, *prohairesis*, a fundamental option in polity and policy that constitutes the very purpose of the speech. In Heidegger's ontological framework, ethos in its display of conviction translates into the particular resolve (*Entschlossensein*) manifested by the speaker in speech, and the way the speaker attempts to bring others to the same resolution regarding the current situation of action, the kairos, this moment of decision in polity and policy (171). And resoluteness is the receptive response to the call of conscience in the Heideggerian framework. To follow up in this framework, then, the politician projects him or herself as the authentic conscience for the other, through prescient insight leaping ahead in order to liberate the particular other. More inauthentically, at the other extreme of how one is for the other, the politician leaps in and dominates the other (SZ 122, 298). Heidegger's choice of words for these options suggests a peculiar combination of politics and pedagogy. The domination and control that comes from "leaping in" for the other comes from taking over the other's proper responsibility to provide for his or her own cares, making the other dependent on such "welfare" (*Fürsorge*), say, in a welfare state.

And what is rhetoric itself, in this framework of resolute response to the call of conscience? It is first of all not an art but a power, *dynamis.* Not immediately the power of persuasion, as the sophists would have it, but rather the cultivated power of situational insight, phronēsis, of being able to see, hear, and feel, in a temporally particular situation of action, what speaks for the matter at issue, "je nach dem" (114). Ethos translated as personal character thus finds deeper roots in the interpersonally shared situation of action to which it must be receptive. Only the later Heidegger will perform the middle-voiced turn on this mode of persuasion, from having to being-had by the situation, that he had earlier performed on logos and pathos. It is the later Heidegger's turn from human being to the situation of being itself. Here, Heidegger can appeal to the older Heraclitean sense of ethos as (1) haunt, abode, and accustomed place, therefore as (2) custom, usage (*Brauch*), the habit of a habitat, the tradition which articulates, restrains, sustains, and guides the character of a speaker as well as the behaving of a people ("German Da-sein") and nourishes its resolve. Accordingly, ethos is (3) the history and destiny of a people in its shared actional *topoi,* which prefigure and prescribe patterns of behavior, its ways of having and holding and taking possession of itself. If the human being is distinguished from the animal by being the shaper and cultivator of worlds for dwelling, this cultivation is achieved by being responsive to the aura of usage, the ways and mores that belong to a particular place and come to us in the *logoi* of fables and myths developed over time and history. This is not as archconservative as it sounds, when we couple it with a sense of being that is always that which "also can be otherwise," especially in the generational exchange at the core of historicity (SZ 385f). It is something that happens to us from the tradition to which we happen to belong, from the historical context into which we in a particular now happen to be thrown, like our character and destiny: the authoritarian-militaristic ethos of Germany in the 1920s and 1930s, the democratic ethos of America in the year of the millennium, Heidegger's romanticized work ethic of peasant building and dwelling, Jünger's heroic ethos combining the hard and earthy military life with technological weaponry of destruction and Nietzschean Dionysianism, the ethos of civic discourse as opposed to propaganda rhetoric typically coupled with threats of force, or the tonalities of political correctness now in currency.

The later Heidegger's move is simply a further reminder that rhetoric's three modes of persuasion are first of all highly intercalated contexts that subtly move and guide us in our situational decisions: the deeply rooted mores and customs of a country looming as a fatality, the sustaining resonances of its language, the mood of the times forced by circumstances of crisis. The intercalated mediating milieus of a community, language, and historically particularized mood (for example, modern versus postmodern) delimit the contexts out of which we can come to better understand the developing persuasions displayed in the case we have followed for only a short stretch, subject recently to so much inflammatory rhetoric and therefore now called "the notorious case of Heidegger."

Authentic doxa. The distinction between the civil rhetoric of the Greeks and the propaganda rhetoric of postwar Weimar Germany reflects a distinction present in 1924, but muted in the text of *Being and Time*, between an authentic and an inauthentic doxa (view, opinion, positing of positions) latent in the ethos of a cultivated language. It appears most clearly in the distinction between (1) the matter-of-course concealment in everyday-routine rhetoric of the folk wisdom of custom and usage incorporated in any language of the world, which for Heidegger and Aristotle provides a partial glimpse and measure of insight into being, and (2) the more malicious concealment of such insight by sophistic rhetoric in its sham usage of the obfuscating catchphrase and cliché. But despite the deceptive machinations to which the doxa of our everyday language is subject, it has for Heidegger, following Aristotle, displayed its "trueing" functions in two ways: as a linguistic source of philosophical insight into the world, and as a partial truth that, by sufficient broadening and reorientation, allows for authentic accord in historical being-with-one-another. Heidegger's ramified Aristotelian account of this primary source of the "tacit major premises" of protorhetoric (130f) is therefore worth a final brief look.

Doxa is "the authentic discoveredness of being-with-one-another in the world" (149). It is the average intelligibility in which the Anyone moves, in what one "on the whole" means about things and about oneself (64). It is the "authentic discoveredness" of being-with-one-another in the world that grows out of speaking with one another in and out of everyday concerns (149). Even though doxa has a certain fixity and solidity in its peculiar familiarity and confidence in what first shows itself, that about which one has an opinion is always open to discussion and thus subject to negotiation (151). For opinion belongs to the realm of "that which always can be otherwise" and is accordingly always capable of revision. In its partiality, it can be true and false, and so must be left open to further discussion. Being-with-one-another thus contains the possibility that one is of this opinion and another of that, which leads to the possibility of speaking-against-one-another (138), disputation, and debate. A basic change in circumstances, say, in the state of a city, may also dictate a change of opinion (161) and reorientation toward its world. That is why doxa incorporates the possibility of negotiating-with-one-another (*Verhandeln*: also "parley, deliberate, plead, discuss, debate"), by which the common ground of a community is actualized and brought to fulfillment. But all such coming-to-an-understanding-and-agreement takes place on a ground of a familiarity which itself is left undiscussed (153). Doxa is thus at once permanent ground and source as well as impetus and end result of speaking-with-one-another (151). A similar "bargaining over opinions" (*Abhandeln*) occurs in the dialectic of a theoretical treatise (*Abhandlung* [152]), which also commonly starts in opinion. But on the practical level, it is the art of rhetoric, which is always conditioned by the politics in which it stands (134), that seeks to guide us to the right opinion and decision needed for resolute action (*entschlossenes Handeln* [145]) in a crisis situation. In such deliberations, the appropriateness of the judgments is to be evaluated not only in terms of the viewpoint being expressed and what speaks for it, the doxic context out of which it arises (162), but also how the opinion is held and presented (ethos of the speaker) and how the auditor stands to the opinion (pathos). Has the speaker, like a good statesman, risen above partial views to an oversight of the whole of the problematic situation, its kairos and full temporal horizon? And if the speaker is fully acquainted with the situation, is the speaker perhaps not saying all, veiling his or her own position and view of the matter? Is the speaker resolute and prudent in his insight into the issues at hand and competing views? Is the speaker attuned to the mood of his audience as well as that of the situation? And so on.

VI. The Fate of Rhetoric in the Later Heidegger

The later Heidegger will develop two additional concepts of the political:

Heidegger's Three Concepts of Polis and the Political

	Period	*Basic Text*	*Basic Concepts*
Phenomenological	1923–25	Aristotle, *Rhetoric*	pathos, ethos, logos of doxic speech situation
Metontological	1933–35	Plato, *The Republic*	leader of people, guardians of state, 3-level service
Archaic-Poietic	1935–43	Sophocles, *Antigone*	*pole-mos* of thinker, poet, and statesman as prepolitical

The present context calls for only a quick tracing of the fate of rhetoric across these remaining concepts of the polis and the political.[9]

VII. The Metontological Polis of National Socialism

The two basic existentials of this concept of the political, a people and its state, are connected as beings to their political being by the crucial political act of historical decision (phronēsis) of the human beings who as a people decide for the state appropriate to its unique tradition (ethos) and freely unite to support and maintain it. The model of national socialism as the basis of organization for that state finds its immediate precedent in the "front community" of World War I, when Germans from all European regions and dialects spontaneously united to defend themselves on the battlefront and at the home front. University Rector Heidegger sees his role in the educational service within this worker state of three services (labor, defense, knowledge), based on the *Führer* principle according to the German tradition of the two Reichs preceding the Third Reich, to be that of political educator of the "guardians" (*Hüter*) who, as future leaders of the nation in whatever profession they had chosen at the university, would be called upon to assist the Führer and share in the responsibility for the state. Such a political education would impart a knowledge of the people and the state destined by its tradition that would aid all individuals to come to meaningful terms with their particular self-responsibility for the people and their state: "The state now rests on our watchfulness and readiness and on our life. Our way of be-ing [our ethos] marks the being of the state. [Accordingly] our task in this historically decisive moment (kairos) includes the cultivation of, and reeducation in, the thought of the state. Each man and woman must learn that their individual lives decides the destiny of the people and the state, supports or rejects it."[10]

The emphasis on human decision as the core and wellspring of the political suggests that it is willpower that founds, sustains, and rules the state and carries out its tasks: first the will of a people, then, through their acknowledgment, the will of the leader (Führer) or leaders, and, by abstract extension, the will of the state enforcing itself by ruling, administering, and other organizational actions bent on maintaining and restoring order. Heidegger's use of this central word of German idealism is conditioned by his understanding of it wholly in terms of Aristotle's political virtue, phronēsis. Will is a striving that puts itself into action by engaging in pursuit of the goal dictated by the situation with a clear sense of the means needed to actualize that goal: "The will deliberatively grasps the situation in the fullness of its time, in it the kairos is at work, calling for resoluteness and action in the full sense." Action is practically technical when it aims to actualize a thing, and practically moral when it aims to actualize the will of another or of an entire group, a community of will, a people's will. It is a people's will, which is not a mere sum of individual wills, that a leader has to contend with and carry out. There are two ways of carrying out such a will, either by persuasion or by coercion.

Persuasion can occur by speech or by deed. The Greeks in particular recognized the power of speech as a political power. Their political instinct made the persuasive power of the speech into a paradigm of politics, like the unforgettable speeches of Thucydides. If nowadays the speeches of the Führer give the impression of "drumming" their points across, in his inimitably forceful style of "propagandizing" (*Trommelnder*), such an impression is but an unconscious acknowledgement of the power of speech that the Greeks had already uncovered politically (in the pisteis of rhetorical politics: see above). But the active will persuades most forcefully through deeds. The doer of deeds and the man of action is at once acknowledged as the power in authority, the ruler, whose Dasein and will is determining through persuasion, that is, by acknowledgment of the superior governing will of the Führer. True rule manifests true knowledge of the goal—the wisdom of a statesman (phronimos) —along with engagement—the active leap toward its realization—and the perseverance, the staying power, to bring this commitment of action to its conclusion.

True effectuation of such a governing will does not come by the dictatorial coercion of commands and orders but by awakening the same willing in the other, that is, commitment to the same goal and its fulfillment. It in effect brings about the re-creation of the others to accord with the mood and temper of the ruling will. It comes about not by way of a momentary yes-saying but by way of a decision on the part of the individual. Important here is not the number of individuals but the qualitative value of the individual decision. This is the way in which the present requirement of political education is to be understood: it is not a matter of learning maxims, opinions, and forms by heart, but of creating a new fundamental attitude of a willful kind.[11]

The will of the leader first of all re-creates the others into a following out of which a community arises. It is from this vital solidarity of followers to leader that the will to mutual sacrifice and service arise, and not from sheer obedience and institutional coercion. Political education is a superlative form of the effectuation of the will of the leader and of the state's will, which is the people's will. Other forms of putting the will of the state into effect, like the administration of governance and of justice, follow from the will of the people on its way to becoming a leader state (*Führerstaat*).

The highest actualization of the human being happens in the state. The leader state that we have signifies a completion of historical development: the actualization of the people in the leader. The Prussian state as it was brought to completion under the tutelage of the Prussian nobility is the preliminary form of the present state. This relationship generates the elective affinity and congeniality that prevailed between Prussiandom and the leader. We come from this great tradition and stand in it when we confess to its sense in the words of the royal elector, spoken in the spirit of Luther: "Si gesturus principatus ut sciam rem esse populi non meam privatam." [To assume the mantle of leadership is for me to understand that the affairs of the people are not my private affair.]

VIII. The Archaic Prepolitical Polis

Heidegger tacitly expresses his growing disenchantment with a Führer turning from statesmanlike to coercive ways to persuade his following, and a total state bent on coercively politicizing all walks of life, allowing no room for the independent counsel of his educated coterie of guardians, by way of a reduction, begun in 1935, of the polis to a prepolitical originarity that is the source of not only the political but also the philosophical, poetic, religious, and other creative human endeavors. In the context of the tragic phronēsis of the conflict between family piety and royal ediction in Sophocles' *Antigone*, Heidegger finds that polis is not merely a geographically located state (*Staat*) or city (*Stadt*) but, more basically, a historical site (*Stätte*) virtually identical to the ontological site of Da-sein in which a unique humankind (for example, Greek being-here, German being-there) "takes place" (*statt-findet, statt-hat*), is "granted stead" (*gestattet*, "permitted"), and in this "leeway" (*Spielraum*) of allotted time and historical place makes its unique "homestead" (*Heimstatt*) befitting its historical destiny. This historical site of Da-sein is the "pole" of the polis, from which human beings receive their stance and status in the state and acquire their stature in each of their historical instantiations. This " 'politics' in the supreme and authentic sense" thus takes place at the supreme site of radical historical transition displayed by the Greek tragedy, which glosses the oxymoronic status of the tragic heroine (Antigone) as *hypsipolis apolis,* at once far beyond and without home and site, unhomely, lonesome, uncanny, singled out for lofty greatness by creating a new home for her people, as well as for the precipitous destruction which was also the fate of Heidegger's more contemporary heroes: Hölderlin, Nietzsche, van Gogh, and Schlageter. Around this core of history, Da-sein as polis, not only statesmen and thinkers, but also poets and prophets are gathered together in unity and lonely, untimely, tragic, and contentious dialogue. Politicians (or better, statesmen) are not the only creators of the polis and so the political. Especially in the "land of poets and thinkers," Hölderlin's "fatherland," politics finds its origins in poetizing and thinking: "It is from these two prior activities that the Dasein of a people is made fully effective as a people through the state—politics."[12]

It is from this archaic vantage of Da-sein that Heidegger now criticizes the Nazi claim of the totalitarian character of the political: "These [Nazi] enthusiasts are now suddenly discovering the 'political' everywhere. . . . But the polis cannot be defined 'politically.' The polis, and precisely it, is therefore not a 'political' concept. . . . Perhaps the name polis is precisely the word for that realm that constantly became questionable anew, remained worthy of question, and necessitated certain decisions whose truth on each occasion displaced the Greeks into the groundless or the inaccessible."[13] Aristotle saw clearly that man was a political animal because he was the animal possessed by speech. But he did not see the full uncanniness that membership in the polis brings, far outstripping the rhetorical as well as the political of a people's state. Hölderlin's poetic words, "Since we are a conversation / and can hear from one another," refer to the thoughtful dialogue among solitary creators (poets, thinkers, statesmen) at the very abysses of being. Language here is the original institution of being in the violent words of poetic origin and not just a means of communication for the sake of quick and easy agreement, rhetoric. The community of creators is a combative community of struggle over the extreme issues of being. Hearing from one another, listening to one another, reciprocally involves radically placing each other in question over the radical issues at stake. Rapprochement here is contention, contestation, war, *pole-mos.* Coming to an understanding is combat: "Conversation here is not communication, but the fundamental happening of radical exposure in the thick of beings."[14]

IX. Arendt's Public Space of Doxa

Hannah Arendt first came to Marburg to study in the winter semester of 1924–25. Her first exposure to Heidegger was accordingly his lecture course on Plato's *Sophist*, which began with a detailed summary of his previous work on Aristotle's practical philosophy. The remainder of the semester was then spent on a detailed exegesis of Plato's Greek texts focusing on the distinction between the philosopher, the rhetorician, and the pseudophilosophical sophist. It is not clear whether Arendt in her Marburg years (1924–26) ever had access to any of the circulated student transcripts of the summer semester 1924 course on Aristotle's ground concepts, from which she could have gleaned, as we have done, Heidegger's phenomenological conception of the protopolitics of the speech situation. But her own work on what can only be called the protopolitics of the human condition is clearly marked by the uniquely phenomenological approach to the Greek polis to which she had already been exposed during her tenure in Marburg. And Aristotle's *Rhetoric* is one of the Greek political writings from which she sometimes draws to make her own protopolitical points, notably in her repeated distinction between the solitary singular *in* which philosophy has traditionally done its thinking and the political plural *between* which public communication takes place and generates its political arena of action. Traditional philosophy tends to speak of "man" in the singular, as if there were such a thing as a single human nature. This impression is conveyed by the genus-species structure of Aristotle's famous definitions of man, even as the early Heidegger interprets them, despite his growing sense of the "temporal particularity" (*Jeweiligkeit*) of Da-sein, which is "in each instantiation mine." Politics, however, does not arise *in* man as political animal but *between* humans, as its very space. Arendt thus interprets the equiprimordiality of definitions of man with this plurality of individuals and public space of interchange in mind: "that man is *zōon politikon* and *logon echon*, that insofar as he is political he has the faculty of speech, the power to understand, *to make himself understood, and to persuade*."[15] To understand by listening to the speech, to persuade by speech, these are the powers of "the highest, the truly political art . . . rhetoric"[16] cultivated by free men in the Greek polis, whose institutionalized speeches are recorded and formally analyzed by Aristotle in his *Rhetoric*. But Arendt's phenomenology of the speech situation is even more protopolitical, reaching back to the "grass-roots politics" of associations that precede institutionalized assemblies and rudimentary judicial systems, thus to spontaneous communications less structured than an authority addressing an auditorium, whose evanescent occurrences are preserved and memorialized in more informal stories than the epideictic speech.

The Human Condition is by Arendt's admission a critical appropriation of Heidegger's Daseins-analytic that she first learned from his lecture courses, seminars, and more private tutorials in her three semesters at the University of Marburg. The Heideggerian antimetaphysical stress on the facticity and contingency of the human condition, its Da-sein—as opposed to anything like a human nature—is overt in Arendt's analysis of the three levels of human activities in the world: of labor in the private world of the household, work in the environing world of things, and action in the interhuman world (*Mitwelt*), where I from birth already find myself thrown together with others. *The Human Condition* reaches its climax in Arendt's unique development of Heidegger's concept of the Mitwelt, of being together with others, that will yield her unique concept of the political. What she does is simply to radicalize Heidegger's occasional use of the plural "others" with which the self from the start finds itself, and articulate its full implications. The basic facts of human plurality and natality constitute for Arendt "the facticity of the entire world of human affairs." One therefore begins with how human beings in their full particularity are in fact situated together in their lifeworld: "Politics is based on the fact of the plurality of human beings. Politics thus has to organize and regulate the being-together of different and not equal beings."[17] But despite their essential differences, human beings share equally in the capacity for mutual communication. This equality of mutuality implies that humans spontaneously engage in nonsovereign relationships with each other. If plurality signifies personal uniqueness, equality enables community. It is not in man as political animal but *between* humans as its very space, that politics arises. What in fact arises in this public space between humans is freedom and spontaneity: "The very content and sense of politics is freedom."[18] It is in this public space of plurality that new beginnings and new initiatives are possible: each new birth inaugurates a new voice which can spontaneously initiate new actions and manifest its virtuosity before others. Natality thus introduces spontaneity into the public space of politics. This is politics in action, its veritable praxis. Politics is the free disclosure of self, through words and deeds, to one's equals in the public realm of *inter-esse*.

Freedom of movement in this public space in fact assumes two forms: (1) the aforementioned freedom to begin something new and unprecedented, the freedom of initiative that comes from the natality of being-there; and (2) the freedom to move among the many and speak with them, thus to experience the many, which in their totality is in each instantiation the world that we share in common, about which we speak and exchange our perspectives with one another and opinions against one another. This is the freedom of speech and unimpeded communication with others ("the many") in expressing our opinions about the actual world in which we live and which we share in common. The freedom to express opinions is "the right to hear others' opinions and to be heard in return." This second freedom, "which became crucial for the organization of the polis, distinguishes itself from the freedom peculiar to action, the freedom to posit a new beginning, in that it is dependent to a far greater degree on the presence of others and being confronted with their opinions."[19]

Constituted by this twofold sense by the freedom of action and freedom of speech, the polis is superbly the public space of freedom, "the realm where freedom is a worldly reality, tangible in words which can be heard, in deeds which can be seen, and in events which are talked about, remembered, and turned into stories before they are finally incorporated into the great storybook of human history."[20]

Arendt tends to call this public space of the many the "space of appearance," of *dokein* or doxa in the twofold Greek sense of "opinion" and "splendor, fame, repute,"[21] *Ansicht* and *Ansehen* in the German, of how things look to me and how I look to others, my public image. This double sense immediately recalls two of the equiprimordial dimensions of persuasion that Aristotle identified in the rhetorical speech situation, namely, the doxic content of the speech itself and the ethos of the speaker himself, how he presents himself in the judgment of his audience. At first, "space of appearance" referred almost exclusively to the domain where "I go public" and "make an appearance," "make my debut, have my coming-out party," as it were. The Greeks established the polis to multiply the opportunities for every free man "to distinguish himself, to show in deed and word who he was in his unique distinctness" and thus to win "immortal fame," or ignoble shame.[22] A sister New Yorker and friend of Arendt, Mary McCarthy, provides a modernized example of this theater of appearance: "Through politics, men reveal not their skill or their products [of work] but themselves in their words and actions, held up to admiration or contempt in the free open space of the agora or forum—a tradition still maintained in the open-air 'forums' of Union Square and Hyde Park. The desire to achieve glory and everlasting remembrance through conspicuous deeds and words has shrunk, however, in modern times, to the right to 'blow off steam'—the most evanescent thing there is."[23] But a major way in which I show myself in the public space, there to be seen and heard by others, is in the expression of opinions. This dimension of doxa multiplies the public world into a vast manifold of appearances (*doxai*), a pluralized "space of appearances" that sometimes threatens to reach anarchic proportions. Each person assumes a position toward the world in accord with that person's particular position in it, and the political realm degenerates into a "battlefield of partial, conflicting interests, where nothing counts but pleasure and profit, partisanship, and the lust for dominion."[24] When this agonal spirit took over, the Greek polis became "an intense and uninterrupted contest of all against all" and the domestic life of the citizens were poisoned with the pathos of mutual hatred and envy, "the national vice of ancient Greece." This agonal spirit eventually brought the Greek city-states to ruin, as in this atmosphere of enmity they were incapable of forming saving alliances. As an antidote to this ultimate threat to the commonweal, Aristotle recommends friendship as the real bond of community and as a political virtue more basic than justice (so in Plato's *Republic*), which is no longer necessary among friends. Friendship makes citizens equal partners in a common world and dispenses with the hierarchical relations of rulership. In the friendly dialogue between equal but radically different persons, one comes to understand the other's point of view to the point of seeing the world as the other in fact sees it, by entering into the other's unique opening to the world. Doxa here is no mere subjective illusion or sophistic distortion, but rather a "true opinion," and therefore an insight, partial as it may be, into the very reality of the common world that constitutes our community.[25]

Such a community of free communication and interchange of opinion among friends, among mutually respected equals who are at once very different and other (often an exile becomes alien resident), may sound a bit utopian—Arendt notes that one prerequisite for such a community would be that each and every citizen "be articulate enough to show his opinion in its truthfulness and therefore to understand his fellow citizens"[26]—but it is precisely such communities that Arendt discovered in the 1940s and 1950s in New York intellectual circles centered around a particular magazine of public opinion, like Dwight Macdonald's short-lived radical magazine, *politics*, or the small but interrelated cluster of periodicals to which Arendt herself was recruited to contribute her uniquely European perspective on current events, thus making her appearance on the pages of *Commentary, Commonweal, Partisan Review, The New York Review of Books*, and so on. These "oases of freedom" and enclaves of participatory democracy constitute the very models that exemplify her phenomenology of protopolitical communities of spontaneous democracy, in which consensus is established by lateral and not hierarchical relationships. The public realm is formed by spontaneous associations like town meetings and voluntary neighborhood associations that constitute the very cells of participatory democracy. "Some public interest concerns a specific group of people, those in a neighborhood or even in just one house or in a city or in some other sort of group. These people will then convene, and they are very capable of acting publicly in these matters, for they have an overview of them."[27] When the public matter at hand is resolved, they disband and dissolve back into their neighborhood life, only to reform into another public forum in the next community crisis. Who we are is thus disclosed in such public convenings in the company of others, in the discharge of our responsibility to others, in the in-betweenness of being-for-the-sake-of-others. Traditional philosophy's sovereign self, cut off from the shared humanity of human beings, is replaced by the person disclosed in action and speech in the face of others.

But what about representative democracy in the space of appearances and multiplicity of often opposing opinions? Arendt invokes the "enlarged mentality" of cosmopolitan "common sense" to guide the prudential judgments of the phronetic statesman who is delegated to represent the views of the entire body politic. This is the common sense that assumes an interpersonal universality for the cosmopolitan Kant, as "a sense common to all . . . a faculty of judgment which, in its reflection, takes account . . . of the mode of representation of all other men."[28] It is the moral imperative of acting in such a way that your principle of action can become a (distributively) universal law: whenever each of us acts rationally, we legislate for all of humanity. Common sense is the ability to look beyond one's own point of view and see things from the perspective of all involved. The outstanding virtue of the statesman is to understand the greatest number of divergent realities "as these realities open themselves up to the various opinions of citizens" and to communicate between the citizens and their opinions in order to bring out the reality of the common world that they share with others.[29] Common sense is therefore the "good sense" of the statesman, in making his judgments and decisions, to look to the nonsubjective and, in this sense, objective world that we share in common. It entails the good will to listen to others in order to reveal the full sense of this "sharing-the-world-with-others" as it bears on the stateman's decisions to represent the fullest possible constituency. It still may not be the most pragmatic decision, but representative thinking is clearly a practice carried out between humans in communication with one another rather than a performance of a single individual who in self-chosen solitude has lost touch with his or her fellow humans and is no longer oriented to their common world. The cosmopolitan ethos of Kant specified for any moral agent and especially for the statesman thus converges with the ethos of the political speaker detailed by Aristotle into the character traits of "good sense, good will, goodness."[30] The application of these character traits of common sense and humanity have no less currency for the contemporary statesman, who must adjudicate the often contradictory advice of expert opinion with the common good in making even more complex decisions of competing national and humanitarian interests at the millennium, like Hiroshima, the Cuban missile crisis, and "9/11-01."[31]

Arendt, the thinker of the origins of totalitarianism, never directly addressed Heidegger's brief but fateful commitment to National Socialism and was probably unaware of the full ontological conceptuality in which that political commitment was philosophically justified. But what she did know of that conceptuality from the published record allowed her to pinpoint precisely where Heidegger's thought had been infected with the bacillus of totalitarianism. In order to cover over his early solipsistic existentialism, in which the authentic Self distances itself from the public Anyone so radically that it departs the common world shared with fellow humans and is now "representative of no one but itself," Heidegger

> later brings in, almost as an afterthought, mythologizing confusions like Folk and Earth in order to supply his isolated Selves with a shared common ground, a kind of social foundation. It is evident that such muddled concepts can only lead us out of philosophy and into some nature-oriented superstition [like the primal myth of the autochthony (Bodenständigkeit) of a landed gentry, of a peasant folk rooted in the earth from which they first sprang and which thus constitutes their native ground]. If it does not belong to the concept of man that he already inhabits the earth together with others of his kind, [the only thing left] is a mechanical reconciliation of atomized selves in a common ground alien to their nature. This results in an organization of selves intent on willing themselves into an Overself in order somehow to make the transition from guilt, accepted in resoluteness, to action.[32]

Notes

1. Martin Heidegger, *Grundbegriffe der aristotelischen Philosophie: Marburger Vorlesung Sommersemester 1924*, Gesamtausgabe vol. 18, ed. Mark Michalski (Frankfurt: Klostermann, 2002), 108. Henceforth all page references not otherwise specified are to this text. The Gesamtausgabe will be cited hereafter as GA, followed by the volume number.

2. Martin Heidegger, *Sein und Zeit* (Tübingen: Niemeyer, 1927, [7]1953, [18]2000), 138, with the German pagination, which is to be found in the margins of both extant English translations of *Being and Time.*

3. Here I have followed, but with numerous modifications, the more detailed elaboration of Heidegger's rhetorical-phenomenological concept of the political found in Theodore Kisiel, "Situating Rhetorical Politics in Heidegger's Protopractical Ontology (1923–1925: The French Occupy the Ruhr)," *International Journal of Philosophical Studies* 8 (2000): 185–208. Another version under the same title is to be found in *Existentia* 9 (1999): 11–30.

4. Guido Schneeberger, *Nachlese zu Heidegger: Dokumente zu seinem Leben und Denken* (Bern: [privately published] Buchdruckerei, 1962), 48. "Gedenkworte

zu Schlageter (26. Mai 1933 vor der Universität)" has recently been reprinted in Martin Heidegger, *Reden und andere Zeugnisse eines Lebensweges (1910–1976)*, GA 16, ed. Hermann Heidegger (Frankfurt: Klostermann, 2000), 759f.

5. Cf. *Rhetoric* 2.21, where Aristotle discusses various examples of the *gnomē*, the maxims (folk sayings, proverbs) pertaining to human comportment that constitute the premises or conclusions of the rhetorical enthymeme, the speech situations in which they are most appropriately employed, and the variations they undergo in such appropriations, for example, "Nor do I approve the maxim 'Nothing in excess,' for one cannot hate the wicked too much" (1395b1).

6. Pierre Bourdieu, *The Political Ontology of Martin Heidegger*, trans. Peter Collier (Stanford: Stanford University Press, 1991), 79. This formalization of existential categories like the one-like-many is at the same time phenomenologically sustained and illustrated by concrete examples out of the tradition like hoi polloi, the "crowd" versus Kierkegaard's "individual," and the masses catered to by the competing mass media of the Weimar Republic. Thus, Herbert Marcuse could see, in the phenomenological description of das Man in *Being and Time,* the implicit cultural sociology of Weimar and a premonition of the disasters of totalitarianism. Herbert Marcuse and Frederick Olafson, "Heidegger's Politics: An Interview," *Graduate Faculty Philosophy Journal* 6 (1977): 28–40.

7. Martin Heidegger, *Die Grundbegriffe der Metaphysik: Welt—Endlichkeit—Einsamkeit*, GA 29/30: lecture course of Winter Semester 1929–30, ed. F. -W. von Herrmann (Frankfurt: Klostermann, 1983), 244. Translated by William McNeill and Nicholas Walker as *The Fundamental Concepts of Metaphysics: World, Finitude, Solitude* (Bloomington: Indiana University Press, 1995), 163.

8. Both citations are translations of Aristotle's trio, *phronēsis kai arete kai eunoia*; *Rhetoric* 2.1, 1378a10. The trio will recur in Arendt's account of the cosmopolitan ethos of the statesman making judgments on the basis of Kantian "common sense."

9. For a more detailed account of the remaining two concepts of the political, see Theodore Kisiel, "In the Middle of Heidegger's Three Concepts of the Political," in *Heidegger and Practical Philosophy* ed. François Raffoul and David Pettigrew (Albany: State University of New York Press, 2002).

10. Citations are from the student protocols of Rektor Heidegger's seminar of the Winter Semester 1933–34, "Vom Wesen und Begriff von Natur, Geschichte und Staat" (unpublished). The concept and essence of the state were treated from the 7th to the 10th and final hour of a seminar that was held once a week.

11. A rectoral greeting addressed to "German Students!" at the beginning of the Winter Semester of 1933–34 concludes with the following statement: "Neither doctrines nor 'ideas' are the rules governing your being. The Führer himself and alone *is* the present and future actuality of Germany and its law." GA 16, 184.

12. Martin Heidegger, *Hölderlins Hymnen "Germanien" und "Der Rhein,"* GA 39: lecture course of Winter Semester 1934–35, ed. Susanne Ziegler (Frankfurt: Klostermann, 1980), 214, 51.

13. Martin Heidegger, *Hölderlins Hymne "Der Ister,"* GA 53: lecture course of Summer Semester 1942, ed. Walter Biemel (Frankfurt: Klostermann, 1982), 98f, 102. Translated by William McNeill and Julia Davis as *Hölderlin's Hymn "The Ister"* (Bloomington: Indiana University Press, 1996), 80, 83.

14. Heidegger, GA 39, 73.

15. Hannah Arendt, "Concern with Politics in Recent European Philosophical Thought" (1954), in *Essays in Understanding* 1930–1954, ed. Jerome Kohn (New York: Harcourt, 1994), 428–447, esp. 442, with my emphases.

16. Hannah Arendt, "Philosophy and Politics" (1954), *Social Research* 57 (1990): 73–103, esp. 74, 79.

17. Hannah Arendt, *Was ist Politik?: Fragmente aus dem Nachlass*, ed. Ursula Ludz, foreword by Kurt Sontheimer (Munich: Piper, 1993), ii.

18. Arendt, *Was ist Politik?*, iii.

19. Ibid., 48–52.

20. Hannah Arendt, *Between Past and Future: Eight Exercises in Political Thought* (New York: Viking, 1968), 154f.

21. Arendt, "Philosophy and Politics," 80.

22. Hannah Arendt, *The Human Condition* (Garden City: Doubleday, 1959), 175; see also 177, 183, 187, 197.

23. Mary McCarthy, "The Vita Activa," in *On the Contrary* (New York: Farrar, Straus and Cudahy, 1961), 155–164, esp. 161. This review of *The Human Condition* first appeared in *The New Yorker*.

24. Arendt, *Between Past and Future*, 263.

25. Arendt, "Philosophy and Politics," 82–84.

26. Ibid., 84.

27. Hannah Arendt, "A Conversation with Günter Gaus" (1964), *Essays in Understanding*, 1–23, esp. 22.

28. Ibid., 21n. citing Kant's *Critique of Judgment*, §40; *Between Past and Future*, 220, 241.

29. Arendt, "Philosophy and Politics," 84.

30. Arendt, *Essays in Understanding*, 441; *Between Past and Future*, 221, 241, cf. note 8 above.

31. Ibid., 21.

32. Hannah Arendt, "What is Existenz Philosophy?," *Partisan Review* 13 (1946): 34–56, esp. 51; *Essays in Understanding*, 181: a composite citation of the two comparable texts.

7

Otto Pöggeler

Translated by John Bailiff

Heidegger's Restricted Conception of Rhetoric

When, in the troubled year 1947, Heidegger found himself indicted on account of his National Socialist entanglement, he privately published *Out of the Experience of Thinking*. Like a convalescent cherishing the simplest of experiences in order to maintain his balance, Heidegger in this work invokes the changes of the days and seasons and relates them to the language of thought. He holds onto the disguised poetic character of thought, as if herding his flock to the shelter of high valleys; he has to separate himself from the excesses of a half-poetic reason. "For a thoughtful poetics is in truth the topology of being [*Seyn*]." This topology calls poetic thinking "the dwelling place [*Ortschaft*] of essence."[1] "Essence," of course, is here understood verbally and historically, so as to differentiate the one place (*Ort*) of thought from any other and so that thought will tend toward producing his poetics.

Ten years later Heidegger published *The Principle of Reason* (*Der Satz vom Grund*),[2] an invited lecture given at the University of Freiburg, in which he no longer sought to articulate the essence of reason in systematic fashion (as he had in his 1929 contribution to the Husserl *Festschrift*[3]). Instead he lets speak the guiding words of Western thought, in order to listen for a language that might indicate a new path for thinking. The principle of reason belongs to these guiding words. According to Wilhelm Dilthey's *Introduction to the Human Sciences*,[4] Leibniz and Hegel, having seen the final formulation of metaphysical thinking in this principle of reason, thereby fail to be open to history. In section 15 of *The*

Birth of Tragedy, Nietzsche pronounces the principle of reason a "supreme metaphysical delusion" which, in its failing, turns thinking into art and poetry, and into their experience of the tragic.[5]

Heidegger traces the principle of reason through the history of Western thought and decides that a single formulation determines its present place (Ort). This "discussion" (*Erörterung*) enables him to carry his thinking beyond the metaphysical tradition. Doesn't this put one in mind of the rhetorical tradition, in which remembrance orients itself by exemplary places (*topoi*)?[6] These topoi are akin to outbreaks of historicism while being committed to history. The Romance scholar Ernst Robert Curtius (though admittedly in connection with medieval Latin literature) speaks of the topoi of researching a place (*Toposforschung*).[7] In his book *Mimesis*, Erich Auerbach presents a version of Western literature and calls it a "topology."[8] Instead of working through the biographies of poets and the history of schools and tendencies, he looks for the guiding relations in short, exemplary texts. In this fashion he could show the way to a particular sort of existential realism. Auerbach thereby indicates the manner in which the understanding of literature expresses itself in terms of guiding words (*Leitworte*) which can be taken up lexically from relevant texts. For example he speaks of "the court and the city" (*La cour et la ville*) as the audience for the French classics.[9]

Might we not regard Heidegger's topology of Being as researching a place, one which takes as its topoi the conceptual ground of Being's place (Ort)?[10] Not incidentally the so-called conceptual history was established after the Second World War. Fixed in the *Historisches Wörterbuch der Philosophie* (*Historical Dictionary of Philosophy*),[11] it made an innocent attachment to their language impossible for philosophers and imposed a linguistic and historical consciousness on thinking. Martin Heidegger himself objected to this attempt to confine his later thought within the dominant methods of the period. Thus, on December 12, 1958, Heidegger wrote me, "I use the term 'topology' quite literally: the speaking of place; that is, thinking the truth (the disclosure of the self-concealed [*das Entbergen des Sichverbergens*]) of being [*des Seyns*]. In using this term I was not aware of the historical connotations that you have suggested."

As was his practice at the time, Heidegger inscribes the word Seyn with a crosswise strikethrough, to indicate thinking the "fourfold" (*Geviert*).[12] Indeed he understood the "topology of being" as searching out a new place for being. Yet it is not just his intentions and self-understanding that are of interest; we must also attend to what he actually did. In his schedule of lectures at Marburg (1923-28) he deals explicitly with rhetoric. Heidegger took up Plato's struggle against sophistry; Plato's polemic, however, no longer accepts the close attachment of rhetoric to words. Contrary to Plato, Aristotle always classified rhetoric and its topics among the intellectual disciplines. In the Roman period Cicero and Quintilian continued this tradition.

Within Roman rhetoric, "topics" belongs to the category of *inventio*, or instructions for the location of arguments. It is related as well to *elocutio* and *memoria*, that is, to work on style of presentation and to the necessity of a wealth of memory. Topoi are thus formal instructions for arriving at arguments. At this point Ernst Robert Curtius addresses the way in which medieval Latin transmits the ancient tradition to European literature, stressing, for example, the importance of Isidore of Seville. In this view topoi become materials for a train of thought, as in the controversial topos of the poet's divine madness.

It is rather astonishing that a Romance scholar like Curtius would not acknowledge Giambattista Vico (whom Auerbach translated and had found useful). By way of contrast, in the field of post-World War II jurisprudence (for example, Theodor Viehweg's 1953 *Topik und Jurisprudenz*[13]), an early speech of Vico—the Neapolitan professor of rhetoric—did lead to a dispute over the fundamental "scientificality" of this practical discipline, which once ranked between medicine and theology. In 1947 the Godesberg publisher Helmut Küpper (formerly the publishing firm of Georg Bondi and once the house of Stefan George) brought out Professor Vico's 1708 lecture *De nostri temporis studiorum ratione*.[14] In it Vico takes up the critical methods of the Cartesians, which aim at *apodictic*—extracting conclusions key to true theories. Vico classifies the assumptions upon which the method depends under the old general category of topics, considered both in its original form and what became traditional. In 1947 this talk on types of study was given the pretentious title *On the Essence and Path of Intellectual Development*. If we compare the opinion of Carl Friedrich von Weizsäcker, published in the same year, which takes a stand in the dispute over whether or not Germany should participate in the development of nuclear technology, then it becomes clear what was actually being talked about: contemporary self-awareness of responsibility!

For philosophers who were formed by classical philology of the Germans, a reevaluation of despised rhetoric remains offensive. But they must sit up and take notice because in the course of the rehabilitation of practical philosophy, rhetoric, and especially topics as a theory of locating and developing argument, will demand it. In 1965 Helmut Kuhn published his polemic *Aristotle and the Methods of Political Science* in the *Zeitschrift für Politik* (*Journal of Politics*). In it he mentions that in 1947 the Romance scholar Fritz Schalk edited Walter F. Otto's translation of Vico's polemical work *De nostri temporis studiorum ratione* as an instructional work for turbulent times. Vico spoke as a teacher of rhetoric and brought topics into play: before we can judge (*dijucatio de veritate* or adjudicate truth), we must be guided by finding the lead arguments (*inventio argumentorum*); in this way we can counter Cartesianism. Curtius (inspired by Bergson rather than Vico) was anti-Cartesian. In addition to this "rhetorical-literary critical preparation," an "ontological bridge" supports the revaluation of topics. In Theodor Viehweg's *Topics and Law*, Nicolai Hartmann's dialectic becomes a "technique for thinking problems." Finally, a Heideggerian like Karl-Otto Apel dares to pass on this "linguistic-philosophical bridge building," especially the Italian humanism of Vico. Heidegger himself was not involved in this "alchemy." "However," writes Kuhn, "his interpreter Otto Pöggeler conjectures that topics as theory of place, which 'held sway from Aristotle and Cicero to Vico,' may be regarded as at least a 'first approximation' to Heidegger's 'discussion of the fundamental words of Western thought.' Topics was to become fundamental ontology."[15]

It is self-evident that the trick of an old tradition cannot do justice to that which is sought as new (the rehabilitation of practical philosophy, or determining the essence of poetry). Doesn't the discussion of topics, however, present a new task? In 1963 Jürgen Habermas still agreed with Wilhelm Hennis that practical philosophy could make its own way and could thereby establish ties to the tradition of rhetoric.[16] In the emotional period of 1968, in an address in Kiel, Karl-Otto Apel adopts the obligation to emancipation in order to validate a quest for an ultimate ground.[17] Hans-Georg Gadamer had to admit the fact that hermeneutics did not originate during the Reformation, thence universalized by Schleiermacher—it had older roots in the tradition of rhetoric. Consequently rhetoric and hermeneutics became a topic for Gadamer too.[18] In Gadamer's *Truth and Method*, Vico's Christian Platonism, with its revelation of common sense, is related back to Aristotle.[19] So the early Vico superseded the author of the *New Science*.[20] The way in which Vico, especially in the works of his middle phase, developed the matter of topics, had to be discussed later. But doesn't this reference to Vico place Heidegger's consideration of Aristotle's *Rhetoric* in a fairer light? It is thus all the more regrettable that Heidegger did not further develop this early exploratory path.

I. The Path to *Being and Time*

As a student of Catholic theology before coming to philosophy, Martin Heidegger naturally saw Aristotle as the predominant Western philosopher. Very soon, however, he would instead look for those more or less excluded by Aristotelianism. During the First World War, Heidegger made Schleiermacher, condemned as the father of reprehensible modernism, a theme of his lectures and conversations within a private circle in

Freiburg. Yet the young Heidegger believed that in Edmund Husserl's phenomenology he had found the starting point for a new philosophizing. Husserl aligned himself against all construction and speculation about the background of the phenomenal; so many regarded his phenomenology as a warrant to take up once again ancient and medieval ontological questions. By the time he came to Freiburg in 1916, Husserl had turned toward modernity and the beginnings of its philosophical transcendentalism: if we are to understand phenomena in their being, then access to that being must be assured in advance. The transcendental "I" becomes the guarantor of access to truth. Quite unlike Husserl, the young Heidegger, roused by the European catastrophe of the First World War, followed those who departed from that transcendental approach to history and its catastrophes. Heidegger came to regard the transcendental "I" as facticity (*Faktizität*), which considers existence something to be taken up, thus placing itself within the integrated sphere of historical articulations.[21]

As a result, the young Heidegger also considered Franz Overbeck, patristic scholar and friend of Nietzsche, to have dissolved the synthesis of antiquity and Christianity. Original Christianity was related to its eschatological manifestations; believers who are prepared for the end of the world do not strive for Greek wisdom or contemporary culture.[22] Heidegger expounded a unique account, presenting in his 1920–21 lectures *Introduction to the Phenomenology of Religion* interpretations of the Pauline letters.[23] While the old hermeneutic had been surpassed in the Protestant sphere by reversion to the stricter interpretation of New Testament gospel (what was therefore called "form history"), Heidegger could still hear "hermeneutic" from within crippled Catholic theology. He resurrected the term *hermeneutic* from Schleiermacher and Dilthey. For his first postwar lecture in 1919, Heidegger combined the "intuition" constructed by Husserl with Bergson's sense of intuition as penetration into the flow of life, to talk about "hermeneutic intuition."[24] Phenomenological philosophy as ontological and transcendental became a hermeneutic; this hermeneutic philosophy had to become justified through an interpretation of Aristotle. Husserl wanted to publish Heidegger's work on Aristotle in his phenomenological studies *Annual*. But Heidegger completed only introductory fragments and for the time being they remained unpublished.

With a view to an appointment, Heidegger in 1922 sketched his work on Aristotle for Natorp in Marburg and Misch in Göttingen. In the first part he would relate book 6 of the *Nicomachean Ethics* to the *Metaphysics* and *Physics*, placing the accent upon *phronēsis*, which he characterized as conscience (*Gewissen*), in so doing discrediting metaphysical reason. This metaphysical reason supports with its philosophical theology only the self-grounding of knowledge (*Wissen*), while passing over actual life as well as its religiosity. Heidegger aimed to confront Aristotle with his opponent Luther, who had called upon actual life and its capacity for faith against philosophy. Heidegger wished, in a second and third section, to deal with book Theta of Aristotle's *Metaphysics*, discussing its notions of possibility and actuality. In this way the relation in *De anima* of the transcendental "I" to being could become a new problem.[25] Heidegger was in conversation at this time with a friend named Julius Ebbinghaus, who espoused a view contrary to that of his father (an empirical psychologist and adversary of Dilthey). Julius Ebbinghaus continued Dilthey's work on the young Hegel with works on Hegel's years at Jena. Heidegger, now at Marburg, wrote to Ebbinghaus on January 4, 1924, about his newfound friend Rudolf Bultmann and then went on to his upcoming lectures: "In the summer semester I read Augustine four hours a week and in winter I will continue with the Hermeneutics of Historical Knowledge."[26]

But Heidegger didn't follow this plan. By going to Marburg in 1923 he had come to a university that had committed itself to the Reformation; theology and philosophy should work in concert. Philosophy was characteristically Neo-Kantian. The Middle Ages were regarded as obscure; for example, Professor Cohen (as Heidegger would claim in his 1926 lecture course) saw Aristotle as a pharmacist, merely pasting labels on what exists. Professor Natorp understood philosophy to be Plato and Kant. So Heidegger sought to discuss anew the definitive philosophical tradition. Accordingly, after his first Marburg lecture course on the origins of modern philosophy[27] he gave to his second course of lectures the provocative title "Aristotle: *Rhetoric*." When he presented the course, he had altered the title to "Basic Concepts of Aristotelian Philosophy" (*Grundbegriffe der aristotelischen Philosophie*).[28]

Aristotle had developed the individual philosophical disciplines—rhetoric and poetics, for example—by differentiating them, while at the same time leaving rhetoric within practical philosophy. (It had to be taught how the Greek orator took a decisive role in the polis.) In the following semester, especially while developing his interpretation of Plato's *Sophist*, Heidegger sharpened the opposition between philosophy and rhetoric: the rhetorician can behave like the sophist, able to do business as a representative of any party. Plato cast rhetoric in a bad light.[29] By the summer semester of 1925, Heidegger had already presented crucial sections of *Being and Time*. In the winter semester of 1925–26 Heidegger made a dramatic break with the announced course dealing with Aristotle, moving over to Kant, because Kant would provide a sharper analysis of the problem of time. In the following semesters his presentation of ancient, as well as medieval and contemporary philosophy had a more didactic character. By 1927 the summer semester lecture course aimed to carry forward fragments of *Being and Time*.

Being and Time was rightly dedicated to Husserl. Yet Heidegger was also indebted to Max Scheler, who had made the realm of the emotional his theme. Feeling was added to knowing and acting; through feelings we turn ourselves toward or away from being-in-the-world in its entirety, bringing into play movement and time. Fear, according to Aristotle, arises from something in the world; in *Being and Time* Heidegger analyzes this experience as flowing from "depression, not to say bewilderment."[30] But, following the Christian tradition, Heidegger links fear with anxiety (*Angst*). With the saying "Neither expectation nor fear" (*Nec spe nec metu*) the Stoics resumed the philosophical tradition in which the brave heart stands up to fear. But the apostle Paul taught us to seek the holy in fear and trembling, from which we can be rescued by hope. Though the moment of panic sounds in the language of anxiety (in claustrophobia, for instance), Heidegger, speaking of the corresponding fear of God, sees the whole of our being-in-the-world becoming questionable in anxiety. Thus anxiety (which is ultimately anxiety over death) awakens the feeling of conscience, which voices a saving call and can lead to faith.

Heidegger knew the passion that can control us and become depravity; like the Church fathers, he engaged in a polemic against the inquisitiveness that the Greeks blamed upon "lust of the eyes." Heidegger analyzed fear and anxiety as feelings, moods (*Stimmungen*), or affects. However, he did not then contrast anxiety with the virtue of courage; instead, he took anxiety itself to be a virtue (but of course without using the apathetic term *virtue*). There are other feelings that can also be virtues: we flush unbidden when shame overcomes us, yet at the same time it is a virtue that claims us. In the 1930s Heidegger distinguished this phenomenon under the name *Scheu* (or *aidōs*, meaning shame, modesty, self-respect in Greek).[31]

Can the matter of philosophy be entrusted to fleeting moods or feelings? From the start, isn't the question of truth absent from feelings? Heidegger contends that the simple sentence must not be regarded as a statement or proposition (*Aussage*), and that the proposition cannot manage the distinction between truth and falsity. *Logos*, as speech, makes something clear, lets something be seen; in contrast to a proposition—a request, for example—logos inserts us into a situation and makes it clear. Heidegger demanded grammar be freed from logic and its orientation to the proposition.[32] Thus Jacob Grimm and Wilhelm von Humboldt come into play. Yet Heidegger is not about to allow his hermeneutic enterprise to be predetermined "by notions and popular concepts." He reverses the customary evaluation of mathematics-based sciences and the humanities: mathematics is not stronger than history, merely stricter. *Being and Time*, however, provides no adequate conceptualization for the question of how language is formed by historical communities. Instead the analysis of historicity is handed over, in an unmediated and striking way, to the concepts of a people and of generation. Since individuals are called to their fates (*Schicksal*), the generation and the people should be delivered over to a common destiny (*Geschick*). The power of destiny arises from communication and struggle. What is communicated is not, in this case, indeterminate information. Rather one is reminded to heed the "communication of words and desires" of which Aristotle speaks in the *Nicomachean Ethics* (1126b12).

Yet it is surprising that Heidegger does not consider the polis as the setting for decisions, treating publicness (*Öffentlichkeit*) only as the mode of being for "they" (*das Man*). So he can say of Aristotle's *Rhetoric*, "Contrary to the traditional orientation of the concept of rhetoric to something like a 'subject,' Aristotle's work must be regarded as the first systematic hermeneutic of the everydayness (*Alltäglichkeit*) of being amongst one another."[33] Does Heidegger assume the political in general to be confined to everydayness and hence just to the businesslike dealings of the "they"? Or does he want to say that the Greeks, in the period of their greatness, could entrust decisions about their course to public assembly, but that this setting for decisions has now been lost? In any case everydayness, to which modern politics appeals, is the realm of the anonymous "they."

Heidegger himself made his first political decisions as he gave himself over to initiating and working out his thoughts on the plan of *Being and Time*. But had he not already restricted crucial dimensions of Aristotle's *Rhetoric* on the path to *Being and Time*? When Heidegger ceases any longer to set passions and feelings over against virtues, then he leaves behind not only Aristotle but, for example, Max Scheler as well. For both of them contrast resentment (analyzed by Nietzsche as *ressentiment*) with virtue.[34] Anyone who would in our time listen for "new rhetoric" must also question what image of justice is speaking. This has been done recently, in the work of Chaim Perelman, for instance.[35] Though it was self-evident for Aristotle and Thomas Aquinas, Heidegger failed to ask this question.

II. From Aristotle to Nietzsche

Being and Time presents its process throughout as "interpretation." In the summer semester of 1924, Heidegger said his lectures did not pursue a philosophical purpose; they asked philological questions about Aristotle's fundamental concepts. And in the lectures Heidegger started from a definition of these concepts. He saw humans as possessing simultaneously a linguistic and a political way of being. Humans are distinguished through speech from other animals, such as bees, whose signals are entirely identical with their society (*Staat*). Aristotle's *Rhetoric* addresses the way in which the polis moves toward decisions. The speaker must set out from a shared opinion (*endoxon*) and return to it. This is a not a matter of scientific proof (*apodeixis*). It is a matter of an orientation such that, while directed toward truth, it sets out from an ability to share the opinions (*doxa*) of others. The speaking person is characterized by *ethos* or attitude (*Haltung*) and by *pathos* or one's feeling of attunement (*Befindlichkeit*).

For the significance of the affects, Heidegger himself can refer to Wilhelm Dilthey's analyses of the Renaissance and the Reformation,[36] but even more to the Christian tradition, such as the Augustinian distinction between holy fear (*timor castus*) and slavish fear (*timor servilis*), between the pure fear of God and the fear of God's punishments in the afterlife. Heidegger presumes that the Greeks did not fundamentally distinguish these experiences. Yet (in contrast to sacred Christian history) they originate not in nature but in the being of what is produced. Thus *eidos* becomes established as appearance (the shoemaker must see the structure of a shoe before making one). Wherever eidos, or appearance, must constantly be invoked, being is relegated to the horizon of the present. When attunement turns toward or away from situational moods, movement and time come into play. What Heidegger represents as Aristotle's definition of time, however, is problematic in the established text.[37] Consequently Heidegger's historical formulation of his guiding question about being and time cannot be considered incorrigible.

At the close of his lectures, Heidegger asserts that movement as *kinēsis* possesses both a *poiētikon* (capacity for creativity) and a *pathētikon* (capacity for feeling). So, with his suggestive brevity, he comes to a conclusion in which his starting point still speaks: Aristotle grasps being-in-the-world (*in-der-Welt-sein*) as *praxis* or practice; but practice for Aristotle is primarily poiesis or creativity. It is no surprise, then, that in *Being and Time* the destruction of traditional ontology proceeds from its analysis of manual activity. This so-called praxis, namely the poiesis of production, aims to proceed beyond being and, accordingly, must cling to the eidos or appearance of being: being as it presents itself. The element of the pathetic or of feeling is relegated to attunement (Befindlichkeit) and mood (Stimmung), in which being-in-the-world suppressed becomes manifest. What the Greeks emphasized—anxiety in the face of death—comes to be analyzed by Heidegger through Christian experiences and with reference to what the finitude of human existence (Dasein) signifies. Each one must confront this finitude in the authentic willingness to have a conscience (*Gewissen-haben-wollen*).

Heidegger's theses have to disturb us. It is difficult to understand how anyone who had likewise carried out an intensive year-long examination of Aristotle could not find praxis in the communication of common issues. Plato the aristocrat, and Aristotle, son of a medical doctor, become for Heidegger craftsmen (nevertheless Socrates asked craftsmen for orientation). Is Plato's Idea a vision of the universal, in which matter seeks form? Does Aristotle apply the matter-form model to the shoemaker, or does he instead find it organically embodied in making shoes? Max Scheler felt it absurd for Heidegger to presume that Plato and Aristotle had involved Western thought in a two-thousand-year-long "ontology of shoemaking."[38] Would the prejudices of the church fathers have led to a philosophy of living (*Lebensphilosophie*) if the Greeks had not assumed a one-sided orientation toward sight, coming to regard eidos and Idea as envisioning form? Oskar Becker, Heidegger's first mentor, also lexically refuted these meanings for the range of words around Idea.

We must credit Heidegger with once again taking Aristotle's *Rhetoric* seriously. But has he grasped the history of rhetoric if he later just finds theories in it and does not even convey the changed tasks and ways of putting questions in Cicero and Quintilian, not to mention Vico? In the fall of 1929, Heidegger turned in a new way to Nietzsche's criticism of tradition. The destruction of the philosophical tradition, which in *Being and Time* was meant to lead to a systematic reconstruction, now unfolded in a completely new fashion. The intent of reason became unfair to life and to history. Hölderlin was placed beside Nietzsche, and together, in Heidegger's 1936–37 Nietzsche lectures, both were set off against Hegel's working-out of the tradition. Then, in his "conversion year" of 1938, Heidegger made Nietzsche jointly responsible for National Socialism and cast him as a representative of merely ornamental Platonism. For Heidegger, Nietzsche became the most excessive representative of so-called metaphysics, who so knotted its motifs that he attended its demise.[39] But because of this Heidegger could not respect, for example, Nietzsche's listening to the Romantics and their theories of irony. When Ernst Behler worked through these connections via Jacques Derrida, he bumped into Nietzsche the rhetorician.[40]

In the fall of 1946, Heidegger wrote his French friends the *Letter on Humanism*, differentiating himself from Sartre's existentialism. When this was published in 1947, many gathered from its strong wording the challenge of an elemental shift (*Kehre*) in thought and existence (Dasein) in general. Heidegger so radicalizes earlier theses in this *Letter* that they become subject to our contrary reflections and contradictions. Startlingly, we frequently also have to ask ourselves whether Heidegger has forgotten how he once worked out a new interpretation of Aristotle. In the very first sentence of the *Letter*, action (*Handeln*) is seen as bringing-to-fulfillment (*Vollbringen*), which is to say as poiēsis. This means, then, that the distinction between theory and practice falls within the technical interpretation of thought. Heidegger, who at the time was unable to confront the published reports of his actions in 1933, polemicizes against the "dictatorship" of publicness (Öffentlichkeit). He understands the humanism of the Renaissance to derive from Rome (a view rejected since Herder). Although the *Letter* appears shortly after the investigations of Ernesto Grassi,[41] Heidegger generally never queries the significant themes of humanism or even the ways in which humanism gave a new role to Aristotle.

Doesn't this polemic leap to the position that the formula *animal rationale* relegates the human to the level of the animal? Hölderlin is enlisted against "Goethe's citizen of the world" (and against the approach of the Romantics as well).[42] It is not surprising that twelve years later, Heidegger (in conversation with me) would not reconsider a thinker like Vico. His judgment on Vico appeared already to be fixed: he wrote in Latin and Italian, therefore following the Roman transformation of the legacy of the ancients. Instead of Vico's Naples turning Heidegger toward an encounter with the cultures of the Mediterranean realm, Heidegger was led to Greece in 1962, in order to read in the cabin of his ship Heraclitus (as he imagined him) and not once to alight in Patmos.[43] This isolated cabin dweller and Naples inhabit contradictory worlds, as do Heidegger's most personal character (*Eigentlichkeit*) and the public-spirited rhetorical tradition. Nevertheless the reader cannot get rid of the impression that, even when it is hidden, Heidegger touches the rhetorical tradition again and again.

Samuel Ijsseling has sought to show that the conflict with rhetoric has been constitutive for the philosophical tradition, in the sense of setting its limits. When the late Heidegger refers to the truth of language and history, and so to unconcealment (*Unverborgenheit*) and ever-renewed self-concealments, he regards them from "a strictly non-Platonic and non-metaphysical standpoint." "At the same time, however," writes Ijsseling, "we cannot fail to recognize that Heidegger's concept adheres strictly to the ancient Greek *understanding of language*, as it is presented, for example, in Isocrates' panegyric on the power of speech and language."[44]

Julius Ebbinghaus remembers Heidegger writing him on November 22, 1950, to recall walks in the winter landscape of the streets of Freiburg and the Immental Valley. In the letter Heidegger says that if he thinks of his philosophical production in general, he finds himself to have been preoccupied by the field of religious questioning. Ebbinghaus replied to these questions by sending him a work on tolerance. In a 1953 essay on Georg Trakl, in the magazine *Merkur*, and in his 1959 collection *On the Way to Language*, Heidegger explains that the word discussion (Erörterung) points to place (Ort); and place gathers in and permeates everything. Because of that the spearhead, or vanishing point (*Speerspitze*) was the first thing to be named by the word "Ort."[45] In the draft of a letter, Ebbinghaus elaborates on this at least a bit: "I do not believe that to discuss (*Erörtern*) has anything do with the vanishing point. It has to be a word of relatively recent invention, which owes its origin to Aristotle's use of topics. To discuss an object means to carry its contemplation through the 'places' [*Örter/loci*] prescribed by the topic—and indeed completely [hence *dis-cuss, er-örtern*]."[46] Later Ebbinghaus appends "a commentary of an earlier date": "For this reason, woodpaths [*Holzwege*] do not mean wood paths because 'wood' is an old word for 'forest,' but because they are paths that have been driven through a wood to carry out timber. They end up, therefore, blind at the places where timber has been made and are, because of this, paths that deceive the traveler." Ebbinghaus then remarks that he always remains stuck at the beginnings of Heidegger's works. "Many times, when I cast my mind over our times together, I think I must run back and say, 'My dear Heidegger, just what is up with you? Don't you actually ever want to be sensible?' But then I think again about what purpose it would serve—if he had had even a trace of willingness to understand my questions, he certainly would not have written what he did write. And then I become dispirited and sad."[47]

Is it sad if philosophers follow diverse paths, eventually being able at best to wave to one another across the intervening distance? Or is it sad when someone clings dogmatically to a philosopher, even a Kant, and so reduces to a minimum his own thinking? Perhaps it is the nature of philosophy that we all proceed from different places on the periphery, aiming at a common center, while still remaining bound by the prejudices of our time to our starting point on that periphery, in our thinking and in our politics. Rhetoric seeks to follow up such binding and development. Heidegger made remarkable contributions to this search, but did not exhaust its tradition and its future possibilities.

Notes

1. Martin Heidegger, *Aus der Erfahrung des Denkens 1910–1976*, Gesamtausgabe vol. 13 (Frankfurt: Klostermann, 1983), 75ff; "The Thinker as Poet," in *Poetry, Language, Thought*, trans. Albert Hofstadter (New York: Harper & Row, 1971). The Gesamtausgabe will be cited hereafter as GA, followed by the volume number.

2. Martin Heidegger, *Der Satz vom Grund*, GA 10 (Frankfurt: Klostermann, 1997); *The Principle of Reason*, trans. Reginald Lilly (Bloomington: Indiana University Press, 1996).

3. Martin Heidegger, "Vom Wesen des Grundes," in *Festschrift für Edmund Husserl zum 70. Geburtstag* (Halle: Niemeyer, 1929); *Vom Wesen des Grundes* (Frankfurt: Klostermann, 1995); translated in *Pathmarks* (Cambridge: Cambridge University Press, 1998).

4. Wilhelm Dilthey, *Einleitung in die Geisteswissenschaften* (Leipzig: Duncker und Humblot, 1883); *Introduction to the Human Sciences*, trans. Ramon J. Betanzos (Detroit: Wayne State University Press, 1988).

5. Friedrich Nietzsche, *Die Geburt der Tragödie. Oder: Griechenthum und Pessimismus. Neue Ausgabe mit dem Versuch einer Selbstkritik* (1886), Werke, Kritische Gesamtausgabe sec. 3, vol. 1 (Berlin: Gruyter, 1972).

6. [*Topos* is "place" or "position" in Greek. "Topology" is the branch of mathematics which studies "positions on geometric configurations unaltered by elastic deformation." The metaphorical use of "topology" here suggests the search for those properties of Being unchanged by historical or other interpretation. Note that the appearance of "place" (Ort) in the German word for "discussion" (Erörterung) cannot be rendered in English. See footnote 46. —Trans.]

7. Ernst Robert Curtius, *Europäische Literatur und Lateinisches Mittelalter* (Bern: Francke, 1948); *European Literature and the Latin Middle Ages,* trans. Willard R. Trask (New York: Pantheon, 1953).

8. Erich Auerbach, *Mimesis: Dargestellte Wirklichkeit in der abendländischen Literatur* (Bern: Francke 1946); *Mimesis: The Representation of Reality in Western Literature*, trans. Willard R. Trask (Princeton: Princeton University Press, 2003).

9. Erich Auerbach, *Vier Untersuchungen zur Geschichte der Französischen Bildung* (Bern: Francke, 1951).

10. For details see my essay "Dichtungstheorie und Toposforschung," *Jahrbuch für Ästhetik und allgemeine Kunstwissenschaft* 5 (1960): 104–201, as well as my *Toposforschung*, ed. Max L. Bäumer (Darmstadt: Wissenschaftliche Buchgesellschaft, 1973), 22–136. Further, cf. Otto Pöggeler, *Der Denkweg Martin Heideggers*, 3rd revised edition (Pfullingen: Neske, 1990), 284f, 431, 438; *Martin Heidegger's Path of Thinking*, trans. Daniel Magurshak and Sigmund Barber (Atlantic Highlands: Humanities Press, 1989), 227–242.

11. *Historisches Wörterbuch der Philosophie*, ed. Joachim Ritter and Karlfried Gründer (Basel: Schwabe, 1971 ff.).

12. [Heidegger introduced the "fourfold" (earth, sky, mortal, and gods) in essays on *Thought and Poetry* (*Denken und Dichten*), written between 1941 and 1947. —Trans.]

13. Theodor Viehweg, *Topik und Jurisprudenz: Ein Beitrag zur rechtswissenschaftlichen Grundlagenforschung* (Munich: Beck, 1953); *Topics and Law: A Contribution to Basic Research in Law*, trans. W. Cole Durham (New York: Lang, 1993).

14. Giambattista Vico, *De nostri temporis studiorum ratione* [*Vom Wesen und Weg der geistigen Bildung*], ed. Fritz Schalk, trans. Walter F. Otto (Bonn-Bad Godesberg: Küpper, 1947).

15. Helmut Kuhn's essay, together with my reply, from the 1970 Hans-Georg Gadamer *Festschrift*, are now reprinted in *Rehabilitierung der praktischen Philosophie* vol. 2, ed. Manfred Riedel (Freiburg: Rombach, 1972), 261–331, cit. 289. The work of Karl-Otto Apel Kuhn refers to is: *Die Idee der Sprache in der Tradition des Humanismus von Dante bis Vico* (Bonn: Bouvier, 1963).

16. Jürgen Habermas, *Theorie und Praxis: Sozialphilosophische Studien* (Neuwied am Rhein: Luchterhand, 1963), 50f; *Theory and Practice*, trans. John Viertel (Boston: Beacon, 1988). On what follows see Otto Pöggeler, "Erklären–Verstehen–Erörtern," in *Transzendentalpragmatik: ein Symposion für Karl-Otto Apel,* ed. Andreas Dorschel et. al. (Frankfurt: Suhrkamp, 1993), 41ff.

17. Karl-Otto Apel, "Szientistik, Hermeneutik, Ideologiekritik: Entwurf einer Wissenschaftslehre in erkenntnisanthropologischer Sicht," *Wiener Jahrbuch für Philosophie* 1 (1968): 15–45.

18. Hans-Georg Gadamer, "Rhetorik, Hermeneutik und Ideologiekritik: Metakritische Erörterungen zu Wahrheit und Methode," in Gesammelte Werke vol. 2 (Tübingen: Mohr Siebeck, 1993), 232–250; "On the Scope and Function of Hermeneutic Reflection," in *Philosophical Hermeneutics*, ed. and trans. David E. Linge (Berkeley: University of California Press, 1976).

19. Hans Georg Gadamer, *Wahrheit und Methode*: *Grundzüge einer philosophischen Hermeneutik*, Gesammelte Werke vol. 1 (Tübingen: Mohr Siebeck 1990), esp. 24–29; *Truth and Method*, 2nd revised edition, trans. Joel Weinsheimer and Donald G. Marshall (New York: Crossroad, 1989).

20. See Otto Pöggeler, "Vico und die humanistische Tradition," in *Humanität und Bildung: Festschrift für Clemens Menze zum 60. Geburtstag*, ed. Johannes Schurr et. al. (Hildesheim: Olms, 1988), 46ff. On what follows see Giambattista Vico, *Liber metaphysicus*, trans. Stephan Otto and Helmut Viechtbauer (Munich: Fink, 1979).

21. For details see Theodore Kisiel, *The Genesis of Heidegger's* Being and Time (Berkeley: University of California Press, 1993).

22. Franz Overbeck, *Christentum und Kultur: Gedanken und Anmerkungen zur modernen Theologie*, ed. Carl Albrecht Bernoulli (Basel: Schwabe, 1919).

23. Martin Heidegger, "Einleitung in die Phänomenologie der Religion (Wintersemester 1920/21)," in *Phänomenologie des religiösen Lebens*, GA 60 (Frankfurt: Klostermann, 1995); translated in *The Phenomenology of Religious Life*, trans. Matthias Fritsch and Jennifer Anna Gosetti-Ferencei (Bloomington, Indiana University Press, 2004).

24. Martin Heidegger, "Die Idee der Philosophie und das Weltanschauungsproblem (Kriegsnotsemester 1919)," in *Zur Bestimmung der Philosophie*, GA 56/57 (Frankfurt: Klostermann, 1999); translated in *Towards the Definition of Philosophy*, trans. Ted Sadler (London: Continuum, 2002).

25. See Martin Heidegger, "Phänomenologische Interpretationen zu Aristoteles" [the so-called Natorp-Bericht], *Dilthey-Jahrbuch* 6 (1989): 235ff.

26. The correspondence between Heidegger and Ebbinghaus is still unpublished. Citations are from a transcript communicated to me by Manfred Baum.

27. Martin Heidegger, *Einführung in die phänomenologische Forschung*, GA 17 (Frankfurt: Klostermann, 1994).

28. Martin Heidegger, *Grundbegriffe der aristotelischen Philosophie*, GA 18 (Frankfurt: Klostermann, 2002); *Basic Concepts of Aristotelian Philosophy* (Bloomington: Indiana University Press, forthcoming).

29. Martin Heidegger, *Platon: Sophistes*, GA 19 (Frankfurt: Klostermann, 1992); *Plato's Sophist*, trans. Richard Rojcewicz and Andre Schuwer (Bloomington: Indiana University Press, 1997).

30. Martin Heidegger, *Sein und Zeit*, 7th edition (Tübingen: Niemeyer, 1953), §30; *Being and Time*, trans. John Macquarrie and Edward Robinson (New York: Harper & Row, 1962); *Being and Time*, trans. Joan Stambaugh (Albany: State University of New York Press, 1996).

31. On this topic see Otto Pöggeler, *Neue Wege mit Heidegger* (Freiburg: Alber, 1992), 142ff; *The Paths of Heidegger's Life and Thought*, trans. John Bailiff (Atlantic Highlands: Humanities Press, 1997), 92ff.

32. Martin Heidegger, *Sein und Zeit*, 32, 165; for what follows, 54, 166, 383, 138; *Being and Time*, trans. Joan Stambaugh, 28–29, 50–51, 130, 154–155, 155–156, 350–351.

33. Martin Heidegger, *Sein und Zeit*, §29.

34. Otto Pöggeler, "Ressentiment und Tugend bei Max Scheler," in *Vom Umsturz der Werte in der Modernen Gesellschaft*, ed. Gerhard Pfafferoth (Bonn: Bouvier, 1997), 7ff. For what follows see my reference to Chaim Perelman in: *Topik: Beiträge zur interdisziplinären Diskussion*, ed. Dieter Breuer and Helmut Schanze (Munich: Fink, 1981), 112f.

35. Chaim Perelman and Lucie Olbrechts-Tyteca, *La nouvelle rhétorique. Traité de l'argumentation* (Paris: Presses Universitaires de France, 1958); *The New Rhetoric: A Treatise on Argumentation,* trans. John Wilkinson and Purcell Weaver (Notre Dame: University of Notre Dame Press, 1969).

36. Wilhelm Dilthey, *Weltanschauung und Analyse des Menschen seit Renaissance und Reformation*, Gesammelte Schriften, vol. 2 (Göttingen: Vandenhoeck und Ruprecht, 1914), 416ff.

37. Otto Pöggeler, *Heidegger in seiner Zeit* (Munich: Fink, 1999), 54f.

38. Martin Heidegger addresses this reproach in *Aristotle, Metaphysics Theta 1–3*, GA 33 (Frankfurt: Klostermann, 1981), 137f. For what follows, see *Die*

Philosophie und die Wissenschaften: Zum Werk Oskar Beckers, ed. Annemarie Gethmann-Siefert and Jürgen Mittelstraß (Munich: Fink, 2002).

39. Otto Pöggeler, *Friedrich Nietzsche und Martin Heidegger* (Bonn: Bouvier, 2002). For what follows, see Otto Pöggeler, "Idealismus und Romantik," *Hegel–Studien* 34 (1999): 135ff.

40. Ernst Behler, *Nietzsche – Derrida, Derrida – Nietzsche* (Munich: Schöningh, 1988).

41. Ernesto Grassi, *Verteidigung des individuellen Lebens: Studia humanitatis als philosophische Überlieferung* (Bern: Francke 1946).

42. Martin Heidegger, *Wegmarken* (Frankfurt: Klostermann, 1967), 145ff; "Letter on Humanism," trans. Frank Capuzzi and J. Glenn Gray, in *Martin Heidegger: Basic Writings*, ed. David Farrell Krell (New York: Harper & Row, 1977), 189ff.

43. Martin Heidegger, *Aufenthalte* (Frankfurt: Klostermann, 1989); *Sojourns: The Journey to Greece*, trans. John-Panteleimon Manoussakis (Albany: State University of New York Press, 2005).

44. Samuel Ijsseling, *Rhetoric und Philosophie: Eine historisch-systematische Einführung*, (Stuttgart-Bad Cannstatt: Frommann, 1988), 5, 42; *Rhetoric and Philosophy in Conflict: An Historical Survey* (The Hague: Nijhoff, 1976).

45. Martin Heidegger, "Georg Trakl: Eine Erörterung seines Gedichts," *Merkur* 61 (1953): 226–258. Reprinted as "Die Sprache im Gedicht," in Martin Heidegger, *Unterwegs zur Sprache* (Pfullingen: Neske, 1959), 35–82, cit. 37; translated in *On the Way to Language*, trans. Peter D. Hertz (New York: Harper & Row, 1962).

46. [The German play on "place" (Ort) in their verb "to discuss" (erörtern) cannot be rendered entirely in English; neither can the Greek sense of "place" (topos) in our word "topic" (see footnote 6). —Trans.]

47. See footnote 26.

Selected Bibliography: Heidegger and Rhetoric

Compiled by Ansgar Kemmann

Key to Abbreviations

GA Martin Heidegger's collected works (Gesamtausgabe), followed by volume number

SS Summer Semester

WS Winter Semester

Rhetoric Defined in Heidegger's Work

The term *rhetoric* can be found in at least eight places. Seven of those come from the Marburg period, when Heidegger makes regular reference to Greek rhetoric from a philosophical perspective. In order to get a full picture of Heidegger's relationship to rhetoric, one must consider rhetoric more broadly as the everydayness of being-with-one-another (Alltäglichkeit des Miteinanderseins). See indexes compiled by Petkovšek and Feick/Ziegler.

Lecture manuscript 1923/24, "Wahrsein und Dasein nach Aristoteles" (unpublished). "Rhetorik" die Fundamentallehre vom *Logos*—die ursprüngliche Logik" (3), following Aristotle's *Rhetoric* 1.2–3.

Lecture Course SS 1924, "Grundbegriffe der aristotelischen Philosophie." GA 18. "Die Auslegung des Daseins des Menschen hinsichtlich der Grundmöglichkeit des Miteinandersprechens am Leitfaden der Rhetorik" (103–267); "Der konkrete Beleg für die Ursprünglichkeit des Sehens [des *Logos*] ist die ganze 'Rhetorik'" (61); "Die Rhetorik ist nichts anderes als die Auslegung des konkreten Daseins, die Hermeneutik des Daseins selbst" (110); "Besinnung über das Sprechen" (113); "Leitfaden" für die Bestimmung der Stellung der "wissenschaftliche[n] Begriffsbildung im Dasein des Menschen" (123f).

Lecture Course WS 1924/25, "Platon: Sophistes." GA 19. Aristotelian rhetoric (200, 219, 337–339, 350–351); Sophistic rhetoric (16, 219, 294, 306–310); Plato on rhetoric, interpretation of the *Phaedrus* (307–351, 625–629).

Lecture Course SS 1925, "Prolegomena zur Geschichte des Zeitbegriffs." GA 20. "Rhetorik ist ein erstes Stück rechtverstandener Logik" (346f).

Lecture Course WS 1925/26, "Logik: Die Frage nach der Wahrheit." GA 21. Aristotle, *De interpretatione* 17a (130).

Lecture Course SS 1926, "Grundbegriffe der antiken Philosophie." GA 22. Mention of rhetoric as the teaching of Protagoras (86) and as a textbook of Aristotle (146).

Sein und Zeit. GA 2. Aristotle's *Rhetoric* as "erste[r] systematische[r] Hermeneutik der Alltäglichkeit des Miteinanderseins" (§29); analysis of mood (*Befindlichkeit*) in the mode of fear, with reference to Aristotle, *Rhetoric* 2.5, 1382a 20 –1383b11 (§§ 30, 68b).

Lecture Course WS 1951/52, "Was heißt Denken?" Published as *Was heißt Denken?* Tübingen: Niemeyer, 1997 (27). "Lateinisch heißt durchsprechen: reor; vgl. das griechische *eirō* (Rhetorik)."

Published and Unpublished Works by Heidegger around SS 1924

"Phänomenologische Interpretationen zu Aristoteles: Anzeige der hermeneutischen Situation" ("Natorp-Bericht," November 1922). *Dilthey-Jahrbuch für Philosophie und Geisteswissenschaften* 6 (1989): 237–269.

Ontologie: Hermeneutik der Faktizität (last early Freiburg lecture course, SS 1923). GA 63.

Einführung in die phänomenologische Forschung (first Marburg lecture course, WS 1923/24). GA 17.

"Der Begriff der Zeit" (lecture for the Marburger Theologenschaft, July 25, 1924). Edited with an afterword by Hartmut Tiedjen. Tübingen: Niemeyer, 1989.

"Der Begriff der Zeit" (essay originally composed in 1924 for the *Deutsche Vierteljahresschrift für Literaturwissenschaft und Geistesgeschichte*, but not published). Projected publication as GA 64.

"Wahrsein und Dasein: Aristoteles, *Ethica Nicomachea Z*" (lecture for the Kant-Gesellschaft Köln, December 2 and 4, 1924, manuscript compiled 1923/24). Projected publication in GA 80.

Platon: Sophistes (third Marburg lecture course, WS 1924/25). GA 19.

"Wilhelm Diltheys Forschungsarbeit und der gegenwärtige Kampf um eine historische Weltanschauung" (ten lectures held in Kassel between April 16 and 21, 1925). *Dilthey-Jahrbuch für Philosophie und Geisteswissenschaften* 8 (1992/93): 143–177. See also the "Kasseler Post" report from April 25, 1925. GA 16.

Prolegomena zur Geschichte des Zeitbegriffs (fourth Marburg lecture course, SS 1925). GA 20.

Reden und andere Zeugnisse eines Lebensweges (1910 –1976). GA 16.

Secondary Literature

Anton, Corey. "Concerning Speech: Heidegger and Performative Intentionality." *Philosophy and Rhetoric* 31 (1998): 131–144.

Apel, Karl-Otto. *Die Idee der Sprache in der Tradition des Humanismus von Dante bis Vico.* Bonn: Bouvier, 1992.

Aubenque, Pierre. "Logos et pathos: Pour une définition dialectique des passions (*De anima* 1.1 et *Rhétorique* B)." In *Corps et ames: Sur le* De anima *d'Aristote*, edited by Cristina Viano. Paris: Vrin, 1996.

Bezzola, Tobia. *Die Rhetorik bei Kant, Fichte und Hegel: Ein Beitrag zur Philosophiegeschichte der Rhetorik.* Tübingen: Niemeyer, 1993.

Braun, Nicolas. "Nachwort." In *Einführung in das Studium des Aristoteles an Hand einer Interpretation seiner Schrift über die Rhetorik* by Josef König, edited by Nicolas Braun. Freiburg: Alber, 2002.

Brogan, Walter. "Plato's Dialectical Soul: Heidegger on Plato's Ambiguous Relationship to Rhetoric." *Research in Phenomenology* 27 (1997): 3–15.

Caravetta, Peter. *Prefaces to the Diaphora: Rhetorics, Allegory, and the Interpretation of Postmodernity.* West Lafayette: Purdue University Press, 1991.

Crosswhite, James. "Mood in Argumentation: Heidegger and the Exordium." In *Philosophy and Rhetoric* 22 (1989): 22–42.

Dilcher, Roman. "Die Einheit der Aristotelischen Rhetorik." *Antike und Abendland* 47 (2001): 66-83.

Dockhorn, Klaus. Review of Hans-Georg Gadamer's *Wahrheit und Methode. Göttingische Gelehrte Anzeigen* 218 (1966): 169–206.

Falzer, Paul R. "On Behalf of Sceptical Rhetoric." *Philosophy and Rhetoric* 24 (1991): 238–254.

Fisher, Walter. *Human Communication as Narration: Toward a Philosophy of Reason, Value and Action.* Columbia: University of South Carolina Press, 1987.

Fumaroli, Marc. Afterword, "Aujourd'hui: facettes d'une renaissance de la rhétorique." In *Histoire de la rhétorique dans l'Europe moderne 1450-1950*, edited by Marc Fumaroli. Paris: Presses universitaires de France, 1999.

Gadamer, Hans-Georg. *Auf dem Rückgang zum Anfang.* Gesammelte Werke 3 (hereafter cited as GW followed by volume number).

———. *Heidegger und die Griechen.* GW 10.

———. *Heidegger und die Sprache.* GW 10.

———. *Hermeneutik und ontologische Differenz.* GW 10.

———. *Die Kehre des Weges.* GW 10.

———. "Die Logik des verbum interius: Hans-Georg Gadamer im Gespräch mit Gudrun Kühne-Bertram und Frithjof Rodi." In *Dilthey-Jahrbuch für Philosophie und Geisteswissenschaften* 11 (1997/98): 19-30.

Grondin, Jean. *Hans-Georg Gadamer: A Biography.* Translated by Joel Weinsheimer. New Haven: Yale University Press, 2003.

———. "Hermeneutik." In: *Historisches Wörterbuch der Rhetorik*, edited by Gert Ueding. vol. 3. Tübingen: Niemeyer, 1996.

Grassi, Ernesto. *Heidegger and the Question of Renaissance Humanism: Four Studies.* Binghamton: Center for Medieval and Early Renaissance Studies, 1983.

———. "Italian Humanism and Heidegger's Thesis of the End of Philosophy." *Philosophy and Rhetoric* 13 (1980): 79–98.

———. "The Original Quality of the Poetic and Rhetorical Word: Heidegger, Ungaretti, and Neruda." *Philosophy and Rhetoric* 20 (1987): 248–260.

———. "La Rehabilitacion del Humanismo Retorico: Considerando el Antihumanismo de Heidegger." *Cuadernos Sobre Vico* 2 (1992): 21-34.

Heidegger-Index (1919–1927). Compiled by Robert Petkovšek. Ljubljana: Universitas Labacensis Facultas Theologia, 1998.

Heim, Michael R. "Philosophy as Ultimate Rhetoric." *Southern Journal of Philosophy* 19 (1981): 181–195.

Hübner, Alfred W. E. *Existenz und Sprache: Überlegungen zur hermeneutischen Sprachauffassung von Martin Heidegger und Hans Lipps*. Berlin: Duncker & Humblot, 2001.

Hyde, Michael J. *The Call of Conscience: Heidegger and Levinas, Rhetoric and the Euthanasia Debate* (Columbia: University of South Carolina Press, 2001).

———. "Contribution to the Debate: Heidegger on Rhetoric." In *Foundations of Morality,* edited by Anna-Teresa Tymieniecka. Dordrecht: Reidel, 1983.

———. "Existentialism as a Basis for the Theory and Practice of Rhetoric." In *Rhetoric and Philosophy*, edited by Richard A. Cherwitz. New Jersey: Erlbaum, 1990.

———. "Heidegger on Rhetoric." *Analecta Husserliana* 15 (1983a): 165–172.

———. "Rethinking 'The Public': The Role of Emotion in Being-With-Others." *Quarterly Journal of Speech* 77 (1991): 446–466.

———. "Rhetorically, Man Dwells: On the Making-Known Function of Discourse." *Communication* 7 (1983b): 146–162.

Hyde, Michael J. and Craig R. Smith. "Aristotle and Heidegger on Emotion and Rhetoric: Questions of Time and Space." In *The Critical Turn: Rhetoric and Philosophy in Postmodern Discourse*, edited by Ian Angus and Lenore Langsdorf. Carbondale: Southern Illinois University Press, 1993.

Ijsseling, Samuel. "Macht, Taal en Begeerte." *Tijdschrift voor Filosofie* 41 (1979): 375–404.

———. *Rhetoric and Philosophy in Conflict: An Historical Survey*. The Hague: Nijhoff, 1976.

Index zu Heideggers Sein und Zeit. Compiled by Hildegard Feick. Fourth updated edition edited by Susanne Ziegler. Tübingen: Niemeyer, 1991.

Jost, Walter and Hyde, Michael J. "Introduction: Rhetoric and Hermeneutics: Places Along the Way." In *Rhetoric and Hermeneutics in Our Time: A Reader*, edited by Walter Jost and Michael J. Hyde. New Haven: Yale University Press, 1997.

Kalariparambil, Tomy S. *Das befindliche Verstehen und die Seinsfrage*. Berlin: Duncker & Humblot, 1999.

Kisiel, Theodore J. *The Genesis of Heidegger's* Being and Time. Berkeley: University of California Press, 1993.

———. "Gibt es eine formale anzeigende Hermeneutik nach der Kehre?" In *Kultur-Kunst-Öffentlichkeit: Philosophische Perspektiven auf praktische Probleme. Festschrift für Otto Pöggeler zum 70. Geburtstag*, edited by Annemarie Gethmann-Siefert and Elisabeth Weisser-Lohmann. Munich: Fink, 2001.

———. "Heideggers Einsetzung der rhetorischen Politik in seine 'urpraktische Ontologie.'" In *Metaphysik der praktischen Welt: Perspektiven im Anschluß an Hegel und Heidegger. Festgabe für Otto Pöggeler*, edited by Andreas Grossmann and Christoph Jamme. Amsterdam: Radopi, 2000.

———. "Situating Rhetorical Politics in Heidegger's Protopractical Ontology. 1923–1925: The French Occupy the Ruhr." In *International Journal of Philosophical Studies* 8 (2000): 185–208.

Knape, Joachim. *Allgemeine Rhetorik: Stationen der Theoriegeschichte*. Stuttgart: Reclam, 2000.

———. *Was ist Rhetorik?* Stuttgart: Reclam, 2000.

Kuhn, Helmut. "Aristoteles und die Methode der Politikwissenschaft." Reprinted in *Rehabilitierung der praktischen Philosophie*, vol. 2, edited by Manfred Riedel. Freiburg: Rombach, 1972.

Marassi, Massimo. "The Hermeneutics of Rhetoric in Heidegger." *Philosophy and Rhetoric* 19 (1986): 79–98.

———. "Rhetoric and Historicity: An Introduction." *Philosophy and Rhetoric* 21 (1988): 245–259.

Megill, Allan. "Heidegger, Wander, and Ideology." *The Central States Speech Journal* 34 (1983): 114–119.

Michalski, Mark. *Fremdwahrnehmung und Mitsein zur Grundlegung der Sozialphilosophie im Denken Max Schelers und Martin Heideggers*. Bonn: Bouvier, 1997.

———. "Nachwort des Herausgebers." In *Martin Heidegger: Grundbegriffe der aristotelischen Philosophie*. GA 18.

Niehues-Pröbsting, Heinrich. *Überredung zur Einsicht: Der Zusammenhang von Philosophie und Rhetorik bei Platon und in der Phänomenologie*. Frankfurt: Klostermann, 1987.

Oesterreich, Peter L. "Die Idee einer existentialontologischen Wendung der Rhetorik in M. Heideggers *Sein und Zeit*." *Zeitschrift für philosophische Forschung* 43 (1989): 656–672.

———. *Fundamentalrhetorik: Untersuchungen zu Person und Rede in der Öffentlichkeit*. Hamburg: Meiner, 1990.

———. "Verborgene persuasive Strategien: Zur rhetorischen Metakritik der Philosophie." In *Rhetorik und Philosophie*, edited by Josef Kopperschmidt and Helmut Schanze. Munich: Fink, 1989.

Patella, Giuseppe. "La metafora di pensare: Metafora, retorica e discorso philosophico." In *Simbolo, Metafora e Linguaggio: Nella elaborazione filosofico-scientifica e giuridico-politica*, edited by Franco Ratto. Bergamo: Edizioni Sestante, 1998.

Pöggeler, Otto. "Dialektik und Topik." In *Hermeneutik und Dialektik: Festschrift für Hans-Georg Gadamer zum 70. Geburtstag*, vol. 2, edited by Rüdiger Bubner. Tübingen: Mohr Siebeck, 1970.

———. "Gadamers philosophische Hermeneutik und die Rhetorik." In *Rhetorik und Philosophie*, edited by Josef Kopperschmidt and Helmut Schanze. Munich: Fink, 1989.

———. *Martin Heidegger's Path of Thinking*. Translated by Daniel Magurshak and Sigmund Barber. Atlantic Highlands: Humanities Press International, 1989).

———. "Metaphysik und Seinstopik bei Heidegger." *Philosophisches Jahrbuch* 70 (1962): 118–137.
———. "Ressentiment und Tugend bei Max Scheler." In *Vom Umsturz der Werte in der modernen Gesellschaft, II. Internationales Kolloquium der Scheler-Gesellschaft*, edited by Gerhard Pfafferott. Bonn: Bouvier, 1997.
———. "Topik und Philosophie." In *Topik: Beiträge zur interdisziplinären Diskussion*, edited by Dieter Breuer and Helmut Schanze. Munich: Fink, 1981.
Ptassek, Peter. *Rhetorische Rationalität: Stationen einer Verdrängungsgeschichte*. Munich: Fink, 1993.
Ramsey, Ramsey Eric. "Listening to Heidegger on Rhetoric." *Philosophy and Rhetoric* 26 (1993): 266–276.
Regehly, Thomas. "'Heideggeriana' im Herbert Marcuse-Archiv der Stadt- und Universitätsbibliothek in Frankfurt am Main." *Heidegger-Studien* 7 (1991): 179–209.
Renaud, François. *Die Resokratisierung Platons: Die platonische Hermeneutik Hans-Georg Gadamers*. Sankt Augustin: Academia Verlag, 1999.
Rese, Friederike. *Praxis und Logos bei Aristoteles: Handlung, Vernunft und Rede in* Nikomachischer Ethik, Rhetorik *und* Politik. Tübingen: Mohr Siebeck, 2003.
Riedel, Manfred. "Seinsverständnis und Sinn für das Tunliche: Der hermeneutische Weg zur 'Rehabilitierung der praktischen Philosophie.'" In *Politik, Philosophie, Praxis: Festschrift für Wilhelm Hennis zum 65. Geburtstag*, edited by Hans Maier, Ulrich Matz, Kurt Sontheimer and Paul-Ludwig Weinacht. Stuttgart: Klett-Cotta, 1988.
Rodi, Frithjof. "Die Bedeutung Diltheys für die Konzeption von Sein und Zeit: Zum Umfeld von Heideggers Kasseler Vorträgen (1925)." *Dilthey-Jahrbuch für Philosophie und Geisteswissenschaften* 4 (1987): 161–177.
Rosenfield, Lawrence W. "Ideological Miasma." *Central States Speech Journal* 34 (1983): 119-121.
———. "The Practical Celebration of Epideictic." In *Rhetoric in Transition: Studies in the Nature and Use of Rhetoric*, edited by Eugene E. White. University Park: Pennsylvania State University Press, 1980.
Schlier, Heinrich. "Denken im Nachdenken." In *Erinnerung an Martin Heidegger*, edited by Günther Neske. Pfullingen: Neske, 1977.
Schrag, Calvin O. "Rhetoric, Hermeneutics, and Communication." In *Communicative Praxis and the Space of Subjectivity*. Bloomington: Indiana University Press, 1986.
Scult, Allen. "Aristotle's Rhetoric as Ontology: A Heideggerian Reading." *Philosophy and Rhetoric* 32 (1999): 146–157.
———. "Heidegger's Hermeneutics and the Rhetoric of Biblical Theology." *Philosophy and Rhetoric* 27 (1994): 397–409.
———. "The Hermeneutics of Heidegger's Speech: A Rhetorical Phenomenology." *The Journal of the British Society for Phenomenology* 29 (1998): 162–173.
Sipiora, Michael P. "Heidegger and Epideictic Discourse: The Rhetorical Performance of Meditative Thinking." *Philosophy Today* (1991): 239–253.
Smith, P. Christopher. *The Hermeneutics of Original Argument: Demonstration, Dialectic, Rhetoric*. Evanston: Northwestern University Press, 1998.

———. "The Uses and Abuses of Aristotle's Rhetoric in Heidegger's Fundamental Ontology: The Lecture Course Summer 1924." In *From Phenomenology to Thought, Errancy, and Desire*, edited by Babette E. Babich. Dordrecht: Kluwer Academic, 1995.

Smith, Craig R. "Martin Heidegger and the Dialogues with Being." *The Central States Speech Journal* 36 (1985): 256–269.

Van Buren, John. *The Young Heidegger: Rumor of the Hidden King*. Bloomington: Indiana University Press, 1994.

Wander, Philip. "The Ideological Turn in Modern Criticism." *The Central States Speech Journal* 34 (1983): 1–18.

Wolzogen, Christian von. "Die eigentlich metaphysische Störung: Zu den Quellen der Ethik bei Heidegger und Levinas." In *Zur Grundlegung einer integrativen Ethik. Für Hans Krämer*, edited by Martin Endreß. Frankfurt: Suhrkamp, 1995.

Van der Walt, Johan. "From Difference to Indifference: Rhetoric in the Thought of Heidegger and Rorty." *South African Journal of Philosophy* 5 (1986): 125–132.

Vattimo, Gianni. "Truth and Rhetoric in Hermeneutic Ontology." In *The End of Modernity: Nihilism and Hermeneutics in Postmodern Culture*, edited by Gianni Vattimo. Translated by Jon R. Snyder. Baltimore: Johns Hopkins University Press, 1988.

Volpi, Franco. "Der Status der Existentialen Analytik." In *Martin Heidegger:* Sein und Zeit, edited by Thomas Rentsch. Berlin: Akademie Verlag, 2001.

Contributors

John Bailiff (1936) is emeritus professor of philosophy, University of Wisconsin, Stevens Point. After undergraduate work at Stanford University he received his PhD in philosophy from Penn State. He taught philosophy for thirty-five years at Penn State, the University of Nevada at Las Vegas, and the University of Wisconsin in Stevens Point. He is a founding member of the North American Heidegger Conference. *The Paths of Heidegger's Life and Thought*, his translation of Otto Pöggeler's *Neue Wege mit Heidegger*, appeared in the series *Contemporary Studies in Philosophy and the Human Sciences*, edited by Hugh Silverman and Graeme Nicholson (Atlantic Highlands: Humanities Press, 1997). *Aesthetic Thinking*, his translation of Wolfgang Welsch's *Ästhetisches Denken* is forthcoming from Humanity Books.

Jamey Findling teaches philosophy at Newman University in Wichita, Kansas. His dissertation, completed at Villanova University, dealt with Gadamer's interpretation of Plato. He is the author of essays on Gadamer and on Greek philosophy, and has previously published a cotranslation (with Snezhina Gabova) of Gadamer's essay, "Plato als Porträtist."

Hans-Georg Gadamer (1900–2002), Dr. phil., was emeritus professor of philosophy at the University of Heidelberg, where he held the chair of Karl Jaspers since 1949. Gadamer began his university studies at Breslau in 1918, continuing at Marburg in 1919, where he received his first doctorate under Paul Natorp in 1922. In 1923 he went to Freiburg to listen to Martin Heidegger. After returning to Marburg with Heidegger in the same year, Gadamer served as his assistant while studying classical philology and completing a second doctorate in 1928 entitled *Platos dialektische Ethik*. His own teaching and research reached a first conclusion in 1960 in his masterwork, *Wahrheit und Methode* (*Truth and Method*). After becoming professor emeritus in 1968, Gadamer continued lecturing as a visiting professor in universities around the world, enjoying a special relationship with Boston College in the United States.

Daniel M. Gross (PhD, Berkeley) has been assistant professor of rhetoric and POROI (Project on Rhetoric of Inquiry) at the University of Iowa since 2000. Previously he studied philosophy and rhetoric in Berlin and Tübingen, and taught comparative literature while on a two-year Mellon postdoctoral fellowship at the UCLA Humanities Consortium, Center for 17th- and 18th-Century Studies. His work on the history and theory of rhetoric appears among other places in the journals *Rhetorica*, *Clio*, *Philosophy and Rhetoric*, and *History of the Human Sciences*, as well as in his book, *The Secret History of Emotion: From Aristotle's* Rhetoric *to Modern Brain Science* (Chicago: University of Chicago Press, 2006).

Michael J. Hyde (PhD, Purdue) is the University Distinguished Professor of Communication Ethics, Department of Communication, Wake Forest University. He is the author of numerous articles and critical reviews appearing in various scholarly journals and texts and is the editor of *Communication Philosophy and the Technological Age* (Alabama: University of Alabama Press, 1982), and *The Ethos of Rhetoric* (South Carolina: University of South Carolina Press, 2004), coeditor of *Rhetoric and Hermeneutics in our Time* (New Haven: Yale University Press, 1997), and author of the award winning *The Call of Conscience: Heidegger and Levinas, Rhetoric and the Euthanasia Debate* (South Carolina: University of South Carolina Press, 2001), as well as *The Life-Giving Gift of Acknowledgment: A Philosophical and Rhetorical Inquiry* (West Lafayette, Purdue University Press, 2005). He is the recipient of the Scholar Award for Communication Excellence in Ethics Education for the Mind, the Heart, and the Soul by the Communication Ethics Center, Department of Communication and Rhetorical Studies, Duquesne University.

Ansgar Kemmann is project manager of the German Federal Contest "Jugend debattiert" ("Youth Debate") at the Hertie Foundation, one of today's largest foundations in Germany. Previously he taught practical rhetoric at the universities of Tübingen and Munich (1992–2003). He is author of various articles in encyclopaedic reference works including the *Historisches Wörterbuch der Rhetorik* (Tübingen: Niemeyer, 1992), *Wörterbuch der antiken Philosophie* (Munich: Beck, 2002), and *Religion in Geschichte und Gegenwart* (Tübingen: Mohr Siebeck, 2003), and he reviews occasionally for the *Frankfurter Allgemeine Zeitung*.

Theodore Kisiel is Distinguished Research Professor of Philosophy at Northern Illinois University. He has translated Martin Heidegger's *History of the Concept of Time: Prolegomena* (Bloomington: Indiana University Press, 1985) and coedited *Reading Heidegger from the Start: Essays in His Earliest Thought* (Albany: State University of New York Press, 1994). His books include *The Genesis of Heidegger's* Being and Time (Berkeley: University of California Press, 1993) and *Heidegger's Way of Thought: Critical and Interpretative Essays* (London: Athlone, 2001), which brings together the uncensored translator's introduction and banned index to *History of the Concept of Time.*

Mark Michalski, Dr. phil., is lecturer at the European Center for the Translation of Literature and the Human Science (EKEMEL) in Athens, Greece, and editor of the central text of this collection: Martin Heidegger's Summer Semester 1924 Marburg Lecture *Grundbegriffe der aristotelischen Philosophie*, vol. 18 of the Gesamtausgabe (Frankfurt: Klostermann, 2002). He studied philosophy and classical philology at the University of Freiburg, Germany, where he first taught philosophy and worked as an instructor in Latin and Greek. In his dissertation *Fremdwahrnehmung und Mitsein* he dealt with the foundation of social philosophy in the thinking of Max Scheler and Martin Heidegger (Bonn: Bouvier, 1997). He has also published the article "Terminologische Neubildungen beim frühen Heidegger" in *Heidegger Studies* 18 (2002).

Otto Pöggeler (1928), Dr. phil., is emeritus professor of philosophy at the Ruhr University in Bochum, Germany. He received his doctorate in German philology at the University of Bonn in 1955, followed by his habilitation in philosophy under Hans-Georg Gadamer at the University of Heidelberg in 1965. Since 1968 he has been professor of philosophy at the Ruhr University in Bochum, and director of its Hegel Archive. He was president of the German Society for Phenomenological Research from 1978 to 1983, and is a member of the Nordrhine-Westfalean Academy of Sciences. His major works include *Der Denkweg Martin Heideggers* (Pfullingen: Neske, 1963), translated as *Martin Heidegger's Path of Thinking* (New York: Humanity Press, 1994), *Hegels Idee einer Phänomenologie des Geistes* (Freiburg: Alber, 1993), *Spur des Worts: Zur Lyrik Paul Celans* (Freiburg: Alber, 1986), *Schritte zu einer hermeneutischen Philosophie* (Freiburg: Alber, 1994), and *Bild und Technik: Heidegger, Klee und die moderne Kunst* (Munich: Fink, 2002).

Lawrence Kennedy Schmidt is professor of philosophy at Hendrix College in Conway, Arkansas. He has organized international conferences and workshops in Heidelberg, Germany to discuss Gadamer's philosophy. In addition to numerous articles on Gadamer and hermeneutics he has published *The Epistemology of Hans-Georg Gadamer* (New York: Lang, 1985), edited *The Specter of Relativism: Truth, Dialogue, and* Phronesis *in Philosophical Hermeneutics* (Evanston: Northwestern University Press, 1995), and *Language and Linguisticality in Gadamer's Hermeneutics* (Lanham: Lexington Books, 2000), and translated many of Gadamer's essays, one set appearing in *Hans-Georg Gadamer on Education, Poetry, and History*, edited by Dieter Misgeld and Graeme Nicholson (Albany: State University of New York Press, 1992).

Nancy S. Struever, professor emerita of Johns Hopkins University, an intellectual historian of the Renaissance, has focussed on the history of rhetoric—its issues and modalities—in her books *The Language of History in the Renaissance* (Princeton: Princeton University Press, 1970), *Theory as Practice: Ethical Inquiry in the Renaissance* (Chicago: University of Chicago Press, 1992), and in several of her articles on Giambattista Vico. She is currently completing a book-length project on rhetoric and politics.

Index of Names

Index of Subject Matter